Kohlhammer

Elmar Stein

Human Resource Development Competencies for HR Business Partners

Verlag W. Kohlhammer

Dieses Werk einschließlich aller seiner Teile ist urheberrechtlich geschützt. Jede Verwendung außerhalb der engen Grenzen des Urheberrechts ist ohne Zustimmung des Verlags unzulässig und strafbar. Das gilt insbesondere für Vervielfältigungen, Übersetzungen, Mikroverfilmungen und für die Einspeicherung und Verarbeitung in elektronischen Systemen.

1. Auflage 2025

Alle Rechte vorbehalten
© W. Kohlhammer GmbH, Stuttgart
Gesamtherstellung:
W. Kohlhammer GmbH, Heßbrühlstr. 69, 70565 Stuttgart
produktsicherheit@kohlhammer.de

Print:
ISBN 978-3-17-045214-5

E-Book-Formate:
pdf: ISBN 978-3-17-045215-2
epub: ISBN 978-3-17-045216-9

Für den Inhalt abgedruckter oder verlinkter Websites ist ausschließlich der jeweilige Betreiber verantwortlich. Die W. Kohlhammer GmbH hat keinen Einfluss auf die verknüpften Seiten und übernimmt hierfür keinerlei Haftung.

Contents

1		Introduction: The Development of Human Resource Management and the Importance of Human Resource Business Partnering	11
2		Ulrich's Intentions and the Initial Model of HR Business Partnering: Human Resource Champions – the Next Agenda for Adding Value and Delivering Results	16
	2.1	The Situation of HR Management and its Necessity for Transformation...	16
	2.2	HR Reorientation and Roles of Business Partners	18
	2.3	The Role and Challenges of Strategic Partners	22
	2.4	Challenges and Responsibilities for Becoming an Administrative Expert	24
	2.5	Challenges and Responsibilities for Becoming an Employee Champion...	25
	2.6	Challenges and Responsibilities for Becoming a Change Agent	25
	2.7	The Challenge and Necessity for Self-Improvement Approaches and Development	27
3		The First Adjustment to the Initial Model – the HR Value Proposition	30
	3.1	The Theory of HR Value and Its Creation....................	30
	3.2	The Consideration of the Business Environment	33
	3.3	The Consideration of External Stakeholders	34
	3.4	The Consideration of Internal Stakeholders..................	35
	3.5	HR Value Adding through the Field of Flow of People and Performance	37
	3.6	HR Value Adding through the Field of Flow of Information and Work	38
	3.7	HR Value Adding through an HR Strategy	39
	3.8	HR Value Adding through HR Organization..................	40
	3.9	HR Roles and Responsibilities	41
		3.9.1 Employee Advocate	44
		3.9.2 Human Capital Developer	45
		3.9.3 Functional Expert.................................	45
		3.9.4 Strategic Partner	46

		3.9.5	HR Leader	47
	3.10		HR Value Contributing Competencies Making a Difference	48
	3.11		HR Professional Development Necessities and HR Transformation Implications.	51

4 The Second Adjustment to the Initial Model – HR Transformation – Building Human Resources from the Outside In 53

4.1	The New Need of HR Transformation	53
4.2	HR Transformation and the Business Context	55
4.3	HR Transformation and Outcome Orientation	57
4.4	HR Transformation and HR Redesign	61
4.5	HR Transformation and the Accountability of HR	67

5 The Third Adjustment to the Initial Model – Victory Through Organization – Why the War for Talent Is Failing Your Company and What You Can Do About It 70

5.1	The Increasing Relevance of HR in the Context of the "War for Talent"		70
5.2	The Nine Roles of Business Partnering and Their Value Creation Contribution		72
5.3	The Relevance of Organization and Its Practices		75
5.4	The Category of Core Drivers		76
	5.4.1	The Credible Activist	76
	5.4.2	The Strategic Positioner	77
	5.4.3	The Paradox Navigator	78
5.5	The Category of Strategic Enablers		79
	5.5.1	The Culture and Change Champion	79
	5.5.2	The Human Capital Curator	80
	5.5.3	The Total Rewards Steward	81
5.6	The Category of Foundational Enablers		82
	5.6.1	The Compliance Manager	82
	5.6.2	The Analytics Designer and Interpreter	82
	5.6.3	The Technology and Media Integrator	83
5.7	HR Capacity Significance and HR Development Relevance		83

6 The Application of the Business Partnering Model and Its Challenges 85

7 The Implications of the "War for Talent" on HR Development and Business Partnering 88

7.1	Talent Shortage and Demographic Shift	88
7.2	The Necessity to Advance Productivity and Commitment	90
7.3	The Challenges with the Generations Y and Z and Their Values and Attitudes	91

	7.4		The Relevance of HR Development in Combination with Superior Business Partner Role Execution	95
8			HR Development Competencies for HR Business Partners in the Latest Competency Model	96
	8.1		Technology and Media Integrator	96
		8.1.1	Virtual Learning	96
		8.1.2	Blended Learning	98
		8.1.3	Individual Learning	102
		8.1.4	Artificial Intelligence in Learning	104
		8.1.5	Gamification	105
		8.1.6	Chances and Challenges of Business Partners in the Role of Technology and Media Integrator	109
	8.2		Analytics Designer and Interpreter	109
		8.2.1	Data Analysis and Identification of Skill Demand	109
		8.2.2	Data-Driven Long-Term Strategic Orientation in HR Development	111
		8.2.3	Data-Driven Integration of HR Development within Organizational Learning and Development	113
		8.2.4	Data Analysis in HR Development for Enhancing Performance	116
		8.2.5	Analyses of Employee Expectations for Performance Improvement	117
		8.2.6	Data-Driven Selection and Development of Coaches and Mentors	119
		8.2.7	Key Performance Indicators in HR Development Effectiveness Evaluation and Improvement	122
	8.3		Compliance Manager	125
		8.3.1	Compliance Management and the Use of Standards	125
		8.3.2	Compliance and the Use of Metrics and Procedures	126
		8.3.3	Assessing and Improvement Methods of HR Development Programs	128
	8.4		Culture and Change Champion	134
		8.4.1	The Integration of HR Development into Organizational Culture	135
		8.4.2	Cooperation of Business Partners and Line Managers to Advance HR Development Marketing	137
		8.4.3	Empowering Change: Agile Leadership and HR Development for Business Success	139
		8.4.4	Enhancing Corporate Culture: The Crucial Role of Performance-Oriented HR Development and Social Learning Strategies	142
	8.5		Human Capital Curator	144

	8.5.1	Elevating Business Partners: The Imperative Role of Human Capital Curators in Strategy and Success........	144
	8.5.2	The Role of Human Capital Curators in Achieving Competitive Advantage	145
	8.5.3	Leveraging Unique Human Capital for Sustainable Competitive Advantage	147
	8.5.4	Leveraging Human Capital: The Key to Sustainable Competitive Advantage Through Unique HR Processes	148
	8.5.5	Strategic Human Capital Management: Navigating the "War for Talent" through Dynamic Capabilities and Evidence-Based HR Strategies	150
	8.5.6	Harnessing Social and Organizational Capital for Business Success	151
	8.5.7	Usage of the Balanced-Scorecard and Its Enterprise Alignment	153
	8.5.8	Unveiling the Strategic Imperatives of Human Capital Curators: Maximizing ROI in Business Partnerships	154
8.6	Total Rewards Steward		156
	8.6.1	Navigating the Complexities of Compensation Design: Challenges and Strategies for Total Rewards Stewards	156
	8.6.2	Striking a Balance: Navigating Procedural Justice in Compensation Systems for Optimal Organizational Dynamic...	158
	8.6.3	Crafting Equitable Compensation: The Complex Role of Total Rewards Stewards in Job Evaluation and Incentive Structures	159
	8.6.4	Balancing Generational Expectations: Crafting Effective Compensation Systems for Today's Workforce	160
	8.6.5	Strategic Integration: Financial Incentives as Catalysts for HR Development Success	161
8.7	Credible Activist		163
	8.7.1	Unlocking Corporate Prosperity in the Role of a Credible Activist: The Strategic Role of HR Development in Today's Business Landscape.......................	164
	8.7.2	Maximizing HR Development Impact: The Imperative of Effective Communication and ROI Integration.......	166
	8.7.3	Strategic Collaboration: Maximizing HR Development Impact Through Synergy Approaches	167
	8.7.4	Strategically Aligned HR Development: Empowering Leadership, Enhancing Competitiveness	169
8.8	Strategic Positioner		170
	8.8.1	Navigating Corporate Development and HR Alignment for Long-Term Success................................	171

		8.8.2	Strategic Positioners: Architects of Organizational Transformation..	172
		8.8.3	Closing the Gap: Integrating Strategic HR Development for Corporate Success	173
		8.8.4	Strategic Positioning of Human Capital: Navigating Scarcity and Development for Corporate Success......	175
		8.8.5	Strategic Positioning in HR: Aligning Business Partnerships for Sustainable Growth and Agility	176
		8.8.6	Strategic HR Development: Navigating VUCA Terrain for Organizational Adaptability and Success	177
		8.8.7	Strategic HR Development: Aligning Competencies Across Temporal Dimensions for Organizational Success	180
		8.8.8	Unlocking Organizational Resilience: Strategic HR Development in a Dynamic Landscape	182
	8.9	Paradox Navigator...		184
		8.9.1	Paradox Navigators: Unraveling Complexity in Strategic HR Development...........................	184
		8.9.2	HR Development in the Age of Paradox: Navigating Technological Advancements and Organizational Dynamics	186
		8.9.3	Unlocking Strategic Synergy: The Crucial Role of Paradox Navigators in HR Development............	187
		8.9.4	Charting the Course: Navigating HR Development in the Complex Business Landscape	188
		8.9.5	Unlocking Success: The Role of Paradox Navigators in Maximizing Value-Added Contribution.............	190
		8.9.6	Empowering Paradox Navigators: Enhancing Collaboration and HR Development for Competitive Advantage	191
9	The Challenge of Competency and Strategic Relatedness of HR Development in HR Business Partnering........................			**194**
	9.1	The Connection between the Roles of the Foundational Enablers and the Additional Categories......................		195
		9.1.1	The Connection between the Technology and Media Integrator and the Other Roles	195
		9.1.2	The Connection between the Analytics Designers and Interpreters and the Other Roles.................	199
		9.1.3	The Connection Between the Compliance Manager and the Other Roles................................	203
	9.2	The Connection between the Roles of the Strategic Enabler and the Other Categories...................................		207
		9.2.1	The Connection between the Culture and Change Champion and the Other Roles......................	207

		9.2.2 The Connection between the Human Capital Curator and the Other Roles	211
		9.2.3 The Connection between the Total Reward Steward and the Other Roles	215
	9.3	The Connection between the Role of the Credible Activist and the Strategic Positioner	217
		9.3.1 The Coordination Function of the Paradox Navigator	219
10	Conclusion		221
References			224

1 Introduction: The Development of Human Resource Management and the Importance of Human Resource Business Partnering

Human resource (HR) management has roots as ancient as the emergence of labor itself, tracing back to the dawn of humanity. Throughout the course of human existence, the regulation and optimization of work, methodologies, procedures, and productivity have been imperative within communal, team, and organizational settings. Historical records reveal a multitude of intricate systems governing work organization, labor allocation, and HR administration, evident in agricultural practices, the governance of the Roman Empire, feudalistic structures, and systems of slavery. The genesis of modern HR management, however, can be traced to the advent of the Industrial Revolution and the subsequent evolution towards contemporary corporate structures.

While the notion of HR management has persisted throughout history, the formalization of a scientific framework can be pinpointed to approximately 1900, coinciding with the publication of Frederic Taylor's seminal work, "The Principles of Scientific Management." Taylor's treatise heralded a paradigm shift by introducing empirical methodologies and objectives into labor management, particularly in the realm of workflow optimization. Central to Taylor's doctrine was the systematic measurement and refinement of work processes through scientific inquiry, with the overarching goal of enhancing organizational efficacy. Fundamental to his approach was the concept of maximizing specialization among workers while delineating distinct spheres for managerial planning and operational execution. This philosophy, encapsulated as "Taylorism," revolutionized labor management practices worldwide.

Embedded within Taylor's model were rudimentary frameworks for HR selection and development, primarily oriented towards fostering specialized skill sets among workers. Additionally, Taylor's framework espoused notions of performance-driven remuneration and competency-based evaluations, underscoring the profound influence of HR on organizational performance (Kolb, Burkart, Zundel, 2010, 12–13).

Before HR management prioritized these aspects, attention was directed towards other domains of activity. Subsequently, the developmental trajectories of HR management, delineated decade by decade starting in the 1950s, are expounded upon. Each new decade witnessed the incorporation of additional responsibilities onto pre-existing ones.

During the 1950s, emphasis was placed on HR administration and societal factors. In the subsequent era of the 1960s, the establishment phase of HR management saw the inclusion of recruitment, a corporate talent development system, and workplace design. Transitioning into the 1970s, a focus on humanization emerged. Augmenting HR management were workplace organization, broadened participation and decision-making scopes, collaborative leadership, and talent development. The 1980s marked the advent of economization within HR management. Key areas of engagement included IT integration, quantitative HR control mechanisms, and the shift towards flexible working hours. In the final decade of the 20th century, the restructuring of HR management took precedence. This restructuring encompassed decentralization, team synergy, goal-oriented leadership, health management, internationalization, qualitative HR methodologies, organizational evolution, and corporate culture enhancement. Dave Ulrich's seminal work in 1997 introduced the concept of Business Partnering, advocating for a heightened focus on HR's contribution to success and the consideration of both internal and external HR customers.

Entering the new millennium, Ulrich's Business Partnering framework gained prominence, emphasizing corporate contribution. Novel HR domains included variable compensation, talent retention strategies (e.g., work-life balance, diversity management), competence mapping, succession planning, process optimization, HR digitalization, crisis management, and human capital optimization. Ulrich's subsequent publications in 2005 and 2009 iterated on the Business Partnering model, refining roles, competencies, and development stages for enhanced value delivery. The 2010s prioritized the establishment of sustainable HR management, aligning with Ulrich's vision of bolstering organizational success through long-term HR strategies and ethical considerations. In 2017, Ulrich's fourth and current book on Business Partnering underscored the significance of the "War for Talent" and its ramifications for HR and business partnerships. While the 2020 decade is ongoing, discernible challenges and focal areas for HR management include the "War for Employees", demographic shifts, talent cultivation, AI utilization, succession planning, adaptability to sudden environmental shifts, digital transformation, mobile work integration, evolving work attitudes, and ethical dilemmas.

Throughout the delineated evolution of HR management, there has been a continual increase in the number of supplementary tasks and challenges, accompanied by a rise in complexity. The process of professionalization within HR management becomes evident when considering the progression and accumulation of tasks and responsibilities. A pivotal aspect of this professionalization has been the shift towards delivering value and contributing to organizational success. This transition marks a departure from a predominantly administrative focus to a robust strategic orientation. Ulrich's seminal work on Business Partnering represents a pivotal moment in HR management's trajectory, introducing a model that revolutionizes the field by prioritizing value delivery and organizational contribution. His model stipulates that all HR endeavors must align with this overarching goal, a principle crucial for establishing credibility and longevity in HR practices. The clarity and practicality of Ulrich's model, detailing roles, tasks, challenges, and their implementation, have led to its widespread adoption across organizations globally. Moreover, Ulrich continually addresses current and future HR management challenges, perpetuating the professionalization of Business Partnering and strategic development.

In 1997, he underscored the imperative for HR management to focus on value delivery and organizational contribution to justify its continued relevance. The delineation of the initial four Business Partner roles and their responsibilities was refined in subsequent years (2005, 2009), emphasizing human capital optimization and customer-centric approaches. In 2017, Ulrich foresaw challenges stemming from talent shortages and advocated for strategic partnerships to address them. He viewed this situation not only as an opportunity but also as a significant obligation for Business Partners and HR management as a whole. Today, an organization's success hinges on the effectiveness and outcomes of its Business Partners, with HR emerging as pivotal success factors. As outlined in foreseeable trends, the importance of HR management, especially Business Partnering, will continue to escalate, becoming strategically indispensable. Strategic planning will increasingly rely on the availability and quality of HR, necessitating adept management of Ulrich's latest Business Partnering model by HR professionals. Challenges such as talent scarcity, the "War for Employees," and evolving skill requirements driven by technological advancements and changing work dynamics will significantly influence Business Partners' work.

Competencies in HR development will thus become paramount for delivering value and fostering organizational success. Consequently, Business Partners must integrate HR development aspects into each role, leveraging existing potential to enhance strategic positioning. However, this incorporation of HR development aspects presents new challenges and expectations, underscoring the need for Business Partners to further refine their strategic acumen and adaptability. By leveraging external challenges, Business Partners can chart a competency development trajectory, elevating their strategic relevance and influence in organizational decision-making processes.

In recent times, HR Management, and consequently Business Partnering, has garnered significance as talent management has emerged as a crucial factor for organizational success. However, in the near future, HR development, encompassing both skills and application, is poised to emerge as the primary strategic determinant due to the burgeoning talent scarcity. As such, the cultivation of Business Partners and their adeptness in HR development will assume heightened importance for value delivery and organizational prosperity.

To operationalize this envisioned paradigm, the objective of this book is to elucidate the HR development competencies and their consequential impact aligned with each Business Partner role. This framework also holds the potential to instigate the subsequent developmental imperatives and phases of Business Partners. Integrating HR development aspects into each Business Partner role introduces a novel consciousness prerequisite, a distinct array of tasks and challenges, as well as developmental requisites for Business Partners.

1 Introduction

The proposed amalgamation of HR development competencies into each role harbors the potential to advance the prevailing state of Ulrich's Business Partner model by incorporating essential facets of value delivery and success-contributing factors within each partnering role. Business Partners must comprehend the interrelation of requisite HR development competencies and systematically assess them. It becomes incumbent upon Business Partners to introspect upon the requisite competencies, identify areas necessitating heightened engagement, and recognize developmental potentials.

Moreover, they may discover more effective means of integrating and enhancing HR development aspects to actualize a greater value contribution. Subsequently, Business Partners can scrutinize their current developmental stage and trajectory, while concurrently aligning their diverse roles to maximize their influence. However, this endeavor necessitates identifying the interconnections between the various roles and the role of HR development aspects through systematic situational analysis.

From this foundational premise, Business Partners can derive viable solutions and discern their developmental imperatives. In essence, the consideration and integration of HR development competencies possess the potential to underpin the subsequent developmental phase of Ulrich's Business Partnering model. Consequently, there exist both practical and theoretical applications by integrating HR development competencies and skills into the existing Business Partnering model.

Given the proposed additional competencies for each Business Partner role, the content of this book accrues benefits for practitioners, students, researchers, and scholars in the domain of Business Partnering due to the fusion of theoretical and practical dimensions.

Prior to delineating the pertinent HR development aspects of each Business Partner role, the objectives of Business Partnering, alongside the initial model and its evolution up to the present scenario, will be expounded upon. Ulrich's aspiration to instigate a novel purpose for HR professionals will be comprehensively summarized, serving as the foundation for his subsequent advancements in 2005, 2009, and 2017. These advancements will also be detailed, as the latest model forms the inception for integrating HR development competencies into each of the nine roles within the extant Business Partnering model.

This approach is adopted for several reasons. Firstly, it furnishes a theoretical underpinning for Business Partnering practitioners, facilitating a deeper understanding of the framework and offering insights for its application. This is advantageous for both neophytes and seasoned practitioners, owing to the proposed integration of HR development aspects into each Business Partner role.

Secondly, theory-oriented readers find a comprehensive summary of the initial postulations and the evolutionary trajectory leading to the current model, along with its proposed integration of HR development competencies. The delineated evolution presents myriad avenues for potential research into each of Ulrich's models, as well as those derivable from the suggested integration of HR development competencies.

Thirdly, this approach is beneficial for students due to the condensed overview of a globally applied model, offering insights into all requisite and forthcoming HR domains, thereby providing a comprehensive understanding of the challenges encountered by Business Partners.

Lastly, this approach is advantageous for novices in the realms of Business Partnering and HR management, elucidating fundamental domains, activities, and challenges within HR management. Additionally, it furnishes an elaborate overview of a globally embraced and implemented model in HR management.

2 Ulrich's Intentions and the Initial Model of HR Business Partnering: Human Resource Champions – the Next Agenda for Adding Value and Delivering Results

2.1 The Situation of HR Management and its Necessity for Transformation

Within this chapter, Ulrich's inaugural model will be elucidated. In 1997, Ulrich authored his pioneering manuscript on Business Partnering, titled "Human Resource Champions: The Next Agenda for Adding Value and Delivering Results." Merely from the title's contemplation, his objectives become readily apparent. The phrase "the next agenda" denotes his aspiration for HR advancement. "Adding value and delivering results" suggests Ulrich's advocacy for HR departments to prioritize tangible outcomes and demonstrate their contributions to organizational efficacy. His aim for HR departments is to enhance their capacity in HR management, achieving true professionalism and embodying the essence of a champion: an individual who ardently advocates, defends, or champions a belief or principle. These deductions, latent in the title, crystallize upon perusal of the preface.

Initiating with the contemporaneously debated inquiry of the era, "Should we do away with HR?" (Ulrich, 1997, vii), Ulrich rebuts this proposition, deeming it futile. He contends, "this is a silly question and a senseless debate. Of course we should do away with HR – if it fails to add value and impedes performance. Of course we should keep HR – if it creates value and delivers results. A more useful question, the question addressed in this book, is 'How can HR create value and deliver results?'" (Ulrich, 1997, vii). He posits a paradigm shift in HR conceptualization as imperative for addressing this inquiry.

Ulrich asserts that HR discourse has remained relatively static over the past four decades, centered on the conventional domains of HR activities: staffing, development, compensation, benefits, communication, organization design, high-performing teams, and the like (Ulrich, 1997, vii). Nevertheless, he acknowledges subtle evolution in HR practices toward innovation, utility, and refinement. Yet, he cautions against complacency, warning that such progression may jeopardize HR's raison d'être and its indispensability.

In the 1990s, HR predominantly bore the stigma of a cost center, preoccupied with routine processes and delineated responsibilities. Ulrich advocates for a radical metamorphosis within HR departments, advocating for a transition from a cost-centric, task-oriented entity to a catalyst for success. He emphasizes, "I want to focus less on what HR professionals do and more on what they deliver" (Ulrich,

1997, vii), championing an outcome-oriented perspective wherein delivery encompasses the tangible results and guarantees of HR endeavors.

To effectuate this transformation, Ulrich delineates four overarching outcomes: strategy execution, administrative efficiency, employee contribution, and capacity for change (Ulrich, 1997, vii). He advocates for a shift from mere task completion to result-oriented deliverables, challenging entrenched beliefs about HR professionals, practices, and departments. HR professionals must assume roles as partners, players, and pioneers, equipped with robust HR management competencies to inform strategic business decisions. A profound comprehension of HR practices and their alignment with both internal and external stakeholder needs is imperative for organizational success (Ulrich, 1997, viii).

Ulrich posits that success in these roles hinges on the visible delivery of value, vital for the perpetuation of HR management and its relevance (Ulrich, 1997, viii). Beyond HR's purview, he discerns its pivotal role in organizational triumph, a realization ahead of its time: "The issues with which HR professionals deal are at the heart of organizational success" (Ulrich, 1997, viii). Overcoming the prevailing perception of HR as solely concerned with administrative, transactional, and policy matters is paramount for its future viability. For the continuity of HR management, Ulrich advocates for the enhancement of capabilities and competencies among HR professionals. They must devise frameworks, ideas, and approaches oriented toward success contribution, supplanting bureaucratic norms with innovative, value-centric, and results-driven methodologies (Ulrich, 1997, ix).

In subsequent sections, Ulrich elucidates his overarching concept and objectives as articulated in the preface. A critical aspect is the collaboration between operational managers and HR practitioners to realize the objective of developing organizations that enhance value for stakeholders, including investors, clients, and employees (Ulrich, 1997, 1). Their collective efforts can architect a competitive enterprise poised for future success (Ulrich, 1997, 1). Central to this endeavor is the transformation of organizational capability into a wellspring of competitive advantage, a feat attainable through adept management by both line managers and HR professionals (Ulrich, 1997, 1). Ulrich delineates eight challenges confronting HR professionals that serve as catalysts for competitiveness (Ulrich, 1997, 1), wherein they can exhibit their indispensability and the imperative of close collaboration with line managers (Ulrich, 1997, 2). Conquering these challenges necessitates a paradigm shift in HR practices and roles, demanding innovative approaches to HR service delivery (Ulrich, 1997, 2). Ulrich underscores the pivotal role of HR management in embracing this developmental trajectory, affirming HR as the linchpin for addressing the eight challenges (Ulrich, 1997, 1). These challenges encompass globalization, optimization of the value chain for business competitiveness and HR services, profitability through cost management and growth, cultivation of organizational capabilities, navigating incessant change, leveraging technology, securing and leveraging competence and intellectual capital, and distinguishing turnaround from transformation (Ulrich, 1997, 2–15).

Ulrich extrapolates business ramifications stemming from surmounting these challenges. In the realm of competition, emphasis must be placed on bolstering organizational capabilities such as agility, responsiveness, relationship-building, and employee proficiency (Ulrich, 1997, 16). Regarding leadership, HR must persuade line managers of the substantive contribution of HR practices to organizational competitive advantage (Ulrich, 1997, 16). The bedrock for addressing the eight challenges lies in the implications for HR as a profession, advocating for a proactive approach centered on value creation and the cultivation of competitive organizations (Ulrich, 1997, 17).

Ulrich posits the feasibility of adapting HR practices to contemporary circumstances, delineating eight imperative actions. First, HR ought to cultivate methodologies enhancing employee competitiveness. Second, HR should synchronize theoretical frameworks with pragmatic applications grounded in robust comprehension. Third, HR must equip itself with tools to gauge the efficacy of HR interventions and correlate them with financial performance. Fourth, HR strategies must not merely aim at cost reduction but rather augment organizational worth by fostering intellectual capital. Fifth, HR is tasked with bolstering line management efforts in fostering employee dedication. Sixth, HR must view its endeavors as an evolutionary trajectory, openly communicated within the organization. Seventh, HR must adopt a stance that is both challenging and supportive in engagements with managerial HR. Eighth, HR must advocate for the recognition of its significance akin to finance and strategy, underscoring its pivotal role in organizational success (Ulrich, 1997, 18).

2.2 HR Reorientation and Roles of Business Partners

The evolution of HR necessitates a departure from existing roles and practices, requiring a redefinition of its functions. Ulrich elucidates that HR management must transcend prevailing perceptions of its role to realize its objectives. Moreover, a reorientation of HR's role is imperative to prioritize value creation and delivery. This necessitates a shift from operational to strategic, qualitative to quantitative, policing to partnering, short-term to long-term, administrative to consultative, functionally oriented to business oriented, internally focused to externally and customer-focused, reactive to proactive, and activity-focused to solutions-focused paradigms (Ulrich, 1997, 23). This metamorphosis entails that HR management must adeptly navigate both operational and strategic spheres within an increasingly complex business environment. Consequently, their responsibilities, challenges, and performance expectations become more intricate. To effectively generate value and yield outcomes, HR professionals must prioritize the delineation of deliverables and their attainment. They can achieve this by focusing on four dimensions: processes, people, operational (day-to-day) concerns, and strategic (future-oriented) considerations (Ulrich, 1997, 24).

Building upon this foundation, Ulrich devises a 2x2 matrix delineating four distinct HR roles crucial for fostering organizational competitiveness. These roles encompass the management of strategic HR, management of transformation and change, management of firm infrastructure, and management of employee contribution (Ulrich, 1997, 24).

	Future / Strategic focus	
Processes	Management of strategic Human Resources	Management of transformation and change	People
	Management of firm infrastructure	Management of employee contribution	
	Day-to-day / Operational focus	

Fig. 2-1: HR Roles in Building a Competitive Organization (Ulrich, 1997, 24)

The upper two roles, namely management of strategic HR and management of transformation and change, primarily center around prospective (strategic) elements. The former emphasizes processes in addition to this focus, whereas the latter prioritizes individuals. In contrast, management of firm infrastructure and management of employee contribution entail an operational (day-to-day) emphasis, with the former encompassing processes and the latter emphasizing individuals (Ulrich, 1997, 24). Ulrich's matrix design unequivocally illustrates that HR professionals are mandated to excel in both operational and strategic dimensions, along with adeptly managing processes and individuals. Ulrich delineates deliverables (outcomes), metaphors, and activities specific to each of these four roles, as outlined in the subsequent table (Ulrich, 1997, 25).

The metaphors represent the four functions of a Business Partner, collectively constituting the components of a Business Partner (Ulrich, 1997, 37). Consequently, the objectives and necessary actions of these four functions are subsequently delineated.

As depicted in the table above, the output of Business Partners in the capacity of strategic HR management is to foster and bolster strategy implementation. In this regard, HR management enhances organizational capabilities by engaging in the delineation of the business strategy process and facilitating the transition from strategy formulation to execution. Anchored in the business strategy, HR delineates priorities aimed at supporting the desired accomplishments. Effective execution necessitates organizational diagnosis, scrutinizing strengths and weaknesses (Ulrich, 1997, 26–27).

Tab. 1: Definition of HR Roles (Ulrich, 1997, 25)

Role/Cell	Deliverable/Outcome	Metaphor	Activity
Management of strategic Human Resources	Executing strategy	Strategic Partner	Aligning HR and business strategy: "Organizational diagnosis"
Management of firm infrastructure	Building an efficient infrastructure	Administrative Expert	Reengineering organization processes: "Shared services"
Management of employee contribution	Increasing employee commitment and capability	Employee Champion	Listening and responding to employees: "Providing resources to employees"
Management of transformation and change	Creating a renewed organization	Change Agent	Managing transformation and change: "Ensuring capacity for change"

The output of Business Partners in the realm of firm infrastructure management is to construct an efficient infrastructure. HR Professionals are tasked with devising streamlined processes across all domains of HR management, harmonizing them with the organizational infrastructure. In this capacity, Business Partners strive to enhance administrative efficiency through ongoing reengineering of administrative workflows. Optimization and refinement of HR and business processes are imperative for contributing to organizational triumph (Ulrich, 1997, 27–28).

The output of Business Partners in the domain of employee contribution management is to enhance employee dedication and proficiency. Given the criticality of intellectual capital as a strategic driver of success, HR professionals are mandated to nurture human capital and correlate employee contribution with organizational success. Even at this nascent stage of human capital scarcity, Ulrich recognized the imperative of establishing stronger links between human capital considerations and thus HR development as pivotal for organizational sustainability. This is manifest in the Business Partner's mandate to persuade line managers of the significant importance of employee training and development. Additionally, Ulrich already incorporates evolving competency requirements at the embryonic stage of his model (Ulrich, 1997, 28–30). Given the markedly adverse trajectory of human capital availability, as subsequently expounded, HR development aspects are assuming greater significance and therefore should be integrated into each Business Partner function.

The output of Business Partners in the domain of transformation and change management is to effectuate organizational renewal. HR management professionals identify the imperative for change and devise implementation strategies accordingly. In this capacity, it is crucial to engage in value discussions to ascertain requisite adjustments for sustaining competitiveness. Effectively managing change is pivotal for HR professionals, necessitating an understanding of critical change processes, the ability to garner commitment, and the facilitation of intended changes to fruition, thereby contributing to organizational success amidst altered circumstances (Ulrich, 1997, 30–31).

Ulrich, in addition to delineating the four prescribed roles, also encompasses the tasks and challenges confronting HR professionals in their endeavor to facilitate and augment organizational triumph. Their duties encompass evaluating the prevailing efficacy of the HR function, scrutinizing its evolutionary trajectory, juxtaposing the perspectives of HR and line managers regarding the function, which encapsulates both alignment and disparities in expectations, distinguishing between the function itself and the individual competencies of HR professionals to leverage the department's capabilities and foster a cohesive vision, and delineating clear-cut responsibilities for each role (Ulrich, 1997, 38–42).

Ulrich posits that HR professionals must effectively discharge the four roles to optimize their organizational contributions. However, he acknowledges the presence of paradoxes inherent in these roles, which HR professionals must navigate adeptly. In their capacity as Strategic Partners, Business Partners collaborate with managerial echelons, thereby assuming an integrated aspect of management. Simultaneously, in their role as Employee Champions, they advocate for employee needs, forwarding them to management. Despite the potential for conflict and paradoxical scenarios, Ulrich contends that representing employee interests, executing management directives, articulating the voices of both employees and management, and fostering a partnership between them are feasible (Ulrich, 1997, 45).

Ulrich identifies another paradox, wherein HR professionals are tasked with reconciling the imperative for change, innovation, and transformation with the necessity for continuity, discipline, and stability (Ulrich, 1997, 46). The envisaged evolution of HR professionals towards a heightened emphasis on delivering value and enhancing organizational success necessitates responsive actions from both line managers and HR professionals. Line managers must:

- "Define the desired and feasible deliverables from HR activities.
  - Operationalize, measure, and communicate the value created by HR.
  - Define who has what responsibility and accountability for HR activities." (Ulrich, 1997, 48)
- HR, however, "must accomplish the following goals:
  - Stop *talking* about being a business partner and *do* it.
  - Define business partner in terms of value created for the business.
  - Profile accurately – with the participation of their clients – the current and the desired quality of their deliverables." (Ulrich, 1997, 48)

Ulrich delineates in meticulous detail the procedures Business Partners can undertake for each of the four designated roles. The prescribed methodologies, essential tasks, and objectives for advancement in each role shall be subsequently elucidated.

2.3 The Role and Challenges of Strategic Partners

Ulrich posits that the attainment of strategic partnership necessitates the manifestation of both fortitude and discipline, in addition to surmounting five distinct challenges:

1. Avoid strategic Plans on Top Shelf (SPOTS).
2. Create a Balanced Scorecard.
3. Align HR Plans to Business Plans.
4. Watch out for quick fixes.
5. Create a capability focus within the firm (Ulrich, 1997, 56).

Challenge one: Ulrich emphasizes that there is a significant disparity between aspirations and execution in the domains of vision, mission, and goals. HR professionals must prioritize the translation of aspirations into actionable plans to engage in the requisite organizational processes and contribute to organizational success. This is optimally achieved through the integration of HR concerns into strategic planning, preempting the exclusive determination of strategy by others (Ulrich, 1997, 56–57).

Challenge two: In crafting a Balanced Scorecard (BSC), Strategic Partners ought to hold themselves to the same standards of accountability as other managerial counterparts by instituting such a system. By employing an economic value-added (EVA), customer value-added (CVA), and people value-added (PVA) framework, HR professionals lay the groundwork for exerting intellectual leadership within the realm of employee management (Ulrich, 1997, 58).

Challenge three: Strategic Partners must vigorously strive to align HR plans with business strategies, endeavoring to secure inclusion and recognition in the business planning process rather than being relegated to a post hoc role. HR considerations should be integrated into the business strategy formulation, ensuring their acknowledgment and incorporation. It is imperative for HR professionals to drive this evolution to add value and elevate the visibility of HR issues in strategy formulation. Through this proactive approach, HR professionals collaborate with line managers to identify HR practices that align with business strategy (Ulrich, 1997, 59–60).

Challenge four: Vigilance against quick fixes is paramount, necessitating HR professionals to acknowledge that progress requires both time and dedication. While short-term solutions may yield immediate benefits, they can impede long-term growth. In the realm of long-term Strategic Partnering, benchmarks must be established and pursued to identify organizational practices, principles, and initiatives conducive to developing effective tools for fostering long-term organizational success (Ulrich, 1997, 60–63).

Challenge five: In fostering a capability-focused culture within the organization, the cultivation of core competencies and capabilities is crucial, enabling the company to execute and fulfill its strategic objectives. The development of these competencies necessitates a deliberate derivation of HR activities aimed at acquiring the requisite skills (Ulrich, 1997, 63–66).

Ulrich underscores that organizational management views the following aspects as pivotal in overcoming the aforementioned challenges in the role of a Strategic Partner:

- "Participation in the *hoshin* (business planning) process.
- Understanding of business issues.
- Participation in business task forces [...].
- Fostering systems thinking. Ensuring program management of workforce planning, skills assessment, succession planning, retraining, and diversity.
- Providing support to group-wide or sector initiatives.
- Championing the company way and management practices." (Ulrich, 1997, 66)

Ulrich posits that the transition from strategy formulation to implementation hinges upon organizational diagnosis, thereby necessitating the capacity to evaluate and subsequently harmonize practices with business objectives. This process entails organizational audits focused on discerning strengths and weaknesses (Ulrich, 1997, 66–67). Ulrich delineates four steps essential for successful auditing.

Firstly, he emphasizes the definition of an organizational architecture, encompassing the design, integration, and operation of systems, which constitutes the core of effective organizations (Ulrich, 1997, 67). This entails establishing the organizational system and processes as the foundational element. While strategy intent and organizational capabilities delineate the organizational trajectory, Ulrich outlines six factors crucial for delineating "how organizations function and identifying systems requiring modification to achieve strategic objectives" (Ulrich, 1997, 68). These factors include shared mindset, competence, consequences, governance, work processes/capacity for change, and leadership (Ulrich, 1997, 68).

Secondly, the auditing process entails developing an assessment mechanism primarily directed at evaluating the identified architectural factors to discern strengths and weaknesses (Ulrich, 1997, 72).

Thirdly, in guiding improvement endeavors, HR professionals are tasked with recommending areas of enhancement for all six aforementioned organizational factors. The objective is to propose, devise, and deliberate upon optimal practices conducive to organizational success (Ulrich, 1997, 75).

Fourthly, and finally, setting priorities is imperative. Acknowledging the inability to address all facets simultaneously is crucial for devising a viable improvement process. HR professionals must consider both impact, involving the alignment of HR practices with strategic realization and customer focus, and implementability, encompassing resource availability and time constraints for HR practice adjustments (Ulrich, 1997, 77–78).

2.4 Challenges and Responsibilities for Becoming an Administrative Expert

In Ulrich's initial model, Business Partners assume a secondary function characterized as the Administrative Expert. This designation connotes the establishment of a streamlined administrative infrastructure for both HR processes and broader business operations, as delineated by Ulrich (1997, 83). Within these domains, Ulrich posits that HR professionals possess the capacity to contribute significant value. Achieving success in this role mandates the application of business reengineering principles through a structured six-step methodology. It is imperative to:

1. "Define the target processes.
2. Develop 'as is' models.
3. Challenge underlying assumptions.
4. Develop 'should be' models.
5. Implement, roll out, market.
6. Measure business impact." (Ulrich, 1997, 88)

Moreover, it is imperative for HR professionals to reassess the process of HR value creation, transcending mere conceptualization and adopting scientific methodologies for HR work accomplishment, as emphasized by Ulrich (1997, 89). In navigating the centralization versus decentralization quandary, HR professionals must discern the optimal administrative organizational structure. Ulrich outlines various organizational paradigms, including corporate centers, brokers of service, service centers, centers of expertise, and integrated solutions (Ulrich, 1997, 89–105). Additionally, HR professionals are mandated to construct a framework concentrating on value creation and delivery modalities, wherein the perception of value from the receiver's standpoint is pivotal (Ulrich, 1997, 89–95).

Following the delineation of the initial two tasks, a value creation process must be extrapolated, with customer requisites occupying a central position as value is delineated by customers (Ulrich, 1997, 106). To achieve optimization, the wants and needs of customers – both line managers and employees – must be diagnosed, followed by the development of delivery mechanisms (Ulrich, 1997, 108). By adopting this approach and engaging customers in defining essential deliverables, a perceived state of value creation can be attained, augmenting credibility (Ulrich, 1997, 110–111). Subsequently, the definition of metrics becomes imperative to establish a foundation for evaluating success, encompassing perceived customer value, cost of HR services, and cycle time for HR services (Ulrich, 1997, 117).

In their capacity as Administrative Experts, HR professionals must remain cognizant of their responsibility to maintain a professionally adept administrative framework, focused on efficacy through appropriate organizational design and efficient processes, thereby ultimately contributing to business success (Ulrich, 1997, 119).

2.5 Challenges and Responsibilities for Becoming an Employee Champion

In Ulrich's original model, the third function of Business Partners is designated as the role of the Employee Champion. According to Ulrich, the pivotal elements of organizational success and commitment lie in the contributions made by each employee. Ulrich identifies a significant challenge, wherein the imperative to enhance output while minimizing HR input underscores the criticality of employee contribution to business operations (Ulrich, 1997, 125). Although Ulrich does not overtly reference talent scarcity at this juncture, HR professionals are pivotal in nurturing the bond between employees and the organization, thereby ensuring sustained high levels of contribution (Ulrich, 1997, 126). To succeed in this endeavor, HR professionals must establish priorities and concentrate on a select few critical activities (Ulrich, 1997, 132).

Early in the model's development, Ulrich underscores the significance of aspects related to work-life balance, noting that project and work commitment, along with challenging tasks, corporate culture, and teamwork, exert substantial influence on goal attainment (Ulrich, 1997, 136–139). Furthermore, Ulrich highlights compensation, communication, individual and procedural fairness, information technology, and competency development through training as key drivers of employee contribution (Ulrich, 1997, 140–145). Ulrich advocates for employee involvement in key decision-making processes, citing its positive impact on fostering commitment and leveraging employee knowledge and emotions to enhance overall performance (Ulrich, 1997, 147).

2.6 Challenges and Responsibilities for Becoming a Change Agent

In Ulrich's initial model, the fourth and ultimate function of Business Partners pertains to their role as Change Agents. This role is necessitated by factors such as globalization, evolving customer demands, technological advancements, and enhanced information accessibility, all of which elevate the tempo at which change is mandated. HR professionals are tasked with facilitating adaptations in HR frameworks by instigating the introduction of novel programs, projects, and procedures (Ulrich, 1997, 151). These adaptations, stemming from strategic planning endeavors, necessitate identification and subsequent implementation. Furthermore, alterations in processes are imperative, with occasional requisites for cultural shifts as companies undergo reconceptualization of their operational paradigms. Amidst the array of change initiatives delineated, HR professionals play a pivotal role in fortifying organizational capabilities, ensuring that initiatives are delineated, developed, and executed punctually (Ulrich, 1997, 152).

The primary challenges faced by HR professionals and change management practitioners revolve around the inability to meet expectations and the failure to execute change initiatives effectively (Ulrich, 1997, 156–157). These challenges are pivotal in understanding the dynamics of change management programs, necessitating HR professionals to cultivate a capacity for change. To address this, Ulrich proposed a framework comprising four developmental stages. The initial stage involves identifying the critical success factors essential for fostering change capacity. This includes activities such as leading change, fostering a shared need, articulating a vision, mobilizing commitment, restructuring systems, monitoring progress, and ensuring sustainability (Ulrich, 1997, 158–159). In addition to acquiring knowledge about change management principles, success hinges on the adeptness to incorporate these critical factors into actionable plans, thereby facilitating business transformation (Ulrich, 1997, 158–159).

The subsequent stage entails assessing the management of these success factors, effectively translating theoretical knowledge into practical managerial tools (Ulrich, 1997, 159). Ulrich advocates for the regular evaluation of each success factor, emphasizing its profound influence on goal achievement. While HR professionals may not directly execute change initiatives, they play a pivotal role in ensuring their realization (Ulrich, 1997, 161).

The third stage involves identifying improvement activities tailored to each success factor. Following the initial assessments, it becomes imperative to gauge the contribution of these activities to performance enhancement, thereby bolstering the implementation of action plans and facilitating the realization of change objectives (Ulrich, 1997, 165–166).

Finally, the fourth and concluding stage underscores the iterative nature of the seven key success factors, emphasizing the importance of continual attention to these factors. Regular progress reviews are strongly recommended to ensure sustained advancement (Ulrich, 1997, 166–168).

Ulrich encounters a formidable challenge in navigating the realm of cultural transformation, wherein the adjustment of values, beliefs, and assumptions is paramount (Ulrich, 1997, 168). Organizational culture, historically deemed a pivotal determinant of success, has transcended its former status as non-imitable (Ulrich, 1997, 168). Ulrich delineates five strategic steps for HR professionals to navigate successful cultural metamorphosis (Ulrich, 1997, 168).

The initial step necessitates the definition and elucidation of the culture change concept, entailing a comprehensive grasp of organizational culture encompassing workflow dynamics, communication modalities, information dissemination, decision-making processes, authority allocation, and HR dynamics. Additionally, an analysis of employee attitudes is imperative to ascertain the prevailing shared mindset and extant organizational culture (Ulrich, 1997, 169–170).

The second phase involves articulating the centrality of culture change to business triumph, predicated on the premise of culture's profound influence on business performance (Ulrich, 1997, 171). Corporate culture profoundly influences employee performance by directing their focus and delineating expected boundaries of conduct (Ulrich, 1997, 176). Moreover, corporate culture significantly impacts external relationships, underscoring the imperative of aligning corporate culture with business imperatives (Ulrich, 1997, 177).

The third step entails devising a framework for evaluating the current culture, envisioning the desired future culture, and discerning the disparity between the two. This necessitates clarifying customer perceptions of the company's identity and reputation, alongside aligning employee and customer expectations (Ulrich, 1997, 178).

In the fourth stage, alternative methodologies for fostering cultural transformation must be identified. Ulrich delineates top-down directive, side-to-side reengineering processes, and bottom-up empowerment as viable approaches for culture creation (Ulrich, 1997, 178–182).

The fifth and final step mandates crafting an integrated action plan incorporating diverse strategies for cultural metamorphosis. Ulrich underscores the rarity and ineffectiveness of singular approaches, emphasizing the pivotal role of HR professionals in orchestrating value-added cultural change initiatives (Ulrich, 1997, 183–184). Effective execution hinges on HR professionals assuming multifaceted roles as catalysts, champions, sponsors, facilitators, designers, and demonstrators of change (Ulrich, 1997, 184–187).

2.7 The Challenge and Necessity for Self-Improvement Approaches and Development

Ulrich underscores the imperative of innovating HR practices for achieving success. His framework posits the necessity for diverse competencies and a paradigm shift in HR management (Ulrich, 1997, 189). To engender value and impact, Ulrich advocates for the establishment of a strategic vision for the HR domain and the structuring of an HR entity primed to execute strategic objectives, thus engendering an iterative process termed "HR for HR" (Ulrich, 1997, 189). Ulrich elucidates that strategic HR aligns HR practices with business strategies, facilitating the translation of business objectives into organizational capabilities (Ulrich, 1997, 189). Conversely, HR strategy delineates the agenda for HR operations, encompassing its vision, mission, and strategic priorities (Ulrich, 1997, 190). Ultimately, the HR organization assumes the role of diagnostician and facilitator, enhancing HR functions to deliver proficient services (Ulrich, 1997, 190). Interconnectedness pervades the triumvirate of strategic HR, HR strategy, and HR organization, ideally evolving sequentially in their conceptualization, design, and execution. Variations in competencies, organizational contexts, overarching strategies, and HR department maturity stages may necessitate adjustments in one realm, exerting substantial influence on the others (Ulrich, 1997, 190).

HR professionals must recognize that strategy formulation delineates the prospective trajectory of the business (vision) and serves as the mechanism for resource allocation. The strategic HR function is tasked with ensuring the comprehensive integration of all strategies and the development of explicit plans for their realization.

The precise delineation and characterization of critical organizational capabilities stand as pivotal elements for achieving success (Ulrich, 1997, 192–193). Within the domain of HR, the defined value to be generated and the resultant deliverables must be actualized. These elements are previously expounded upon in the HR strategy, which also encompasses priority establishment and resource allocation (Ulrich, 1997, 195–196).

A fundamental prerequisite for HR organizational success lies in HR professionals' ability to employ the organizational diagnosis process, as delineated above, within their own department. This constitutes a fundamental requirement for aligning HR with the HR function (Ulrich, 1997, 212).

Ulrich emphasizes that HR management should prioritize the assessment of future developmental potential and factors conducive to value addition and outcomes. According to Ulrich (1997, 231), HR management harbors significant potential in enhancing competitiveness. He posits that pivotal elements for sustaining competitiveness include the organization itself, core competencies, HR, their knowledge and learning capabilities, as well as organizational culture and values. Ulrich asserts that HR, HR practices, and particularly the alignment of HR with business strategy are paramount (Ulrich, 1997, 232). Business Partners are tasked with crafting organizational frameworks that ensure a focus on people, processes, and practices from the standpoint of value creation and results delivery (Ulrich, 1997, 233).

In his seminal work on Business Partnering, Ulrich underscores the pivotal role of HR in enhancing organizational efficacy and competitiveness. Consequently, Business Partners are tasked with assuming the mantle of HR advocates, compelling line managers to similarly invest in this domain. This collective responsibility entails the translation of strategic directives into actionable initiatives, prioritizing outcomes over mere procedural adherence (Ulrich, 1997, 234–235).

This necessitates that line managers cultivate a profound comprehension of organizational capacity and its ramifications for competitive advantage (Ulrich, 1997, 236). Through a symbiotic process, line managers and Business Partners are tasked with forging a collaborative framework wherein knowledge dissemination is prioritized, fostering a collective effort towards achieving tangible outcomes. For Business Partners, this entails proficiency in HR theory, practical application, and conceptual acumen, facilitating heightened efficacy and fostering the requisite rapport, endorsement, and collaboration with line managers. According to Ulrich,

2.7 The Challenge and Necessity for Self-Improvement Approaches and Development

this represents the inaugural challenge for Business Partners seeking to assume the role he prescribes.

The subsequent challenge involves the ongoing evolution of the HR management process. Ulrich emphasizes the imperative to enhance HR competencies in fundamental domains, including executive development, recruitment and placement, training and development, reward systems, performance appraisal, employee relations, labor relations, and diversity initiatives (Ulrich, 1997, 240). This evolution aims to yield benefits for employees. Employees ought to recognize that the endeavors of Business Partners and line managers are synchronized and bolster their capacity for adaptation to meet customer demands, ensuring that all efforts are concentrated on enhancing customer value (Ulrich, 1997, 245).

From this premise, challenges three to seven arise, encompassing HR capabilities, HR value proposition, HR governance, HR careers, and HR competencies. These factors must achieve alignment to foster business acumen, optimize HR delivery, and facilitate adept management of change processes.

Business acumen stands as a fundamental cornerstone, serving as the bedrock for harmonizing HR functions with organizational dynamics amid shifting business landscapes. It empowers Business Partners to meaningfully engage in strategic dialogues and spearhead change initiatives proficiently.

The efficacy of HR practices, discerned by line managers, substantiates perceived competence, thereby enhancing the likelihood of collaborative partnerships. This effect is particularly pronounced when the design and execution prowess of HR systems are deemed equally efficacious.

Given the accelerated pace of business transformation, adept change management capabilities assume heightened significance. These capabilities are indispensable for driving business evolution while factoring in HR dynamics and ensuring organizational coherence.

Collectively, these facets contribute to cultivating and perpetuating the personal credibility of Business Partners. Credibility serves as a pivotal cornerstone for the effective evolution of Business Partners, thereby underpinning the delivery of outcomes and the generation of value. Ulrich emphasizes the imperative for Business Partners to prioritize their development in the forthcoming period (Ulrich, 1997, 245–254).

3 The First Adjustment to the Initial Model – the HR Value Proposition

3.1 The Theory of HR Value and Its Creation

Drawing upon their seminal work of 1997, Dave Ulrich and Wayne Brockbank initiated the first modifications to the foundational model of Business Partnering in the year 2005. Evident from the title of their publication, "The HR Value Proposition," the adapted model distinctly centers on value provision. The imperative of Business Partnering lies in the assurance of value generation for stakeholders including investors, customers, line managers, and employees, through a focus on personal competencies and outcome orientation (Ulrich & Brockbank, 2005, x). The objective of their publication is to furnish HR professionals with an integrated methodology to achieve sustainable value creation (Ulrich & Brockbank, 2005, x).

Drawing from their observations of prior developments, Ulrich and Brockbank underscored the imperative of advancing Business Partner evolution to enhance alignment with organizational strategies (Ulrich & Brockbank, 2005, 1). The focal point for Business Partners must intensify on the perceived value delivered to stakeholders. In their discourse, Ulrich and Brockbank hinted at the growing scarcity of resources, though specifics were absent at that juncture. Notably, there was no mention of shortages in talent or employees, either in quantitative or qualitative terms, leading to the inference of a broader resource challenge identified by Ulrich and Brockbank at that time. Early on and with precision, Ulrich and Brockbank highlighted that emphasizing value delivery and results orientation would not only benefit the organization but also catalyze the development potential of Business Partners. By demonstrating perceived value through their actions, HR professionals and Business Partners enhance their credibility, garner respect, and wield influence (Ulrich & Brockbank, 2005, 2). To catalyze the envisaged developmental trajectory, Business Partners must instigate an HR transformation aimed at reshaping the HR role, value proposition, and results orientation. The evolution of HR management, particularly the delineated evolution of Business Partnering, necessitates the allocation of financial resources, which HR and Business Partners must secure. Securing these resources is contingent upon Business Partners persuading stakeholders of the benefits of such investments, a likelihood bolstered by improvements in stakeholder welfare and development (Ulrich & Brockbank, 2005, 2). Ulrich and Brockbank advocate for the integration and alignment of diverse HR activities, emphasizing the compulsory shift toward a new agenda. Central to this agenda is the definition of HR value (Ulrich & Brockbank, 2005, 3). They assert that since value is ascribed by recipients rather than providers, any value proposition must prioritize the perspectives of recipients (Ulrich & Brockbank, 2005, 4). The HR transformation necessitated by this revised value proposition engenders six critical implications for HR professionals, according to Ulrich and Brockbank (Ulrich & Brockbank, 2005, 4).

Primarily, this suggests that HR and Business Partners comprehend the aspirations of various stakeholders. Business Partners and thus HR's endeavors must adopt an alternative viewpoint. It is not about their perceived benefits but rather what others deem advantageous. HR's activities and initiatives commence with a business-centric approach. Consequently, Business Partners must intimately grasp business operations and tailor their initiatives accordingly. Embracing this perspective shift necessitates Business Partners to align activities with stakeholders' interests and benefits (Ulrich & Brockbank, 2005, 4–5).

Secondly, Ulrich and Brockbank underscore the paramount importance of considering the ultimate beneficiaries of business endeavors: the customers served by the company. In addition to attaining a profound understanding of internal customers, Business Partners must also enhance their comprehension of external customers to facilitate value creation and results orientation aligning with human and organizational capabilities according to customer and market demand (Ulrich & Brockbank, 2005, 5).

Thirdly, HR professionals must forge a competitive advantage for their organization by focusing on perceived value and delivering commensurate results. This directly ties to the fourth aspect, which is aligning HR programs and activities with the demands and expectations of both internal and external customers (Ulrich & Brockbank, 2005, 6).

Fourthly, HR professionals must equip themselves with the knowledge, skills, and experience to correlate HR programs and activities with perceived stakeholder value. However, this can only materialize if HR professionals cultivate an extensive understanding of internal and external customers and stakeholders, shareholders, business strategy, and the latest developments in HR processes. Only then can HR professionals derive implications for their initiatives and align them with organizational strategy and objectives (Ulrich & Brockbank, 2005, 7).

Sixthly, HR professionals can only secure financial resources from organizational management if they demonstrably add substantial value through their programs and activities, as outlined in the fifth aspect. They must be recognized as distinctive and influential in their contributions to stakeholders (Ulrich & Brockbank, 2005, 8).

Similar to other departments, an HR department must substantiate their value addition through actions, programs, and activities while also comprehending and bolstering value creation across other departments. Uniqueness is attained by establishing and fostering a link between business objectives and employee commitment, customer perceptions, and investor expectations. Through this, HR

3 The First Adjustment to the Initial Model – the HR Value Proposition

professionals bridge the gap between management and employees and contribute to aligning customer and investor anticipations (Ulrich & Brockbank, 2005, 8).

By cultivating their distinctive and influential perspective, HR professionals significantly enhance value addition and focus on delivering results by integrating aspects that other departments may overlook. This development necessitates HR professionals to ensure they are heard and can substantiate value creation and results orientation by understanding which HR and organizational capabilities are essential for meeting customers' demands in terms of quantity and quality of products and services (Ulrich & Brockbank, 2005, 8-9). Ultimately, this underscores that discussions with managers should revolve around how value can be efficiently created and acquired from HR services. To adopt a proactive stance, HR professionals must possess superior knowledge about how they can add value for investors, customers, managers, and employees alike. Ulrich and Brockbank conclude that these six aspects are fundamental for ensuring the development potential and the trajectory of HR professionals' progress (Ulrich & Brockbank, 2005, 18).

Ulrich and Brockbank delineate five domains for the HR value proposition. These encompass knowing external business realities, serving external and internal stakeholders, crafting HR practices focusing on people, performance, information and work on the one hand, and HR strategy and organization on the other, while also ensuring HR professionalism (Ulrich & Brockbank, 2005, 10). These five facets of HR transformation serve as the foundation for this book and the requisite adjustments to the initial model. The subsequent figure illustrates the five aspects of the HR value proposition.

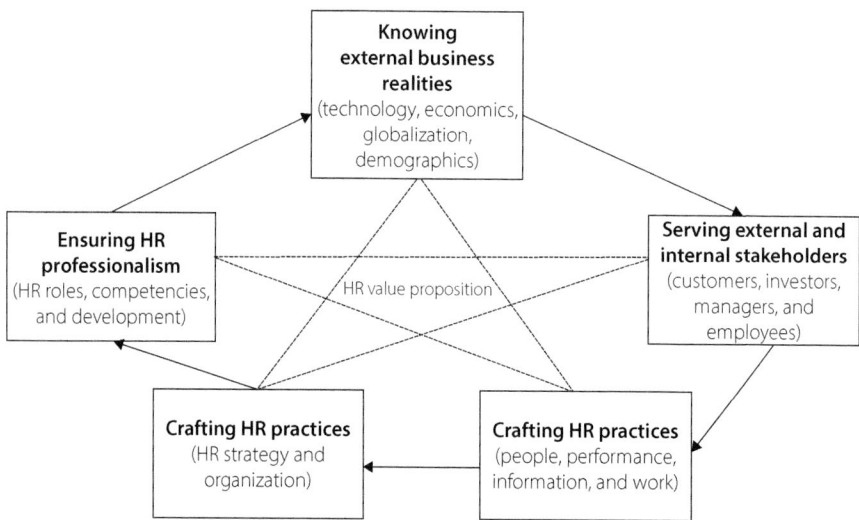

Fig. 3-1: The HR Value Proposition (Ulrich & Brockbank, 2005, 10)

3.2 The Consideration of the Business Environment

In the realm of external business dynamics, Business Partners are tasked with ensuring and facilitating support in key areas deemed critical by stakeholders. This objective, however, can solely be realized by Business Partners upon attaining credibility and advanced comprehension across four pivotal trend domains. These encompass technological advancements, economic and regulatory landscapes, workforce demographics, and the phenomenon of globalization, which significantly influences the former three realms (Ulrich & Brockbank, 2005, 21).

Within the domain of technology, HR professionals are mandated to conduct an in-depth analysis of technological progress and its applicability in enhancing business processes, thus maintaining a competitive edge (Ulrich & Brockbank, 2005, 22). Essential factors to assess include velocity, efficacy, connectivity, and customization, as they profoundly impact operational processes and workflows (Ulrich & Brockbank, 2005, 23).

In the domain of economic and regulatory affairs, HR professionals engage in a systematic analysis of the organizational milieu, thereby elucidating the contextual framework within which the organization operates. Early detection and proactive preparation for both ongoing and prospective alterations are imperative, providing the foundational groundwork for timely adjustments, thereby satisfying the expectations of clientele, stakeholders, executives, and staff (Ulrich & Brockbank, 2005, 27). Ulrich and Brockbank underscore the significance of various factors such as workforce quality, flexibility, investment, health, escalating wage differentials, productivity enhancement, and long-term economic sanguinity in their assessment. Particularly noteworthy is the relatively limited prevalence of the enumerated HR facets during that period. The authors include topics that subsequently emerge as pivotal aspects (Ulrich & Brockbank, 2005, 28-29). They further expound on the pertinence of economic considerations in the context of globalization, which proffers abundant opportunities owing to the concomitant deregulatory trends, while simultaneously posing formidable challenges (Ulrich & Brockbank, 2005, 30-32). Ulrich and Brockbank posit that a comprehensive comprehension of prevailing and prospective economic and regulatory landscapes forms the bedrock for augmenting strategic deliberations and evolution, and for aligning HR strategies, practices, endeavors, and initiatives therewith in a timely, precise, and efficient manner (Ulrich & Brockbank, 2005, 34).

Ulrich and Brockbank underscore the significance of HR assets, as evidenced by their inclusion of workforce demographics alongside previously outlined HR dimensions within the technological domain. The authors prognosticate a forthcoming decline in workforce availability, along with ensuing challenges (Ulrich & Brockbank, 2005, 36). Specifically delineated are trends such as the advancing age of the workforce, shifting gender distributions, escalating ethnic heterogeneity, and declining economic welfare within families (Ulrich & Brockbank, 2005, 36-40).

Ulrich and Brockbank assert that globalization exerts an influence on workforce dynamics, as evidenced by the proliferation of globally oriented enterprises and a more internationally diverse workforce, a trend expected to persist (Ulrich & Brockbank, 2005, 40–41). HR practitioners must meticulously evaluate these trends and advancements in workforce dynamics to effectively integrate them into strategic workforce planning, thereby enhancing value in strategic deliberations.

A primary hurdle for HR professionals lies in comprehensively assessing both direct impacts on employees and indirect ramifications on and contributions from customers, shareholders, management, and employees. Armed with this foundational understanding, HR professionals empower themselves to harmonize HR strategies, activities, programs, practices, and interventions in a timely, precise, and efficacious manner (Ulrich & Brockbank, 2005, 43).

3.3   The Consideration of External Stakeholders

The secondary aspect of HR value proposition pertains to interactions with external stakeholders. HR strategies, endeavors, undertakings, and schemes should primarily concentrate on generating value and prioritizing outcomes to contribute to and attain a sustainable competitive advantage (Ulrich & Brockbank, 2005, 45). Adapting to (the perceived) stakeholder value necessitates that every HR operation transcends compartmentalized thinking and harmonizes internal organizational dynamics with external occurrences (Ulrich & Brockbank, 2005, 46). Ultimately, it is imperative for HR practitioners to be evaluated and assessed based on the effects and achievements they generate for external stakeholders, taking into account the business milieu and its evolution (Ulrich & Brockbank, 2005, 46).

For management investing in the HR department, allocating financial resources represents an essential avenue for enhancing opportunities and potential within an organization. Similarly, investors, through the provision of financial resources, significantly influence shareholder value, a pivotal metric in corporate evaluation. HR professionals and departments are tasked with ensuring the judicious allocation of investments and resources, a task accomplished by demonstrating their contribution to value creation. This demonstration hinges on the strategic alignment of HR activities with stakeholder interests, as highlighted by Ulrich and Brockbank (2005, 46).

Ulrich and Brockbank delineate six crucial actions for HR professionals, beginning with fostering investor literacy and understanding the significance of intangible assets. Subsequently, HR activities should be tailored to enhance intangible value and underscore its relevance to shareholder returns. Intangible audits, designed to evaluate and measure intangible assets, further cement the link between HR actions and organizational value creation (2005, 46–47).

The growing importance of intangible assets, forecasted by Ulrich and Brockbank in 2005, underscores the need for HR practices to contribute to organizational capability. This capability, rooted in intangible resources, defines a company's potential to leverage its assets effectively and align its actions with strategic objectives. HR practices play a pivotal role in nurturing organizational learning, trust, and cooperation, thus augmenting human capital and facilitating processes beneficial to external stakeholders (Ulrich & Brockbank, 2005, 48–49).

By shifting focus from mere quality improvement to quantifiable shareholder value, leaders are empowered to delve deeper into the impact of HR practices on organizational performance (Ulrich & Brockbank, 2005, 50–52). Building upon this foundation, HR professionals can adopt an investor-centric approach in formulating and executing HR strategies, thereby addressing core business concerns more effectively (Ulrich & Brockbank, 2005, 56–57).

In addition to catering to internal stakeholders, HR practices must also align with customer perspectives, particularly concerning value propositions. This customer-centric approach ensures that HR initiatives resonate with purchasing motivations and contribute directly to organizational success (Ulrich & Brockbank, 2005, 60–68).

3.4 The Consideration of Internal Stakeholders

In the realm of internal stakeholders, Ulrich and Brockbank emphasize the imperative for HR professionals to enhance the capability and aptitude of said stakeholders (Ulrich & Brockbank, 2005, 69). Within this domain, Ulrich and Brockbank postulate an increasing frequency of HR professionals' communication with line managers concerning strategies for business leaders to achieve desired objectives and outcomes. Four distinct methodologies are delineated through which HR professionals can augment value generation. Primarily, misconceptions regarding HR's purview must be rectified. Secondly, the cultivation of trust-based relationships is essential. Thirdly, an emphasis on tangible deliverables is paramount. Fourthly and lastly, a prioritization of capabilities is mandated, encompassing the formulation of an action plan designed to yield desired results (Ulrich & Brockbank, 2005, 70). Line managers must be notably persuaded of HR's centrality to their success and disabused of the notion that HR bears sole responsibility for HR-related activities and outcomes. For HR professionals, the dual obligation and challenge persist in demonstrating that their initiatives, programs, and support engender favorable behavioral shifts in practical contexts, thereby exerting tangible influence on attained outcomes (Ulrich & Brockbank, 2005, 71–73). Trust and trustful cooperation, alongside teamwork, exert a pivotal influence on the outcomes attained within organizational settings.

To enhance the integration of HR aspects within the purview of line managers' responsibilities and to facilitate the alignment of HR initiatives with both internal and external stakeholders, it is imperative for HR professionals to adeptly employ the language, logic, and conceptual framework inherent to business operations. HR practitioners must cultivate their proficiency in this domain to furnish recommendations that effectively aid line managers in accomplishing their objectives. Additionally, HR professionals need to equip themselves with the capacity to discern the requisite competencies of line managers necessary for the realization of organizational goals and strategic imperatives (Ulrich & Brockbank, 2005, 73–75). As posited by Ulrich and Brockbank, "capabilities assist line managers in strategy execution, investors in garnering intangible value, customers in sustaining connectivity, and employees in fostering engagement" (Ulrich & Brockbank, 2005, 75).

To ensure a perpetually efficient workflow, HR professionals must possess the acumen to comprehend the essential competencies indispensable for achieving business objectives. Subsequently, prioritization becomes indispensable, with precedence accorded to the development of the most crucial capabilities foremost. This process entails four sequential steps: delineating the objectives of capability, making decisions conducive to enhancing capability, executing actions that fortify capability, and establishing metrics to monitor capability. Furthermore, for augmenting organizational effectiveness, HR professionals must orchestrate strategic coherence, thereby fostering alignment among disparate departments and resource allocations (Ulrich & Brockbank, 2005, 80–81).

In the realm of HR, it is imperative that professionals develop a comprehensive value proposition tailored to employees, thereby acknowledging the human dimension within HR. This necessitates fostering a sense of appreciation and significance among employees, emphasizing their contribution to the organizational fabric. Such objectives are optimally realized through the delineation of clearly articulated standards and expectations, underpinned by an employee value proposition (EVP). Conceptually, EVP encompasses a spectrum of elements including visionary outlooks, opportunities for growth, incentivization mechanisms, demonstrable impacts, communal engagement, effective communication channels, and avenues for experimental initiatives (Ulrich & Brockbank, 2005, 82–83).

Moreover, HR professionals must actively advocate for the interests of employees to cultivate trust and foster perceptions of visibility and approachability. When coupled with the imperative of ensuring equitable treatment for all staff members, these efforts yield substantial benefits for organizational cohesion and employee satisfaction (Ulrich & Brockbank, 2005, 85–86). Furthermore, the provision of administrative support necessitates a conscientious approach to addressing employee needs and expectations, thereby necessitating a well-structured administrative infrastructure. Key objectives within this framework include personalizing services, facilitating swift responses to inquiries, ensuring user-friendly interfaces, executing tasks with precision, and maintaining a high degree of responsiveness (Ulrich & Brockbank, 2005, 80–89).

Within the domain of internal stakeholders, HR professionals are tasked with ensuring that employees possess a heightened level of cognitive and behavioral competencies. This involves integrating various facets of talent management, as elucidated by Ulrich and Brockbank, who observe the emergence of a "War for Talent" among organizations, precipitating a competitive milieu for skilled individuals.

Mere quantitative sufficiency in talent acquisition is inadequate for fostering competitiveness; concurrent emphasis on employee commitment is imperative for achieving organizational success. Optimal outcomes are facilitated through the explicit delineation and characterization of requisite knowledge, competencies, and behavioral patterns essential for meeting customer expectations, as posited by Ulrich and Brockbank (2005, 89–90).

Moreover, factors such as agility, shared cognitive frameworks, individual and collective responsibility, collaborative dynamics, continuous learning paradigms, adept leadership, customer-centric orientation, propensity for innovation, strategic coherence, and operational efficacy are acknowledged to exert substantial influence on employee capabilities, job satisfaction, motivational propensities, retention rates, developmental trajectories, and thereby, ultimate business performance (Ulrich & Brockbank, 2005, 90–94).

3.5 HR Value Adding through the Field of Flow of People and Performance

The third aspect of the HR value proposition pertains to HR practices aimed at augmenting value, directly interlinked with elements discussed in the preceding domain, notably catering to both external and internal stakeholders. HR practices are mandated to concentrate on the fluidity of HR, performance metrics, informational exchange, and task execution to foster value generation and pinpoint a strategic focus (Ulrich & Brockbank, 2005, 95–96). Within these operational currents, HR professionals are tasked with elucidating the value addition for key stakeholders and furnishing an array of HR practices alongside their evaluated value contribution (Ulrich & Brockbank, 2005, 96). Ideally, this is accomplished through the implementation of an action plan encompassing five fundamental components: action items, resource allocation, delineation of responsibilities, temporal scheduling, and performance monitoring, with collaborative engagement with line management proving advantageous (Ulrich & Brockbank, 2005, 96–97).

Regarding the HR stream, it is posited that proficient individuals must be recruited into the organization and subsequently nurtured, honed, and maneuvered within the organizational framework to optimize knowledge utilization and skill deployment. This encompasses not only the elevation of employees to higher echelons within the organization but also the culling of underperforming HR. This approach is underpinned by the premise that enterprises boasting superior talent pools, skill sets, competencies, motivation levels, and retention rates are predisposed to achieve superior outcomes. Thus, the HR continuum commences with endeavors to enlist top-tier HR and extends to HR development initiatives (Ulrich & Brockbank, 2005, 98–109).

Ulrich and Brockbank assert that performance management serves as a pivotal catalyst for both managers and organizations, thus holding substantial significance. The pursuit of robust performance necessitates the implementation of practices, activities, and programs fostering performance enhancement and long-term viability. HR functions and organizational frameworks necessitate resource allocation and leadership endorsement to ensure the generation of intangible value and a results-driven orientation. In the realm of HR practices, this entails driving performance through the establishment of benchmarks, provision of both financial and non-financial incentives, and fostering developmental initiatives.

The effectiveness of standards, programs, activities, and strategy implementation hinges upon systematic measurement to facilitate performance analysis and enhancement through adaptive modifications. Ulrich and Brockbank critique the prevalent tendency to measure what is convenient rather than what is aligned with strategic objectives. Consequently, HR professionals are enjoined to prioritize the alignment of standards with strategic objectives, harmonize behavioral and output standards for individual and team evaluations, prioritize metrics, identify leading indicators, establish ambitious performance targets, and focus on measurable variables within their control.

It is imperative for HR practitioners to recognize the necessity of effective communication in the decision-making process regarding performance metrics. Moreover, adherence to standards in the establishment and monitoring process is crucial. This encompasses the delineation and tracking of standards, identification of tracking methodologies, result evaluation, and frequency of feedback. Following each tracking interval, a comprehensive follow-up process should ensue, aimed at identifying critical performance aspects. This process should entail informal discussions, provision of pertinent data, opportunities for individual reflection, elucidation of the underlying rationale, and adjustment initiation based on insights gleaned from the evaluation process.

Ulrich and Brockbank elucidate that the management of information flow represents an emergent activity within the domain of HR, wielding significant influence over human-centric facets and consequently impacting stakeholder value enhancement. Information pertaining to shifts in customer demographics, shareholder dynamics, economic fluctuations, regulatory frameworks, technological advancements, and HR landscapes assumes critical importance for organizational adaptation.

3.6 HR Value Adding through the Field of Flow of Information and Work

The challenge intrinsic to information flow lies in its requisite management across both horizontal and vertical axes, ensuring its precise dissemination to designated recipients (Ulrich & Brockbank, 2005, 121–122). Given the profound impact of information on organizational objectives, strategic alignment, supply chain dynamics, workflow optimization, and resultant value generation, the establishment of a communication strategy and an information transmission infrastructure becomes imperative. This infrastructure should predominantly focus on reaching the appropriate recipients to facilitate accurate inference drawing (Ulrich & Brockbank, 2005, 122–123).

Enhancing the efficacy of information dissemination necessitates the formulation of a comprehensive communication strategy. This strategy, both during its inception phase and subsequent execution, mandates congruence between communicated messages and actualities, codification of universally understood concepts, language standardization, integration control mechanisms, cultivation of audience-centric communication competencies, establishment of accountability frameworks, and continual measurement and enhancement of communication effectiveness (Ulrich & Brockbank, 2005, 123–125). The development and implementation of an information system necessitates meticulous analysis of the influx of data across various hierarchical tiers. Consequently, information dissemination exhibits distinct modalities including top-down, bottom-up, and lateral orientations. As data permeates through the organizational hierarchy, these modalities engender diverse circulation patterns, necessitating coordinated communication strategies (Ulrich & Brockbank, 2005, 125–131).

The culmination of HR practices in enhancing organizational value manifests in the orchestration of work processes. Workflow, being the focal point, facilitates the conversion of conceptualizations and resources into tangible outputs. Enterprises leverage both human capital and other resources through work and workflows to attain desired objectives. Given that HR, including employees and their workflows, contribute value to organizations and stakeholders, it is imperative for HR professionals to actively engage in orchestrating and optimizing work processes within the organizational framework. This necessitates the management of interdepartmental relationships and alignment to maximize value creation and outcome orientation (Ulrich & Brockbank, 2005, 133). Considerations encompass the organizational structure, its evolution, and human interaction dynamics (Ulrich & Brockbank, 2005, 134–144).

3.7 HR Value Adding through an HR Strategy

In the realm of HR management, the fourth dimension of the HR value proposition pertains to the formulation of an HR strategy. HR practitioners are tasked with crafting a strategic process aimed at aligning business objectives with HR priorities, facilitating the realization of desired outcomes (Ulrich & Brockbank, 2005, 149).

Within the construct of the HR strategy, a pivotal focus lies on fostering organizational capability and, consequently, shaping organizational culture. This entails cultivating a collective mindset characterized by shared cognitive patterns and modes of thinking. These factors exert significant influence on behavioral dynamics, information processing, and the generation of knowledge (Ulrich & Brockbank, 2005, 150).

Ulrich and Brockbank delineate a framework for an HR strategy anchored in culture and capability. This framework hinges on a robust comprehension of prevailing trends within the business landscape, which impact both strategic business decisions and the cultural competencies essential for achieving success. Notably, it is imperative to acknowledge the reciprocal relationship between business trends, strategic imperatives, and cultural capabilities, as they mutually influence each other (Ulrich & Brockbank, 2005, 151).

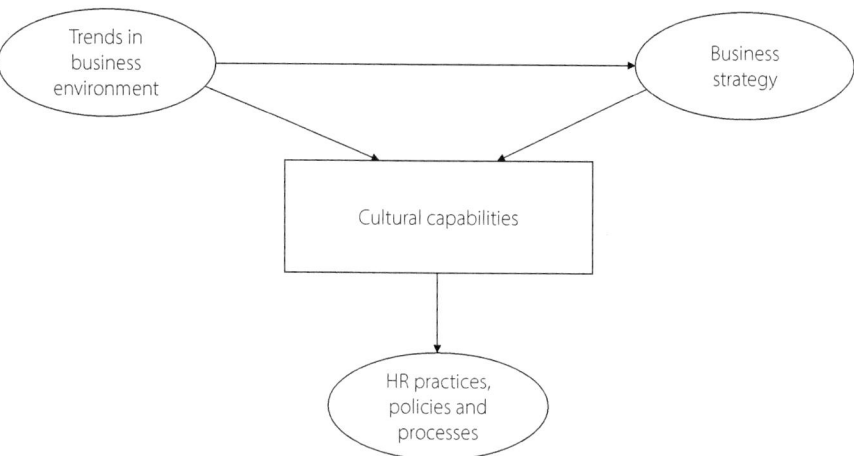

Fig. 3-2: Framework for a Culture-Capability-Based HR Strategy (Ulrich & Brockbank, 2005, 151)

The foundational premise of commencing an HR strategy development procedure lies in acknowledging that historical success does not necessarily ensure future success. In order to facilitate adaptations to the HR strategy, the developmental process delineated by Ulrich and Brockbank comprises six sequential steps. These steps encompass:

1. "Identify the organizational unit and organize the workshop.
2. Prioritize the trends in the business environment.
3. Specify the sources of competitive advantage and the measurements for each source of competitive advantage.
4. Define the desired cultural capabilities together with the behavioral expressions of these cultural capabilities.
5. Identify the HR practices that will have greatest influence on creating and sustaining the desired culture.
6. Develop an overall implementation plan." (Ulrich & Brockbank, 2005, 152–153).

3.8 HR Value Adding through HR Organization

In the fourth domain of the HR value proposition, the establishment of HR resources entails the HR organization. It is imperative for HR professionals to assess the extent to which the HR organization aligns with the business strategy (Ulrich & Brockbank, 2005, 177). The primary objective of HR professionals within the realm of HR organization is to ensure that the company's outcomes exceed the sum of its individual components. The challenge faced by HR professionals is to institute practices that support business strategies and contribute to shareholder value and corporate image. At the level of business units, HR professionals must concentrate on strategic objectives, target customers, shareholder value, and the delivery of the employee value proposition (Ulrich & Brockbank, 2005, 177). The core of value creation lies in the matching and alignment of HR organization with business organization (Ulrich & Brockbank, 2005, 179). Within the HR strategy, it is essential to incorporate the design and implementation of process tools that foster robust value creation and business-oriented HR agendas (Ulrich & Brockbank, 2005, 181). Ulrich and Brockbank advocate for achieving this through HR transformation efforts, focusing on the four sources of HR delivery: corporate HR, embedded HR, centers of expertise, and line managers (Ulrich & Brockbank, 2005, 190).

Key objectives include emphasizing values and principles, enabling line managers to attain their strategic objectives with HR support, facilitating transitions into new roles, integrating HR professionals into strategic business discussions, identifying investments conducive to success in the business environment, developing strategic communication translated into actionable plans, ensuring HR delivers on strategy with its own strategy, budget, and business plan, overseeing achievable goals, holding line managers accountable for HR matters, fostering reliance of line managers on HR professionals for pertinent HR issues, challenges, and progress, securing commitment from line managers on HR issues, enhancing visibility and innovation among HR professionals, and providing relevant data for informed decision-making alongside line managers (Ulrich & Brockbank, 2005, 191–196). To achieve these objectives, Ulrich and Brockbank outline seven HR transformational steps:

1. "Diagnose business strategy and organization.
2. Align HR and business organization structures.
3. Differentiate transaction and transformation work.
4. Create a project team.
5. Build transaction efficiencies.
6. Develop transformational effectiveness.
7. Monitor progress." (Ulrich & Brockbank, 2005, 196)

3.9 HR Roles and Responsibilities

HR professionals must attain a high level of expertise and specialization within their respective HR functions to effectively execute the designated developmental objectives and thereby significantly enhance value generation and outcome orientation (Ulrich & Brockbank, 2005, 199). A cacophony of HR roles is depicted in the following figure.

3 The First Adjustment to the Initial Model – the HR Value Proposition

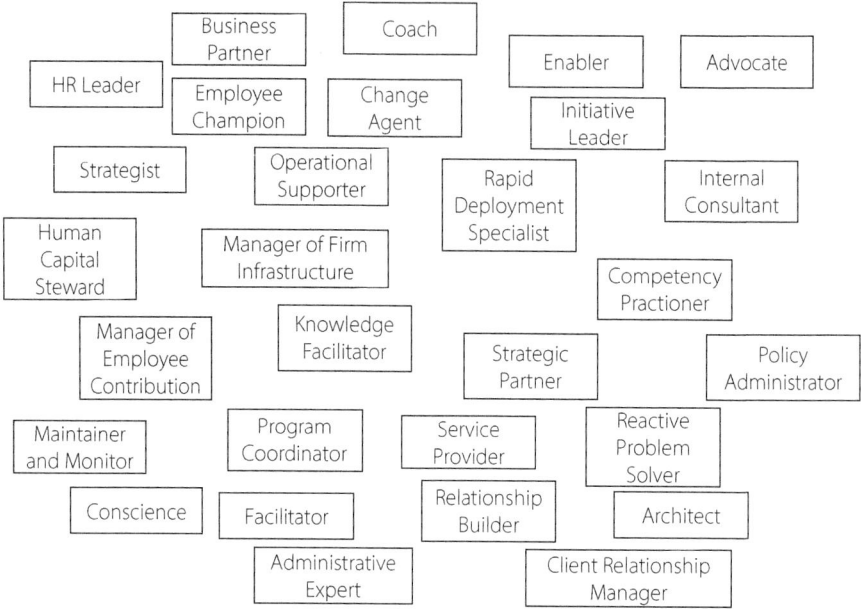

Fig. 3-3: A Cacophony of HR Roles (Ulrich & Brockbank, 2005, 200)

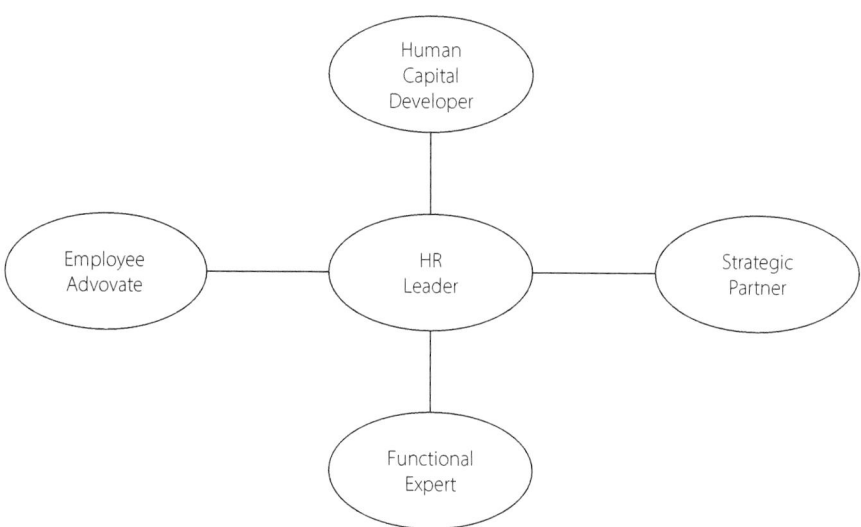

Fig. 3-4: Synthesis of Roles of HR Professionals (Ulrich & Brockbank, 2005, 200)

Comprehending the concept of (perceived) value from the perspective of its recipients is imperative for HR professionals. Ulrich and Brockbank introduced a revised framework delineating the pivotal responsibilities of HR practitioners. This model assigns HR professionals five distinct roles which are shown in the following figure. They comprise:

1. Employee Advocate
2. Human Capital Developer
3. Functional Expert
4. Strategic Partner and
5. HR Leader (Ulrich & Brockbank, 2005, 199–201).

The evolution of the HR roles is presented in the following table.

Tab. 2: Evolution of HR Roles (Ulrich & Brockbank, 2005, 201)

Evolution of HR roles		
Mid – 1990s	Mid – 2000s	Evolution of thinking
Employee Champion	Employee Advocate (EA), Human Capital (HC) Developer	Employees are increasingly critical to the success of organizations. EA focuses on today's employees; HC developer focuses on how employees prepare for the future.
Administrative Expert	Functional Expert	HR practices are central to HR value. Some HR practices are delivered through administrative efficiency (such as technology), and others through policies, menus, and interventions, expanding the "Functional Expert" role.
Change Agent	Strategic Partner	Being a Strategic Partner has multiple dimensions: Business Expert, Change Agent, Knowledge Manager, and consultant. Being a Change Agent represents only part of the Strategic Partner role.
Strategic Partner	Strategic Partner	As above.
	Leader	The sum of the first four roles equals leadership, but being an HR Leader also has implications for leading the HR function, collaborating with other functions, ensuring corporate governance, and monitoring the HR community.

From the data depicted in the aforementioned table and elucidated within the subsequent discourse on the five roles, a noticeable convergence of functions is discernible alongside the adaptations implemented towards the original framework and its designated roles. The erstwhile designation of "Employee Champion" has been bifurcated into two distinct roles, namely the "Employee Advocate" and the "Human Capital Developer". The role previously denoted as the "Administrative Expert" has been rechristened as the "Functional Expert". The erstwhile entity termed the "Change Agent" has now amalgamated with the "Strategic Partner" and is henceforth referred to as the "Strategic Partner". Lastly, the addition of the "HR Leader" complements the erstwhile quartet of roles designated as HR Business Partners. Hereinafter, the quintet of Business Partnering roles according to Ulrich and Brockbank's 2005 model shall be expounded upon.

3.9.1 Employee Advocate

In the capacity of advocating for employees, HR professionals play a crucial role in establishing a symbiotic relationship between employees and employers (Ulrich & Brockbank, 2005, 199). Ulrich and Brockbank highlight within the advocacy role the pivotal significance of attending to employees' needs, actively listening, and providing responsive support, constituting core tenets of HR responsibilities. It is imperative for HR professionals to empathetically comprehend employees' apprehensions, anxieties, and anticipations, while also aligning with managerial perspectives to effectively convey essential requisites and demands. HR professionals must exhibit accessibility and empathy towards employees, notwithstanding the diverse viewpoints they encounter, assuming responsibility for fostering assimilation through effective communication and empathic comprehension.

Acknowledging the significance of this role is paramount, as employee welfare profoundly impacts organizational dynamics, given that employees are the principal assets of enterprises. In fulfilling the role of Employee Advocate, HR professionals wield influence over employee loyalty and retention, underscoring not only the ethical imperative but also the organizational benefits of comprehending and addressing employees' concerns, apprehensions, needs, and circumstances. Ulrich and Brockbank further posit that the treatment of employees influences their interactions with customers, thereby accruing benefits for stakeholders and investors. Amidst impending organizational transformations, advocates for employees must carefully consider the ramifications for employees and advocate for their interests proactively.

Advocating for fairness and equity influences the corporate reputation, thereby impacting its attractiveness in the labor market, as well as employee morale and retention rates. This advocacy encompasses addressing subpar performance and subsequent reactions (Ulrich & Brockbank, 2005, 201–203). The role of an Employee Advocate contributes to value generation for both employees and stakeholders by positively influencing tangible and intangible capacities. Moreover, monitoring and reporting productivity enhances shareholder value by attracting investments based on perceived employee contribution. Additionally, enhancing intangible assets fortifies competence, dedication, and strategic execution capabilities (Ulrich & Brockbank, 2005, 204). Line managers must also prioritize employee advocacy as their conduct significantly influences the behavior, emotions, and sentiments of their subordinates (Ulrich & Brockbank, 2005, 205).

3.9.2 Human Capital Developer

In their capacity as developers of human capital, HR professionals bear the responsibility of cultivating the prospective workforce for the organization (Ulrich & Brockbank, 2005, 199). This domain of accountability entails HR professionals focusing on the individual augmentation of competencies, skills, and knowledge from the standpoint of organizational wealth creation. They formulate strategies, initiatives, and engagements aimed at harmonizing employee opportunities with the cultivation of forthcoming proficiencies, consonant with aspirations and feasibilities. Such endeavors are crucial not only for internal advancement but also for adapting to evolving work environments, encompassing shifts in requisite skills, knowledge, competencies, and expertise.

Functioning as Human Capital Developers, HR professionals act as mentors, fostering performance enhancement and team dynamics management. In this capacity, they notably augment value for both employees and line managers by fostering an atmosphere of progress, thereby enhancing individual career prospects and contentment. Consequently, a discernible correlation exists between the objectives of a Human Capital Developer and those of an Employee Advocate.

Beyond benefiting employees, stakeholders, and investors, Human Capital Developers also enhance customer welfare, as employees bolster customer relations and service experiences (Ulrich & Brockbank, 2005, 205–208).

3.9.3 Functional Expert

In the capacity of Functional Experts, HR professionals bear the responsibility of formulating and implementing HR methodologies that bolster both individual aptitude and organizational proficiency (Ulrich & Brockbank, 2005, 199–200). Functioning as experts within their domain, HR professionals are mandated to adeptly oversee their own occupational duties and performance within the HR sphere, ensuring their viability as dependable and effective collaborators for organizational administration and line managers. Drawing from this foundation, HR professionals are empowered to contribute to the analysis of business requirements, subsequently facilitating the formulation and refinement of HR methodologies for the provision of value.

In their role as Functional Experts, HR professionals must possess comprehensive expertise across four distinct realms of operation (Ulrich & Brockbank, 2005, 208–209). These realms include:

1. the creation of solutions to routine HR problems,
2. the creation of menus of choices, drawing on theory, research, and best practices within other companies,
3. the consulting with the business and adaption of programs to unique business needs, and
4. the setting of the overall policy and direction of HR practices in special areas (Ulrich & Brockbank, 2005, 208–209).

As the workload in HR escalates, a heightened necessity arises for specialized expertise and continual knowledge augmentation. It is imperative for HR practitioners to acknowledge the inherent limitations in instantly possessing solutions to all potential facets, thus necessitating an understanding of constraints. Nevertheless, proficiency lies in the adeptness to discern avenues for acquiring requisite information and data. The primary objective of Functional Experts resides in furnishing business alternatives grounded in experiential insight, diverse information sources, and an understanding of business domain exigencies. This encompasses the perpetual identification of enhancement prospects within operational methodologies. Emphasis should be placed on the formulation of procedural frameworks that fortify organizational infrastructure to enhance the feasibility of executing envisioned strategies. A comprehensive comprehension of processes, principles, and resources is indispensable for devising a repertoire of designs to meet prevailing and future procedural requisites (Ulrich & Brockbank, 2005, 209–210).

Functional expertise is instrumental in augmenting stakeholder value by translating business directives into organizational protocols. Moreover, HR professionals contribute value to various stakeholder cohorts through this endeavor. Customers derive benefit from the endeavors of Functional Experts owing to the desired harmonization of HR protocols with business imperatives and consequent organizational procedures. Finally, employees experience a positive impact as HR practices are formulated considering competency and commitment, thereby fostering enhancements in ability and conduct consistent with delineated strategies (Ulrich & Brockbank, 2005, 210–212).

3.9.4 Strategic Partner

In their capacity as Strategic Partners, HR practitioners facilitate the achievement of objectives by line managers across all tiers (Ulrich & Brockbank, 2005, 201). They amalgamate expertise in business, change management, consultancy, and learning methodologies to engage in symbiotic relationships with line managers, fostering value creation. This entails possessing a robust comprehension of business operations and dynamics, essential for guiding and supporting line managers in goal attainment. Such proficiency encompasses the examination of organizational resources and their harmonization with strategic objectives and customer demands. Moreover, HR professionals are tasked with ensuring the alignment of strategy implementation with HR frameworks, thereby contributing to the realization of organizational vision and mission. This necessitates the integration and coordination of strategies, as well as active involvement of pertinent stakeholders in strategy formulation. Achieving this mandate requires membership within the management cadre and a profound understanding of human capital dynamics and organizational structures (Ulrich & Brockbank, 2005, 212).

In their capacity as Strategic Partners, HR professionals assume the role of Change Agents alongside their expertise in business affairs. The amalgamation of these dual facets empowers them to identify and analyze organizational dilemmas, subsequently formulating an agenda and strategy for future readiness and proactive action. Armed with this knowledge foundation, HR professionals transition into Internal Consultants, providing guidance to leaders on requisite actions and facilitating the management of the change process.

Functioning as knowledge custodians, HR professionals contribute significantly to strategic advantages by identifying and disseminating the knowledge essential for adapting to evolving requirements (Ulrich & Brockbank, 2005, 212–213). In their Strategic Partner role, HR professionals evidently enhance value generation and outcomes delivery, concurrently bolstering organizational reputation and fostering intangible value creation. This symbiotic relationship proves advantageous for stakeholders and customers alike, as it integrates their preferences into strategic deliberations. Ultimately, employees also reap the benefits of this role, as their interests and developmental capacities are incorporated throughout the phases of strategy formulation and execution (Ulrich & Brockbank, 2005, 214).

3.9.5 HR Leader

In the capacity of HR Leaders, HR professionals bear the responsibility of establishing credible connections between their HR functions and business domains (Ulrich & Brockbank, 2005, 201). To achieve potential success, HR professionals must embody leadership qualities within their domain and prioritize values ahead of line managers and organizational management's acknowledgment of them as significant Internal Consultants. This necessitates HR professionals to elevate the importance of HR matters and institute more efficacious practices, thereby enhancing their credibility with line managers, who typically gauge understanding more through observation than verbal communication. A proficient grasp of leadership theory coupled with a resolute commitment to achieving knowledge-driven and action-oriented results is imperative for HR professionals. Effective HR leadership entails delineating clear objectives, employing robust communication strategies, managing change, and defining desired outcomes to add perceived value for investors, customers, line managers, and employees.

HR Leaders are tasked with identifying talent and fostering development capabilities across the organization and transcending silos. Collaborating with other departments facilitates the creation of intangible value through enhanced customer connectivity, productivity, and information technology, thereby augmenting business decision-making. Additionally, HR Leaders integrate the efforts of other departments by accessing and assimilating pertinent information about them. Consequently, HR Leaders play a pivotal role in corporate governance and oversee the HR community within the organization.

Moreover, HR leadership extends beyond organizational perspectives to encompass personal leadership and accountability for meeting future HR needs (Ulrich & Brockbank, 2005, 214–216). Given the crucial role of leadership in organizational success, HR Leaders significantly contribute to value creation and enhancement. They serve as exemplars in HR domains such as recruitment, development, compensation model design, and information sharing, thereby bolstering intangible value.

By conducting demand analysis and meeting expectations, HR Leaders contribute to value creation for both customers and line managers. Furthermore, HR professionals assist line managers in enhancing business performance. The competence level and perceived performance of HR Leaders profoundly influence credibility, consequently impacting employee satisfaction and commitment (Ulrich & Brockbank, 2005, 217–218).

Despite the slight adjustments made by Ulrich and Brockbank to the roles of HR professionals as Business Partners, it is evident that a close interrelation and reliance between these roles persists. The 2005 model accentuates the significance of the Strategic Partner role of Business Partners and the diverse domains of HR operations within it. In this model, HR Leaders assume a more central and conspicuous position in HR management. This is discernible through the delineated activities of HR Leaders and their positioning within the model diagram. Moreover, it is apparent that HR professionals are required to acquire and enhance new competencies to effectively contribute and add value to their roles (Ulrich & Brockbank, 2005, 218–219).

3.10 HR Value Contributing Competencies Making a Difference

Ulrich and Brockbank delineate competency domains pertinent to HR professionals necessitating assessment across various objectives. These encompass:

- "To specify what people need to do to improve performance
- To predict performance in complex jobs
- To match individuals with jobs
- To drive strategy and integrate management practices

- To measure and develop effectiveness of professionals, processes, and functions." (Ulrich & Brockbank, 2005, 221–222)

Ulrich and Brockbank pioneered the construction of a competency model aimed at delineating the HR value proposition. This model encompasses strategic contribution, personal credibility, HR delivery, business knowledge, and HR technology, as illustrated in the subsequent figure (Ulrich & Brockbank, 2005, 222).

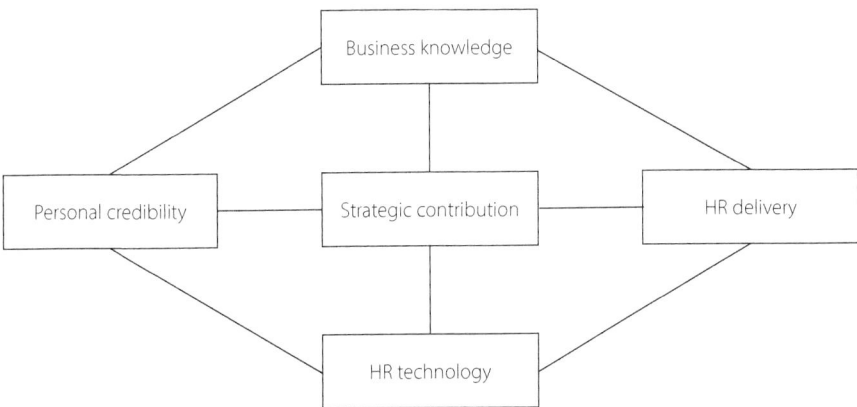

Fig. 3-5: Competency Model for the HR Value Proposition (Ulrich & Brockbank, 2005, 222)

After conducting a comprehensive study, Ulrich and Brockbank discerned the efficacy of competency categories and their consequential influence on business performance, as delineated in the subsequent tabular representation.

Tab. 3: HR Effectiveness and Influence on Business Performance (Ulrich & Brockbank, 2005, 223)

Competency category	HR effectiveness (1 = low; 5 = high)	Impact on business performance
Strategic contribution	3.65	43 %
Personal credibility	4.13	23 %
HR delivery	3.69	18 %
Business knowledge	3.44	11 %
HR technology	3.02	5 %

In the analysis of business performance impact, strategic contribution manifests a superior influence compared to the combined effects of personal credibility and HR delivery, despite the latter two exhibiting the second and third most substantial impacts, respectively. Findings elucidate that HR practitioners should broaden their scope beyond personal credibility, HR delivery, and business knowledge, as these factors collectively account for approximately half of the business performance impact. While these elements may serve as foundational aspects for strategic contribution, HR professionals can amplify their influence on business performance by prioritizing the latter, namely strategic contribution.

Ulrich and Brockbank's study and subsequent analysis delineate four distinct categories within strategic contribution: culture management, rapid change, strategic decision-making, and market-driven connectivity (Ulrich & Brockbank, 2005, 224). Within the realm of culture management, HR practitioners are tasked with ensuring the alignment of organizational culture with the multifaceted demands of external customers, business strategy, and employee engagement. The capacity for swift change, encompassing both potential and capabilities, emerges as a pivotal determinant of corporate success. HR professionals are enjoined to monitor and enhance their adeptness in executing change initiatives, thereby fortifying the organization's preparedness for future transformations. This facet also intersects with strategic decision-making, wherein HR professionals wield influence in delineating directional shifts, leveraging their comprehensive grasp of the business landscape to foster strategic thinking among stakeholders. Furthermore, HR professionals assume a reactive stance in strategic decision-making processes. A robust market-driven connectivity is imperative, empowering HR practitioners to discern and address customer-centric facets while disseminating pertinent information to relevant stakeholders. Such connectivity facilitates the concentration of resources on critical issues essential for meeting the exigencies of customers and shareholders alike (Ulrich & Brockbank, 2005, 224–225).

Ulrich and Brockbank categorize three pivotal dimensions crucial for establishing personal credibility, encompassing the documentation of outcomes, interpersonal adeptness, and communication proficiency. These dimensions respectively contribute to approximately 50 %, 33 %, and the remainder of credibility acquisition. Owing to the significance of these facets, HR practitioners necessitate cognizance thereof.

In the realm of outcome tracking, HR practitioners should strive to cultivate a robust reputation for fulfilling obligations and adhering to verbal commitments. Additionally, fostering personal integrity necessitates that not only the attainment of results is acknowledged by line managers, but also the manner in which such accomplishments are attained.

Concerning interpersonal skills, HR professionals must hone competencies vital for effective collaboration with organizational management and line managers within an environment of mutual trust. Regarding communication skills, HR professionals must cultivate an awareness of how to convey messages clearly and effectively to message recipients, particularly concerning content critical to organizational success (Ulrich & Brockbank, 2005, 226–227).

Although HR delivery exerts a lesser influence on business performance, proficiency in this domain remains imperative for HR professionals. Ulrich and Brockbank underscore that the utilization of HR tools yields a significantly heightened impact on business performance (43 %) when accompanied by a culture-centric HR strategy. Moreover, HR delivery exerts a substantial influence on trust and credibility. Inability to furnish (strategic) value contribution within their own sphere significantly undermines the rationale for entrusting HR professionals with similar responsibilities elsewhere. Thus, excelling within their domain stands as a pivotal determinant for garnering influence and credibility in other realms (Ulrich & Brockbank, 2005, 228).

Through organizational, structural, process, and strategic configurations, HR professionals can validate their value creation, foster sustainable corporate development, and ensure the enhancement of organizational capabilities alongside a culture oriented towards market and strategy. Additionally, HR professionals must acknowledge the mutually reinforcing relationship between heightened HR practices and culture, ultimately facilitating strategy execution (Ulrich & Brockbank, 2005, 228–232).

Although business knowledge may exert a modest impact on performance, HR professionals can only ascend to partnership status if they possess a robust comprehension of the company's clientele and industry. This knowledge serves as the cornerstone, empowering HR professionals to strategically contribute and foster a corporate ethos that harmonizes with customer expectations, thereby facilitating organizational triumph. Additionally, the ability to pose pertinent inquiries, garner acceptance for contributions during the strategic formulation process, and execute the company's vision and mission hinges upon a profound grasp of the business landscape. As posited by Ulrich and Brockbank, familiarity with the value chain and value proposition significantly shape the efficacy of HR professionals, with labor knowledge exerting comparatively less influence (Ulrich & Brockbank, 2005, 235–236).

Ultimately, HR technology exerts a discernible impact on performance, albeit of modest magnitude. Nevertheless, HR technology possesses the capacity to substantially enhance HR methodologies and operations. Consequently, HR practitioners are advised to vigilantly seek out applications and procedural refinements conducive to augmenting efficiency and efficacy. In summary, Ulrich and Brockbank assert that HR technology constitutes a fundamental HR determinant necessitating continual advancement, notwithstanding its relatively minor influence on financial performance (Ulrich & Brockbank, 2005, 238–239).

3.11 HR Professional Development Necessities and HR Transformation Implications

In order to significantly contribute to value creation and outcome orientation, HR professionals must cultivate competencies requisite for fulfilling designated roles and for enhancing proficiency in corresponding fields (Ulrich & Brockbank, 2005, 242). HR practitioners are compelled to enhance their capabilities to ultimately align HR strategy, operations, procedures, and methodologies with business strategy and objectives. They must ground novel concepts in business actuality and within their developmental framework. The articulation of the aforementioned precise objectives is indispensable, while the acquisition and establishment of trust are also pertinent (Ulrich & Brockbank, 2005, 243-245). Central to their advancement is the capacity to discern topics and issues necessitating immediate intervention versus those necessitating long-term deliberation. Additionally, they must equip themselves to grasp business strategy and extrapolate HR strategy, actions, practices, which encompasses continuous recalibration as necessary, to deliver value (Ulrich & Brockbank, 2005, 263).

The evolution into a Strategic Partner necessitates a developmental trajectory for HR professionals. As posited by Ulrich and Brockbank, this encompasses four distinct phases: conceptualization, evaluation, investment, and subsequent monitoring. In the conceptualization phase, HR professionals must deepen their theoretical understanding to discern actions required and their rationales for enhancing value delivery and outcome orientation. Subsequently, an evaluation is imperative to pinpoint areas requiring advancement. In the investment phase, resources must be allocated to bridge identified gaps between the current state and the desired state. To secure financial backing, HR professionals should articulate their intentions and anticipated outcomes as clearly as possible. This should be encapsulated in a goal statement focusing on the intended impact and resultant value creation. Early demonstration of developmental progress yields significant benefits. Outcomes, thus modified processes and activities, should be promptly assimilated to demonstrate their impact to line managers and senior management, initiating visible value addition expeditiously. Follow-up procedures are essential to regularly assess progress and enact timely adjustments (Ulrich & Brockbank, 2005, 265-278).

In the realm of HR management, it is imperative for HR professionals to scientifically establish the perceived value of their contributions, both in terms of their own efforts and the human capital they manage. Line managers must be unequivocally assured that HR professionals are adept at generating and enhancing organizational capabilities, thereby justifying the allocation of investments, temporal resources, financial resources, and cognitive resources. The formulation of an HR strategy serves as a blueprint wherein HR professionals systematically delineate how they intend to operationalize the overarching business strategy into tangible HR activities. In their conclusive assertion, Ulrich and Brockbank underscore the increasingly pivotal role of HR in driving business success, positing that the HR value proposition stands as a linchpin for the future progression and professional evolution of HR (Ulrich & Brockbank, 2005, 278-281).

4 The Second Adjustment to the Initial Model – HR Transformation – Building Human Resources from the Outside In

4.1 The New Need of HR Transformation

In 2009, Ulrich, Allen, Brockbank, Younger, and Nyman, collectively referred to as Ulrich et al., expanded upon the dimensions of Business Partnering, integrating additional facets concerning its evolution, intentions, and objectives. Concurrently, they undertook a reconfiguration of the roles inherent in Business Partnering. The central concern regarding Business Partnering is encapsulated in the assertion: "The heightened strategic role of HR is less about mere inclusion at decision-making tables and more about adept management of talent and organizational issues to achieve business objectives. When HR professionals facilitate the delivery of value to investors, customers, and communities by business leaders, HR inherently generates value" (Ulrich et al., 2009, xii). Moreover, Ulrich et al. underscore the imperative for HR professionals to overhaul their operational paradigms to facilitate value creation (Ulrich et al., 2009, xii).

Consequently, from the outset and thus inferred from the title, HR transformation – shaping HR from an external perspective – emerges as the primary aim of their 2009 work. Through the proposed HR transformation framework and methodology, the aim is to meet escalating expectations and confront challenging business developmental landscapes (Ulrich et al., 2009, 3). While HR professionals are tasked with ensuring alignment between HR practices, programs, and activities to drive business outcomes, they are additionally expected to actively engage in the formulation of business strategies. Ulrich et al. assert that their proposed approach and model should also be familiar to line management, as "talent management, organizational capability enhancement, strategy execution, and leadership are pivotal to organizational success" (Ulrich et al., 2009, 4). Furthermore, staffing functions are acknowledged for their role in orchestrating process and practice transformations to address business challenges within a turbulent operational milieu, ultimately benefiting the enterprise (Ulrich et al., 2009, 5).

Central to this transformation is the evolution of HR professionals into business partners aligned with the company's objectives, necessitating a pronounced emphasis on strategic and business-centric endeavors. For HR to achieve its desired goals, certain aspects require particular attention. Firstly, value creation should extend beyond internal operations to encompass the attraction, servicing, and retention of customers and investors. Secondly, HR organizational structures must be predicated upon business imperatives and objectives, rather than solely HR-centric considerations. This underscores the interdependence between HR strategy and business strategy, with a concerted focus on value addition superseding the optimization of HR functions exclusively. This naturally leads to the third aspect: HR transformation must transcend the mere execution of HR tasks and instead concentrate primarily on fostering business success (Ulrich et al., 2009, 6–7).

As a logical culmination of these delineated principles, Ulrich et al. delineate their model for HR transformation, illustrated in the subsequent figure.

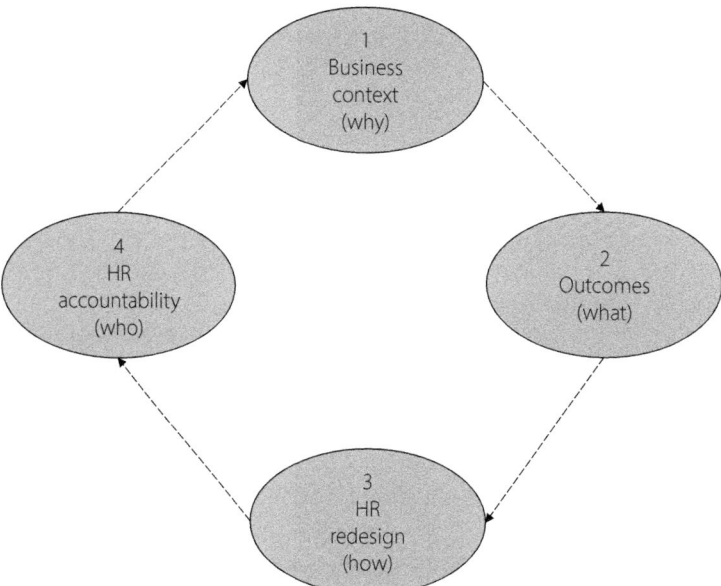

Fig. 4-1: Model for HR Transformation (Ulrich et al., 2009, 10)

The business context (why) will be dealt with first.

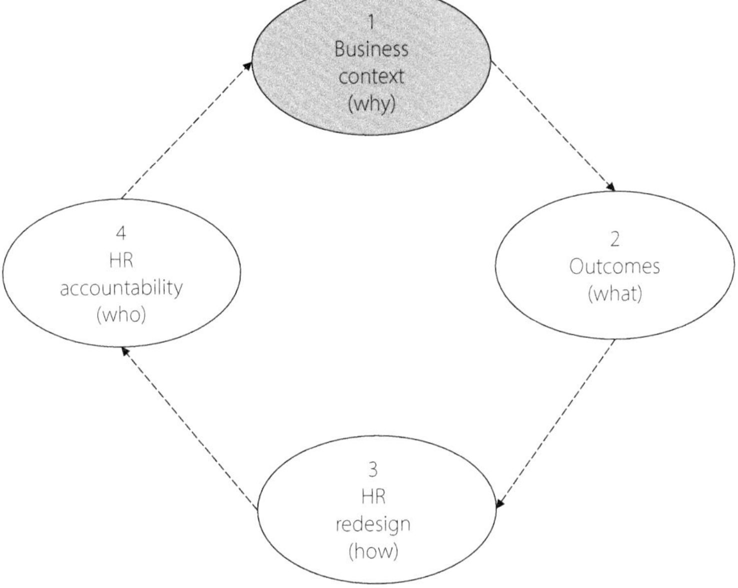

Fig. 4-2: The Business Context in the Transformation Process (Ulrich et al., 2009, 13)

4.2 HR Transformation and the Business Context

In the depicted graph, the genesis of the transformation process lies within the business context, serving as the genesis due to its contribution to the acceptance of transformative concepts. This origin is pivotal, as it fosters alignment between business strategy, shaped by environmental determinants, and HR initiatives encompassing practices, programs, and activities (Ulrich et al., 2009, 15).

Effective commencement of the transformation endeavor hinges upon HR professionals' comprehension of overarching business conditions and their consequential impact on business strategy. Such comprehension is imperative for justifying and harmonizing subsequent developmental trajectories (Ulrich et al., 2009, 18). The global milieu and dynamic shifts within the business landscape, including fluctuations in natural resource costs, alterations in global trade patterns, geopolitical shifts, and demographic transitions, exert a profound influence on both corporate entities and the corresponding HR methodologies. Hence, HR professionals must maintain a nuanced understanding of these factors, which significantly influence a company's market positioning and its performance potential (Ulrich et al., 2009, 18–20).

Ulrich et al. emphasize the imperative consideration of all stakeholders, along with their situational contexts and vested interests, for comprehending the foundational principles and milieu of the HR transformation process. Within the realm of employee stakeholders, HR professionals are tasked with scrutinizing the influence and resultant impact of both internal and external demographic factors on present and future talent pools, as well as on talent development and attraction dynamics. Consequently, discerning and implementing suitable responses becomes paramount.

In the domain of line managers, HR professionals must secure ingress into business deliberations, thereby fostering active participation that garners recognition and validation. This entails a meticulous exploration and grasp of the line manager's spheres of accountability and the corresponding objectives to be achieved.

Within the customer sector, HR professionals are mandated to cultivate enduring and intimate relationships with clientele, recognizing their pivotal role in influencing customer satisfaction and fostering enduring collaboration, particularly concerning target demographics. Conversely, in the sphere of investors, there exists a discernible inclination towards evaluating leadership efficacy and organizational prowess. HR professionals must thus incorporate leadership-driven value creation strategies to meet investor expectations, while also enhancing intangible value generation through adept strategy execution and alignment of core competencies with organizational capabilities.

Amidst the landscape of competitors, a comprehensive understanding of the present and future trajectories of rival entities becomes indispensable for devising strategies and aligning HR initiatives, programs, and practices accordingly. As organizational and by extension, customer value, constitute the primary objectives of HR professionals, this dimension assumes paramount significance. Regarding global suppliers, HR professionals are enjoined to contribute towards sustainable service provision and business operations. In respect to regulators, HR professionals should demonstrate keen awareness regarding potential changes in regulatory frameworks and their implications for business operations and HR practices. Within the community realm, safeguarding reputation emerges as a pivotal concern, given its ramifications on talent acquisition and business potential (Ulrich et al., 2009, 21–25).

In advising HR professionals, it is prudent to adopt an approach centered on the creation of value for stakeholders, as perceived value forms the foundation for garnering support in the HR transformation process and acquiring necessary resources (Ulrich et al., 2009, 25). As depicted in the subsequent illustration, HR transformation commences with an assessment of the business context, emphasizing key stakeholder orientation. These elements establish the groundwork for HR transformation. Subsequently, alignment with the business strategy and adaptation of HR design ensue. This progression must build upon existing and traditional HR design frameworks (Ulrich et al., 2009, 26–27).

Commencing from the business domain HR practitioners ought to subsequently focus on outcomes, thereby directing their attention towards the "what" of the transformational procedure.

4.3 HR Transformation and Outcome Orientation

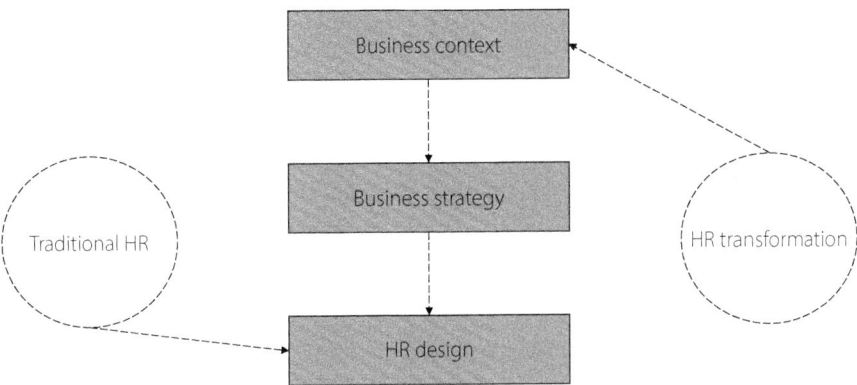

Fig. 4-3: Traditional Versus Transformative HR (Ulrich et al., 2009, 26)

4.3 HR Transformation and Outcome Orientation

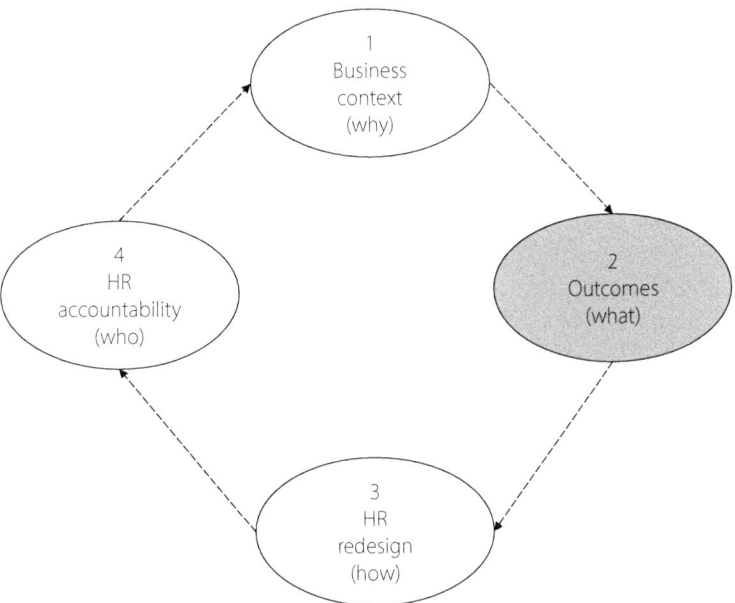

Fig. 4-4: The Outcomes in the Transformation Process (Ulrich et al., 2009, 31)

The paramount objective of the HR transformation process should center on discerning stakeholder outcomes, with due consideration to the evaluation of HR activities' impacts, as emphasized by Ulrich et al. (2009, 33). This focus is imperative as it necessitates an understanding of the outcomes pertinent to each key stakeholder. Throughout this process of transformation, particular attention must be paid to those stakeholders most significantly impacted by the changes (Ulrich et al., 2009, 34).

Measurement of capabilities holds pivotal importance owing to the dynamic nature of factors such as identity, culture, and image, thereby influencing organizational capability and behavior (Ulrich et al., 2009, 36). Assessing and fostering capability, along with its interrelations and evolution, stand as critical yardsticks for gauging a company's present status and potential for growth. Ulrich et al. enumerate several crucial aspects defining well-managed companies, including talent management, agility, fostering a shared mindset, and fostering accountability (Ulrich et al., 2009, 36–38). Additionally, factors like collaboration, continuous learning, effective leadership, customer engagement, innovation drive, strategic coherence, operational simplicity, social responsibility, risk management, and efficiency are underscored as essential elements (Ulrich et al., 2009, 36–38).

Ulrich et al. underscore the paramount importance of talent in organizational dynamics, elucidating its pivotal role in shaping organizational capability and efficacy. Within the realm of talent management, the imperative lies in the acquisition, motivation, and retention of HR who exhibit both dedication and proficiency. Leadership assumes a critical function in this domain, tasked with the recruitment, development, progression, integration, and, when necessary, expulsion of talent. Concurrently, the ongoing evaluation of employee competence and productivity, alongside alignment with corporate strategy and ethos, serves as a linchpin in optimizing organizational performance (Ulrich et al., 2009, 38–39).

In the sphere of agility, adeptness in organizational identification and adaptability emerges as paramount for maintaining competitive edge. The ability to effectuate rapid change necessitates a robust emphasis on expeditious decision-making and the establishment of conducive structural frameworks. Quantifying agility extends to discerning the temporal gap between issue identification and implementation of viable remedial strategies (Ulrich et al., 2009, 39–40).

Within the domain of shared cognitive frameworks, cultivating a positive corporate image among clientele and employees assumes paramount importance. HR practitioners play a pivotal role in actualizing the desired corporate identity, both among prospective and current clients, thereby influencing demand-side dynamics and labor market attractiveness (Ulrich et al., 2009, 40).

Accountability constitutes a cornerstone of organizational performance, underlining the imperative of a performance-driven ethos. Embedded within organizational capability, accountability hinges on the mutual comprehension between employees and leaders regarding performance expectations. This can be fostered through the establishment of performance benchmarks coupled with incentivization mechanisms tied to performance metrics, ensuring alignment between effort and compensation (Ulrich et al., 2009, 41).

In the arena of collaboration, HR professionals shoulder the responsibility of fostering cross-boundary teamwork to enhance operational efficiency and leverage. Central to this paradigm is the aspiration for synergy, wherein the collective outcome transcends the sum of individual contributions. Facilitating an environment conducive to learning, fostering interdepartmental knowledge sharing, and optimizing resource allocation and utilization collectively contribute to efficiency gains and the development of synergistic approaches (Ulrich et al., 2009, 42).

In the domain of learning, collaboration serves as a conduit for the identification and resolution of challenges through the implementation of viable solutions. This collaborative learning process extends beyond boundaries, encompassing intra-departmental and intra-team scenarios. The dissemination of solutions among departments, teams, and groups facing similar challenges yields substantial benefits. By sharing insights with pertinent individuals, organizational learning is substantially augmented, consequently enhancing the velocity of adaptation and problem-solving (Ulrich et al., 2009, 42–43).

Within the realm of leadership, leaders are tasked not only with embodying the organizational leadership ethos but also with ensuring the realization of desired outcomes in an appropriate manner and timeframe. They bear the responsibility of meeting customer expectations and effecting suitable employee actions. However, the significance of employee expectations, contentment, and satisfaction cannot be understated (Ulrich et al., 2009, 43–44).

Regarding customer engagement, Ulrich et al. underscore the importance of cultivating enduring relationships with key customers. Central to this engagement is the identification of significant customers based on a thorough analysis of customer value. A robust customer relationship is best fostered when employees develop a strong rapport with customers (Ulrich et al., 2009, 44).

In the arena of innovation, the evolution and refinement of both content and processes are paramount. A steadfast emphasis on innovation is imperative, as it enables a company to maintain a competitive edge and reevaluate resource utilization and application methodologies crucial for enhancing the quality of services, products, and processes. Business and HR Leaders must continually reassess forthcoming innovation steps. In certain instances, evaluating innovation capability and its metrics may necessitate adjustments to business strategies and a reevaluation of resource allocation and competencies, consequently impacting HR activities, programs, and processes that must align with evolving conditions (Ulrich et al., 2009, 45).

Strategic coherence demands the establishment of a robust articulation and dissemination of the strategic viewpoint. Attainment of lofty objectives is contingent upon a shared understanding across four key agendas: the intellectual agenda, which necessitates a common comprehension of the strategy's significance; the behavioral agenda, which mandates alignment of leadership and employee behavior with the established strategy; the process agenda, which emphasizes synchronization of organizational processes with the overarching strategy; and finally, the measurement agenda, which dictates the parameters for gauging progress towards strategic objectives (Ulrich et al., 2009, 45–46).

In pursuit of simplicity, strategies, processes, products, and services should be streamlined for ease of management. Business and HR Leaders advocate for simplification of workflows, facilitating not only HR process management but also enhancing customer-centric aspects, product design, administrative functions, and technological infrastructure (Ulrich et al., 2009, 46–47).

In the realm of social responsibility, the primary focus lies in the nexus between community contribution, organizational reputation, and resultant effects, such as talent acquisition and retention potential, within the operational sphere (Ulrich et al., 2009, 47–48).

In the realm of risk analysis, the proactive assessment and mitigation of potential risk factors stand as pivotal elements. Advancements in this domain facilitate the capability of organizations to prognosticate the likelihoods associated with risk factors and subsequent future scenarios, predicated upon the present circumstances and their evaluated and presumed evolution (Ulrich et al., 2009, 48).

Efficiency optimization pertains to the adept management of operational expenditures and the yields derived from activities. Stakeholders such as management, leadership, and HR professionals ought to advocate for cost reduction through enhancements in processes, projects, and HR functions utilizing technological advancements, collaborative endeavors, and task streamlining. Moreover, resource allocation should prioritize sectors exhibiting potential growth. Singular emphasis on cost reduction proves unpromising, as efficiency enhancement overwhelmingly proves more efficacious. Efficiency quantification commonly relies on the examination of balance sheets and income statements, yet HR metrics pose a challenge due to their primarily qualitative nature (Ulrich et al., 2009, 48–49).

Fig. 4-5: Diagram of Stakeholder Measures (Ulrich et al., 2009, 50)

The process of HR transformation necessitates a foundation rooted in measurement and metrics, employing a capability assessment approach. Within this framework, the identification of pivotal areas essential for future organizational triumph, given prevailing and forthcoming business circumstances and strategies, assumes paramount importance. Hence, it is advantageous to encapsulate the opportunities and hurdles within the aforementioned domains. For this purpose, the subsequent diagram proves instrumental.

This methodology guarantees the robust integration and centralization of organizational value generation and result-focused endeavors. Moreover, it serves as a pivotal foundation for the third stage of the HR transformational continuum, namely, the HR design phase, which addresses the "how" aspect and is elucidated subsequently.

4.4   HR Transformation and HR Redesign

The initiation of the HR redesign process commences by prioritizing the restructuring of the HR department, as both HR strategy and structure necessitate reconfiguration to attain robust alignment with the prevailing business context and the facilitation of value creation (Ulrich et al., 2009, 55). This initial phase aims to establish a foundation for success, as asserted by Ulrich et al., necessitating the specification of a vision (identity), a mission (objective), and the desired outcomes (purpose) of the HR transformation endeavor. The vision articulates the intended offerings of the HR strategy, necessitating a direct correlation with the exigencies of the business milieu. The formulation of the envisioned identity is to be a collaborative endeavor, involving line managers as they represent pivotal stakeholders of HR services. Within the mission statement, HR practitioners must delineate the requisite competencies essential for achieving success. Subsequently, in the outcome-oriented approach, HR professionals are mandated to articulate comprehensive objectives, inclusive of provisions for progress monitoring and evaluation (Ulrich et al., 2009, 55–57).

To effectuate a successful overhaul of the HR organization, Ulrich et al. propose a tripartite methodology. Firstly, the HR organization should prioritize alignment with business objectives and HR strategy. Secondly, it must adhere to the operational dynamics typical of a professional service entity. Thirdly and lastly, a clear demarcation between transactional and transformational HR functions is imperative (Ulrich et al., 2009, 58). Tailoring practices to align with the imperatives of business requirements and optimizing synergies across business units are deemed indispensable. HR professionals must recognize their pivotal role in empowering line managers to enhance productivity (Ulrich et al., 2009, 58–61).

In their 2009 publication, Ulrich et al. extensively examine the four domains of HR practices, namely the flow of HR, flow of performance management, flow of information, and flow of work (Ulrich et al., 2009, 80–81). They underscore the imperative of disentangling these domains to effectively oversee transformative

4 The Second Adjustment to the Initial Model

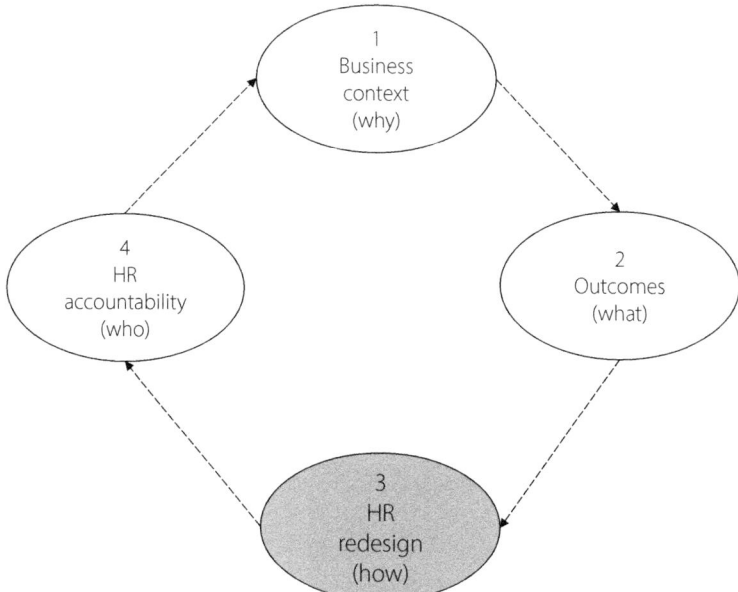

Fig. 4-6: The HR Design in the Transformation Process (Ulrich et al., 2009, 53)

processes. Moreover, they advocate for a thorough consideration of alignment, integration, and innovation across all four domains (Ulrich et al., 2009, 81). To establish a closer nexus with the latter three aspects, the principal focal points of the four categories are reiterated herein.

Ulrich et al. stipulate the fundamental importance of attracting, retaining, and enhancing talent within the realm of HR flow. Talent, however, is conceptualized as a product of competence, commitment, and contribution – as depicted in the talent equation formula (Ulrich et al., 2009, 82):

TALENT = COMPETENCE × COMMITMENT × CONTRIBUTION

Ulrich et al. conceptualize competence as the amalgamation of knowledge, skills, and values requisite for current and forthcoming occupational demands. Consequently, organizations strive to ensure the presence of individuals possessing optimal aptitude, situated appropriately within the organizational framework. To bridge the chasm between extant requisites and competencies, as well as preempt future discordance, HR practitioners must discern the requisite proficiencies for each temporal epoch. This necessitates a comprehensive evaluation of organizational dynamics and employee proficiencies. Addressing presumed lacunae demands investments in talent augmentation, finely calibrated to present and prospective exigencies. Ultimately, a monitoring mechanism is indispensable to gauge the evolution and efficacy of competency development processes (Ulrich et al., 2009, 82–84).

Commitment denotes the robust dedication of HR toward the attainment of organizational objectives. Compared to the delineation presented in the 2005 edition, slight adjustments have been made to emphasize salient considerations. Key determinants encompass vision, opportunity, incentive structure, impact, communal cohesion, communication efficacy, and entrepreneurial spirit or adaptability. Consequently, erstwhile experimentation is supplanted by an accentuation on the latter attribute (Ulrich et al., 2009, 85).

In the realm of organizational contribution, Ulrich et al. accentuate the heightened imperative for companies to fulfill the needs and interests of their workforce, as this is significantly correlated with motivation, performance, and developmental outcomes (Ulrich et al., 2009, 86). Within the framework of performance management, minimal adjustments are warranted. Desired outcomes necessitate translation into quantifiable objectives and incentives designed to stimulate goal attainment. HR practitioners must integrate principles of accountability, transparency, comprehensiveness, and equity to ensure the generation of value. According to Ulrich et al., a four-step process is essential to cultivate effective performance management. These four steps entail:

1. Clarify strategy and priorities: be clear about what is wanted
2. Set standards: define what to measure
3. Design rewards: build in welcome and unwelcome consequences
4. Follow up: make sure that performance management endures (Ulrich et al., 2009, 88–92)

Within the flow of information, Ulrich et al. offer a more refined delineation of factors pertinent to information management compared to preceding models. The primary objective of information governance is to ensure adaptive responses to extrinsic stimuli. To establish an effective information transmission infrastructure, Ulrich et al. advocate the formulation of a communication strategy. They emphasize the importance of considering five sequential stages. Firstly, simplification and focus of the message are paramount. Secondly, identification of the intended recipient(s) is essential. Thirdly, comprehension of the target audience's characteristics is imperative. Fourthly, determination of the optimal temporal context for message delivery is crucial. Fifthly, the mode of message dissemination must be carefully deliberated (Ulrich et al., 2009, 92–93).

In the flow of work, analogous observations apply to the extent of adaptations within the updated framework. Operational dynamics entail the dispersion of organizational objectives to individual agents, necessitating the pervasive integration of organizational frameworks, which encompasses organizational architecture. Pertaining to the evolution of HR, practitioners in this domain are tasked with concentrating on procedural workflows, governance mechanisms, and the physical environment (Ulrich et al., 2009, 93–95).

The novel aspect introduced in this model adjustment involves the incorporation of alignment, integration, and innovation into the HR transformation process to maximize its impact. Alignment underscores the imperative for HR practices to closely align with organizational strategy. HR professionals must assess the extent to which each practice contributes to the development of desired capabilities, while considering the rate of change and existing processes. It is imperative to ensure that HR practices propel strategy realization through capability enhancement (Ulrich et al., 2009, 95–96).

In the realm of integration, the primary objective is to cultivate HR systems that function cohesively and are formulated with a cohesive strategic focus. Ultimately, the integration of processes aims to yield a significant impact on business outcomes. This integration process necessitates stakeholder engagement and a thorough examination of how individuals within the organization allocate their time and energy (Ulrich et al., 2009, 96–98).

In the domain of innovation, HR professionals are chiefly concerned with staying abreast of evolving HR practices. Emerging trends must be analyzed and incorporated into the organization where beneficial. It is evident that HR practice innovation is intricately linked to alignment and integration. Adopting new innovations into existing systems demands an analysis of their impact on current practices and the ensuing consequences (Ulrich et al., 2009, 98).

To attain the desired objectives, Ulrich et al. delineate the essential competencies of HR practitioners and their cultivation. Initiating a developmental trajectory, there is a pronounced adherence to Ulrich et al.'s (2009, 101) four-step model of competency establishment, evincing substantial internal coherence within the model. The ensuing steps, as enumerated below, comprise:

1. Articulate a theory or set a standard
2. Assess individuals and organizations
3. Invest in talent improvement
4. Follow up and track competence (Ulrich et al., 2009, 101)

Initially, HR professionals are tasked with elucidating and delineating their conceptualization of success. From this foundational understanding, they can discern the areas within HR roles, activities, and competencies that necessitate enhancement. By scrutinizing HR roles and activities, the requisite HR competencies can be deduced (Ulrich et al., 2009, 102). Ulrich et al. expound upon four activities undertaken by HR professionals, namely coaching, architecting, designing and delivering, and facilitating.

HR professionals engage in coaching business leaders to enhance performance. Crucial responsibilities in this domain include establishing credibility, attentively listening, and providing astute counsel (Ulrich et al., 2009, 105). During the process of architecting, there is a paramount need to meticulously consider the strategic orientation of the company. The ramifications for organizational design must be comprehended and subsequently aligned with the business strategy (Ulrich et al., 2009, 105–106). Subsequent to identifying organizational design imperatives, HR professionals must also assess the implications for the design of HR practices to

4.4 HR Transformation and HR Redesign

ensure maximal value. This can be best achieved through the pursuit of an approach emphasizing alignment, integration, and innovation, albeit contingent upon HR professionals staying abreast of HR theory, research, and practice (Ulrich et al., 2009, 106). To facilitate organizational adaptations, HR professionals concentrate on delineating the nature and structure of change processes, while concurrently fostering acceptance and support for these changes. Through this proactive stance, HR professionals transition from being reactive to proactive contributors to business endeavors (Ulrich et al., 2009, 106).

In order to optimize value delivery and fulfill their objectives, Ulrich et al. propose a redesign of the business partner role model. In the 2009 iteration of the role model, six business partner roles are delineated, as illustrated in the accompanying figure.

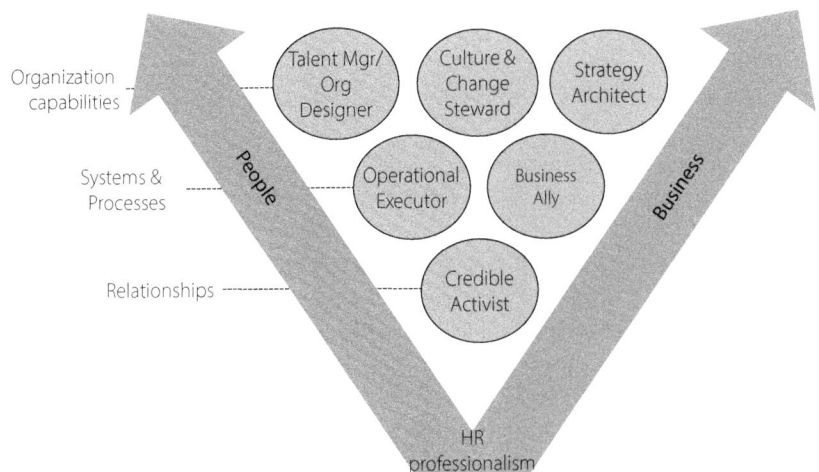

Fig. 4-7: Key Attributes of HR (Ulrich et al., 2009, 107)

Through the process of designing adaptation inspired by role modeling, it becomes evident that the roles of business partners exhibit a correlation with both business-centric and human-centric aspects. Moreover, the vertical segregation signifies the alignment of these roles with relationships, systems, processes, and organizational capabilities.

The persona of a Credible Activist is closely associated with both the human-centric and business-centric focuses. The Operational Executor and the Business Ally are situated within the realm of systems and processes. Although the Operational Executor tends to prioritize human interactions, the Business Ally, as implied by the title, leans more towards business-oriented activities. At the organizational capabilities level, three distinct roles emerge. The Talent Manager and Organizational Designer exhibit a stronger inclination towards human-centric endeavors, whereas the Strategy Architect displays a greater affinity for business-centric endeavors. Occupying a middle ground is the Culture and Change Steward (Ulrich et al., 2009, 107).

The subsequent elucidation entails a delineation of the tasks, responsibilities, and accountabilities pertinent to each of these six roles. Ulrich et al. delineate the obligations of the Credible Activist as being agents of business outcomes through the nexus of human capital and organizational efficacy. Their mandate, requiring both credibility and proactivity, can be construed as foundational to other roles. It is underscored that advancement along the human capital and business effectiveness continuum hinges upon these dual facets (Ulrich et al., 2009, 108).

In the capacity of a Culture and Change Steward, HR practitioners engage with and shape organizational culture. They transmute expectations into employee conduct and organizational ethos. They facilitate cultural metamorphoses and additionally aid managers in discerning how their actions influence and are influenced by organizational culture (Ulrich et al., 2009, 108).

In the capacity of Talent Managers and Organizational Designers, HR professionals direct their focus predominantly towards the human element as competence requisites and workforce mobility, including potential exits, are central. Of particular significance is the alignment of talent management endeavors with organizational strategy, ensuring efficacy and efficiency (Ulrich et al., 2009, 109).

In the capacity of Strategy Architects, HR professionals bear primary responsibility for envisioning the desired organizational performance for success. They also wield considerable influence in crafting strategy and contribute to its realization through HR practices. Furthermore, they are tasked with bridging these strategies to employee engagement (Ulrich et al., 2009, 109).

In the capacity of Operational Executors, HR professionals are entrusted with the management and oversight of HR within the organization, encompassing policy formulation and administrative duties. These activities are to be efficiently managed leveraging technology and organizational alignment. Feedback mechanisms and close collaboration facilitate the process of identifying areas for improvement (Ulrich et al., 2009, 109–110).

In the capacity of business allies, delineating and articulating goals and objectives is imperative to ensure proactive responses to opportunities and threats. Coupled with a robust comprehension of the business landscape and a keen focus on the value chain, this forms a solid foundation for staunchly supporting sustainable success and preemptively identifying potential adaptations (Ulrich et al., 2009, 110).

The second stage, akin to the four-step competency building framework, pertains to assessment. Ulrich et al. emphasize the pivotal role of HR professionals in ensuring alignment between the assessment process and expectations, along with a continuous feedback loop based on outcomes (Ulrich et al., 2009, 111). This feedback mechanism should encompass diverse sources to encompass all pertinent stakeholders and establish a direct link to performance. Any discerned disparities between expectations and actual outcomes should prompt a thorough search for strategies to mitigate them (Ulrich et al., 2009, 111–114).

The third phase, labeled as investments, primarily centers on enhancing the competencies of HR professionals through educational initiatives. The allocation of resources towards HR training and development should be geared towards maximizing efficacy. This optimization is best achieved through the integration of the following five components:

1. A close connection of HR training to strategy as well as to customers and investors
2. A preparation of an integrated HR development model
3. The consideration of training as an experience rather than an event
4. The integration of real work in training programs and hence an action learning approach
5. An analysis of training

The pursuit of this methodology significantly enhances the potential for effective training and ultimately the resultant impact, as posited by Ulrich et al. (2009, 114–119).

In the concluding step, namely measurement and follow-up, it is pivotal to quantitatively assess the efficacy of HR investments. This necessitates an examination of the extent to which individuals are facilitated in their career progression, how their growth contributes to organizational efficacy and strategic alignment, and the extent to which specific organizational capabilities are cultivated and perpetuated. To achieve this, the integration of HR development into HR performance management is imperative, alongside transparent communication of the HR transformation process. These measures are indispensable for optimizing organizational structure and fostering a robust orientation towards value delivery and tangible outcomes (Ulrich et al., 2009, 120–121).

4.5 HR Transformation and the Accountability of HR

The ultimate phase of the HR transformation process delineated by Ulrich et al. delves into the concept of HR accountability. Success in this transformative journey and adherence to the six delineated HR professional roles within this framework necessitates the establishment of a collective accountability among HR professionals, fostering heightened dedication and engagement. Stakeholders imbued with a sense of accountability and consequent responsibility towards the developmental trajectory exhibit greater support and interest in surmounting challenges encountered therein. The four pivotal stakeholder cohorts tasked with assuming responsibility encompass HR Leaders and professionals, line managers, external customers and investors, as well as consultants and advisers.

The cohort comprising HR Leaders and professionals represents a pivotal entity, given their primary aim of instigating and proficiently executing the delineated HR transformational endeavor. Absent a robust intent and aptitude in skills and compe-

4 The Second Adjustment to the Initial Model

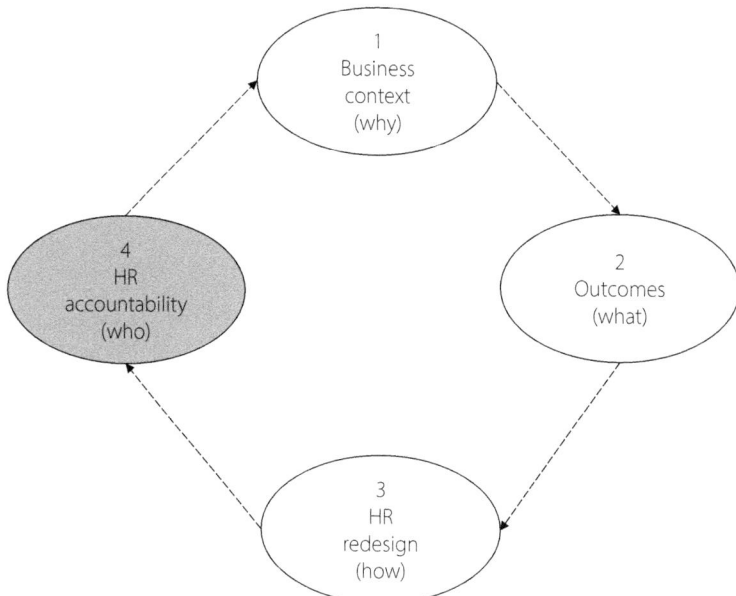

Fig. 4-8: HR Accountability in the Transformation Process (Ulrich et al., 2009, 123)

tencies, the trajectory of the transformational journey is predisposed to failure. HR professionals, particularly those in leadership roles, are obliged to fervently endorse the transformational initiative by investing considerable time and effort therein. Beyond merely instigating the process, it falls within their purview to assume leadership, orchestrate, and evaluate the evolutionary trajectory.

For line managers, it is generally imperative to possess the appropriate talent, at the precise time, and in the optimal quantity. Line managers may be held responsible for the transformational process owing to their vested interest and capacity for enhancement in achieving their objectives. HR professionals are advised to elucidate the advantages of the transformational process to line managers, thereby increasing their likelihood of actively supporting the process for their own benefit. When line managers perceive themselves benefiting from the transformational process, they are more inclined to engage actively and assume ownership. Moreover, establishing a trusting relationship and being perceived as Credible Activists becomes easier for HR professionals. Nevertheless, HR professionals should clarify from the outset, as well as throughout the process, that they also serve as coaches aiming to propel the process forward through inquiry.

Crucially, HR professionals must dispel misconceptions regarding HR and clarify that they are not solely accountable for the success of the transformational process. Instead, they must emphasize that the benefits of HR transformation and its intended outcomes are ultimately not for HR's sake but for customer benefit, hence value creation. Line managers do not receive benefits without obligation; they are mandated to contribute to a successful transformational process. As external customers and, indirectly, investors are the recipients of the transformational process, their intentions and expectations must be duly considered. Their experiences and ideas for improvement are critical for value creation and, consequently, for the developmental trajectories of the transformational process.

The involvement of consultants and advisors in the transformational process is advantageous, as this cohort can significantly contribute to its advancement and management. They can leverage their expertise and insights to surmount typical challenges encountered in transformation processes. In addition to articulating clear rationales for the transformational process and its objectives, HR professionals and other stakeholder groups must collaboratively devise a coherent developmental framework. This framework should encompass milestones delineating what needs to be accomplished, activities specifying how tasks should be executed, and outcome monitoring to evaluate progress (Ulrich et al., 2009, 125–143).

5 The Third Adjustment to the Initial Model – Victory Through Organization – Why the War for Talent Is Failing Your Company and What You Can Do About It

5.1 The Increasing Relevance of HR in the Context of the "War for Talent"

In 2017, Ulrich et al. published the most recent iteration of HR Business Partnering, which is a model often cited in organizational management. Comparable to the seminal work, the title of their publication, "Victory Through Organization: Why the War for Talent Is Failing Your Company and What You Can Do About It," succinctly conveys its primary objective. This title serves as an initial indicator of the model's focus on the deficiencies observed in talent acquisition strategies within contemporary business environments.

From the outset, Ulrich et al. underscore the necessity for significant adjustments to their model, prompted by the escalating intensity of the "War for Talent." This phrase denotes the competitive landscape characterized by fierce recruitment and retention battles among organizations. Ulrich et al. assert the profound influence of talent-related issues on organizational performance. They posit that mishandling employee concerns could precipitate the downfall of a company, thus emphasizing the criticality of effective HR management practices. Consequently, it is readily apparent that HR professionals bear a weighty responsibility amidst the escalating significance of HR matters. However, this heightened responsibility also presents a dual challenge and opportunity. Ulrich et al. contend that HR professionals can navigate these challenges by enhancing the quality and efficacy of their practices, thereby adapting to the evolving demands of HR work.

HR professionals must broaden their perspective beyond the paradigm of the "War for Talent" to recognize it merely as the inception of their endeavors. The possession of skilled HR serves as a pivotal foundation for success; however, effective HR operations necessitate congruence with suitable organizational structures and strategies. Failure to align with these elements results in missed opportunities, as elucidated by Ulrich et al. (2017, ix). Ulrich et al. assert an ameliorated landscape for HR professionals, with heightened prospects for implementing proposed models within corporate frameworks. Organizations and their leaders increasingly acknowledge the pivotal role of HR efforts in determining their overall success. Consequently, there is a heightened emphasis on HR issues, which have metamorphosed into crucial business imperatives (Ulrich et al., 2017, 5).

Moreover, companies and their managers have grasped the intrinsic link between intangibles, leadership, and resultant financial outcomes. As a corollary, HR professionals find themselves not only more frequently included in strategic discussions but also entrusted with greater expectations to provide strategic insights. This paradigm shift empowers HR professionals to fulfill their envisioned roles and enhance both individual and organizational capabilities. The significance of HR issues transcends the confines of the "War for Talent" and is underscored by four additional factors. Firstly, there is the emergence of a dynamic business context encapsulated by the acronym STEPED, denoting social, technological, economic, political, environmental, and demographic trends. Secondly, there is a pronounced acceleration in the pace of change typified by the term VUCA (volatility, uncertainty, complexity, and ambiguity). These first two factors underscore the presence of opportunities and threats within the business milieu, characterized by heightened intensity and velocity of change. Thirdly, stakeholders articulate their expectations of HR professionals, thereby delineating essential tasks for maintaining success. These expectations vary contingent upon stakeholders' affiliations and are delineated comprehensively in the subsequent figure (Ulrich et al., 2017, 5).

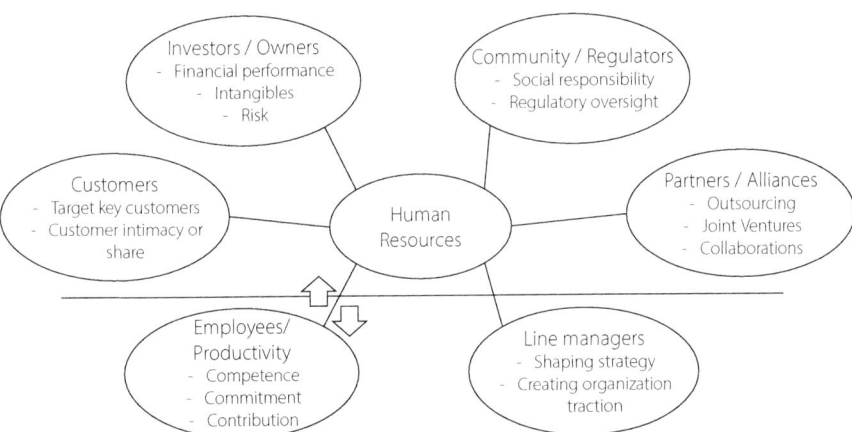

Fig. 5-1: Key Stakeholders to HR and Their Needs and Expectations (Ulrich et al., 2017, 12)

HR professionals exhibit heightened engagement in enhancing customer share, investor intangible, community reputation, and partnership cooperation delivery, thereby accruing significance in realizing these outcomes. It is incumbent upon HR professionals to facilitate the strategic development of leaders, concomitantly with the enhancement of employee productivity.

This progression leads to the fourth determinant, which encompasses the reaction of employees to alterations in the work milieu and consequent behavioral shifts. Of particular note, six societal shifts exert influence on workplace dynamics, collectively termed the six I's: intensity, individuation, isolation, indifference, immediacy, and in-group dynamics. For HR professionals to achieve success, they must possess a deeper comprehension of the requisites for organizational success both presently and in the future. Furthermore, an effective preparatory process necessitates a comprehensive understanding of contextual factors, procedural intricacies, stakeholder dynamics, and personal attributes impacting competitiveness. It is imperative for HR professionals to recognize that the competitiveness of organizations hinges upon their efforts and accomplishments (Ulrich et al., 2017, 12–15).

In contrast to their prior works, Ulrich et al. adopt a distinct approach in their latest publication. They initially delineate the adjustments made to the roles of Business Partners before elaborating on the underlying causes and rationales. This method is aimed at providing a comprehensive overview spanning from the original model to the current iteration of Business Partnering.

5.2 The Nine Roles of Business Partnering and Their Value Creation Contribution

The first category is Core Drivers, which includes the following three roles:

- "Strategic Positioner: Able to position a business to win in its market
- Credible Activist: Able to build relationships of trust by having a proactive point of view
- Paradox Navigator: Able to manage tensions inherent in making change happen (e. g., be both long and short term, be both top down and bottom up)" (Ulrich et al., 2017, 34)

The second category is Strategic Enablers, which includes the following three roles:

- "Culture and Change Champion: Able to make change happen and to weave change initiatives into culture change
- Human Capital Curator: Able to manage the flow of talent by developing people and leaders, driving individual performance, and building technical talent
- Total Rewards Steward: Able to manage employee well-being through financial and nonfinancial rewards" (Ulrich et al., 2017, 34)

The third category is Foundational Enablers, which includes the following three roles:

- "Technology and Media Integrator: Able to use technology and social media to drive high-performing organizations
- Analytics Designer and Interpreter: Able to use analytics to improve decision making
- Compliance Manager: Able to manage the processes related to compliance by following regulatory guidelines" (Ulrich et al., 2017, 35)

5.2 The Nine Roles of Business Partnering and Their Value Creation Contribution

Ulrich et al. have transitioned away from assigning roles solely based on individuals and business accessibility, opting instead to classify them into three distinct categories. Moreover, they have introduced three additional roles, resulting in a total of nine roles. With an equitable distribution, each category encompasses three roles apiece.

The delineated taxonomies and their respective functional roles are visually represented in the subsequent figure.

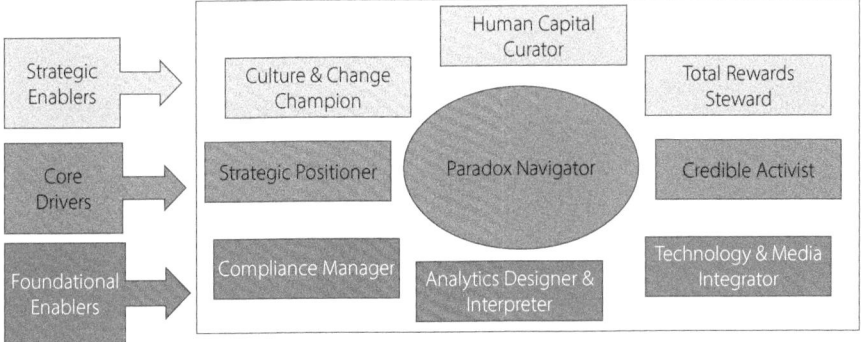

Fig. 5-2: 2016 HR Competency Model: Round 7 (Ulrich et al., 2017, 35)

Ulrich et al. have adopted a novel empirical methodology in their 2017 publication. This approach emphasizes observational data and quantitative analysis. As an instance of this methodological shift, they have incorporated a comprehensive competency domain average for each rating group across the nine delineated roles, as illustrated in the subsequent figure.

Tab. 4: Round 7 Competency Domain Averages by Rater Type (Ulrich et al., 2017, 37)

	1 All raters (non-self ratings)	2 Self-ratings	3 Supervisor ratings	4 HR Associate ratings	5 Non-HR Associate ratings
Number of raters	27,904	3,964	3,738	13,168	10,998
Strategic Positioner	4.13	4.05	3.94	4.13	4.21
Credible Activist	4.33	4.35	4.27	4.29	4.42
Paradox Navigator	3.99	3.87	3.86	3.98	4.08
Culture and Change Champion	4.03	3.96	3.88	4.02	4.11
Human Capital Curator	4.01	3.90	3.88	4.01	4.08

5 The Third Adjustment to the Initial Model

Tab. 4 Round 7 Competency Domain Averages by Rater Type (Ulrich et al., 2017, 37) – continued

	1 All raters (non-self ratings)	2 Self-ratings	3 Supervisor ratings	4 HR Associate ratings	5 Non-HR Associate ratings
Analytics Designer and Interpreter	4.01	3.89	3.78	4.04	4.06
Total Rewards Steward	3.88	3.76	3.81	3.86	3.95
Technology and Media Integrator	3.92	3.77	3.78	3.93	3.96
Compliance Manager	4.32	4.34	4.31	4.30	4.38
Overall averages	**4.07**	**3.99**	**3.94**	**4.06**	**4.14**

Comparing the mean values, it becomes evident that the self-assessments of HR professionals exhibit higher scores than those of supervisors, albeit both are inferior in comparison to the mean score of all assessors. There exist several potential explanations for these findings. It is plausible that HR professionals possess a heightened awareness of their limitations compared to their evaluators. Additionally, HR professionals may exhibit lower self-assurance in their competencies than the confidence others have in them. However, a more likely scenario is that external raters perceive HR professionals as capable of achieving more. Overall, there appears to be a trend indicating that the perceived self-image and self-assurance regarding their own competencies may impede the enhancement of HR professional effectiveness and contribution to value (Ulrich et al., 2017, 36–37).

Ulrich et al. conducted an analysis to assess the extent to which each of the nine roles can elucidate overall effectiveness. Their findings are illustrated in the subsequent table.

Tab. 5: Independent Impact of Each HR Competency on Overall Individual Effectiveness (Ulrich et al., 2017, 41) (In all tables, bold numbers are statistically significant at 0.05 level; scores in brackets are negative)

	Percentage of overall effectiveness explained by each competency domain (adds up to 100 %)
Strategic Positioner	14.5
Credible Activist	19.3
Paradox Navigator	11.7
Culture and Change Champion	14.2

Tab. 5: Independent Impact of Each HR Competency on Overall Individual Effectiveness (Ulrich et al., 2017, 41) (In all tables, bold numbers are statistically significant at 0.05 level; scores in brackets are negative) – continued

	Percentage of overall effectiveness explained by each competency domain (adds up to 100 %)
Human Capital Curator	13.1
Analytics Designer and Interpreter	8.2
Total Rewards Steward	(6.2)
Technology and Media Integrator	(4.9)
Compliance Manager	7.9
Percentage of effectiveness R^2 explained by competencies	83.4

The data demonstrates that all nine competencies exert influence on effectiveness, with the Credible Activist role identified as paramount. Following this, the Strategic Positioner exhibits the second most significant impact, succeeded by the Culture and Change Champion, the Human Capital Curator, and the Paradox Navigator, in respective order, all contributing to the outcomes (Ulrich et al., 2017, 41).

In their analysis, Ulrich et al. ascertain that Business Partners engaged in strategic discussions should prioritize embodying the attributes of a Credible Activist and carefully consider their affiliations. Moreover, they establish a strong correlation between the Paradox Navigator and the Strategic Positioner with preceding business performance, attributing this phenomenon to the dynamic nature of the business landscape. Despite the acknowledged importance of individual competencies among HR professionals, the collective competencies within the HR department wield a considerably greater impact. Consequently, it is deduced that while enhancing the proficiency of HR professionals is crucial, augmenting the capabilities of the HR department holds greater significance (Ulrich et al., 2017, 41–48).

5.3 The Relevance of Organization and Its Practices

The prioritization of organizational capability over individual talent acquisition is advocated by Ulrich et al. for enhancing competitive advantage (Ulrich et al., 2017, 55). They accentuate this perspective by highlighting that HR departments integrated into the organizational framework yield a fourfold enhancement in business performance compared to individual HR professional competencies. Notably, the organizational HR function generates double the value for external customers in contrast to individual HR professionals, while for line managers, the value creation is quadrupled when compared to individual contributions (Ulrich et al., 2017, 55–58).

In spite of the recently emphasized shift towards enhancing the overall capabilities of the HR department rather than focusing on individual HR talents and skills, there is a noticeable dearth of novel insights regarding organizational capability compared to the preceding developmental paradigm. However, the impact of human capital factors on business performance remains relatively insignificant, thus making only a marginal contribution to the establishment of competitive advantage (Ulrich et al., 2017, 69).

Moreover, there is an observable transition occurring in the domain of technological proficiencies. While possessing technical expertise and maintaining its currency are crucial, the primary imperative lies in the effective utilization of technological knowledge and the cultivation of organizational capability (Ulrich et al., 2017, 70).

Ulrich et al. delineate the avenues through which activities and HR departments influence business performance. In the short term, HR departments are tasked with prioritizing employee performance, encompassing metrics, incentives, training, and empowerment. However, the enhancement of value for regulators, line managers, and employees is optimally achieved through the deployment of integrated HR services, aligning with a facet of the book's title: "Victory Through Organization" (Ulrich et al., 2017, 79–83).

The optimal realization of integrated HR services and activities occurs when HR departments are adept at devising practices that account for culture and core competencies, alongside a concerted focus on implementing a high-performing work system, strategic HR management, and effective HR systems (Ulrich et al., 2017, 100).

In order to optimize value delivery and prioritize outcome orientation, it is imperative for HR practitioners to establish cohesive methodologies and offerings grounded in proficient execution across the nine delineated roles within the existing framework. This necessitates a comprehensive understanding of the requisites, commitments, anticipations, duties, and liabilities associated with each role.

These aforementioned attributes will be delineated for each of the nine roles henceforth. Initially, emphasis will be placed on elucidating the functions of the Core Drivers. Subsequently, attention will shift towards the Strategic Enablers and Foundational Enablers.

5.4   The Category of Core Drivers

5.4.1   The Credible Activist

In the first category, the primary role is that of the Credible Activist, serving as a Core Driver within the organizational framework. The logical derivation of this role's significance lies in its capacity to generate value for the business entity. Consequently, the integration of HR professionals into strategic discourse becomes imperative. This integration hinges upon their portrayal as trusted and adept advisors, facilitating their involvement in critical business deliberations. Drawing from robust knowledge reservoirs and experiential insights, HR professionals must adopt a proactive stance, offering credible and comprehensible recommendations to propel progress. Establishing robust and trust-based alliances with partners is essential, accompanied by an inherent inclination to identify and advocate for improvement opportunities within the organizational fabric. Furthermore, an openness to discern and contribute to evolving organizational strategies and priorities is crucial.

The articulation of potential avenues for value creation, coupled with their effective execution, serves to fortify credibility. Only through the cultivation of trust and proactive engagement can HR professionals realize their full potential value within the organizational milieu. Thus, personal credibility and a steadfast commitment to strategic input emerge as focal points of HR competency.

The principal challenge faced by HR professionals in assuming and sustaining the role of Credible Activists revolves around strategically situating their organization and its HR endeavors amidst dynamic market dynamics. The cultivation of business acumen and adept communication skills is paramount in this endeavor, alongside a dedication to continuous self-improvement. To ensure this progression, HR professionals are encouraged to formulate and pursue a structured self-improvement regimen encompassing five fundamental steps, as delineated by Ulrich et al. (2017, 131–144):

1. "Recognition of the need for change
2. A specific goal, time frame, and plan of action for changing
3. Support before, during, and after taking action
4. Rigorous monitoring progress
5. Help from a spotter or admired individual who reinforces and supports change motivation and commitment" (Ulrich et al., 2017, 144)

To evolve as a Credible Activist, it is imperative to exhibit personal integrity and ethical conduct, as these serve as the foundational elements for establishing credibility and engendering trust, thereby fostering efficacy in HR management. Optimal attainment of these objectives can be realized through the generation of favorable outcomes (Ulrich et al., 2017, 144–149). Moreover, HR professionals ought to authentically delineate achievable objectives and subsequently fulfill them. This practice not only reinforces a value-driven approach but also fosters the cultivation of trust.

5.4.2 The Strategic Positioner

In their capacity as Strategic Positioners, HR professionals are tasked with integrating distinctive data, insights, and recommendations regarding talent, leadership, and organizational dynamics, thereby fostering a competitive edge. This competence fortifies their standing and visibility within deliberations while fostering organizational advancement (Ulrich et al., 2017, 151). The pivotal element for HR professionals to accomplish this feat lies in possessing a robust comprehension of the business ecosystem and its dynamics. A profound understanding of the business environment facilitates the discernment of nascent trends and alterations, imperative for delineating developmental imperatives and potentials, thereby steering the future trajectory of the enterprise.

Furthermore, HR professionals must instigate the metamorphic process to seize these opportunities. They must proficiently extrapolate talent, leadership, and organizational endeavors from the business strategy, ensuring alignment with developmental prospects. Hence, these elements are intricately intertwined, with HR professionals serving as conduits. Through this intricate nexus, HR professionals contribute to crafting a forward-looking vision for organizational evolution (Ulrich et al., 2017, 151–155). To evolve into genuine Strategic Partners, Ulrich et al. outline four distinct phases:

1. "Master the language and flow of business.
2. Recognize and deliver strategy and sources of competitive advantage.
3. Understand and co-create with external stakeholders.
4. Anticipate and react to external business trends and context." (Ulrich et al., 2017, 155)

The Strategic Positioner plays a pivotal role in enhancing the efficacy of HR and catalyzing business outcomes. HR practitioners are tasked with augmenting their competencies in deciphering the commercial landscape, comprehending stakeholder anticipations, and internal business mechanics (Ulrich et al., 2017, 160). Collaboration and synergy with line managers are pivotal for HR professionals functioning as Strategic Positioners to grasp a unit's contribution to value generation within the enterprise and discern its strategic direction and vulnerabilities. To genuinely embody a strategic role, HR professionals must conduct risk analyses and discern which HR initiatives, schemes, and methodologies can mitigate these risks. Such endeavors are often indispensable for organizational value augmentation. Ulrich et al. delineate three pivotal facets crucial for strategy implementation. Firstly, HR professionals must adeptly narrate stories, which involves comprehending the overarching vision and strategy. Secondly, they must interpret strategies, translating them into actionable measures concerning talent, organizational culture, and leadership. Thirdly, they must facilitate strategies, ensuring alignment of processes to bolster the likelihood of successful strategy execution (Ulrich et al., 2017, 160–175).

5.4.3 The Paradox Navigator

As the Paradox Navigator, HR professionals face the primary challenge of harmonizing seemingly contradictory activities, as well as those occurring concurrently which demand coordination. This is notably evident across operational versus inspirational, administrative versus strategic, and transactional versus transformational realms. Navigating paradoxes presents formidable hurdles, compounded by the rapid and unpredictable shifts in the business landscape, as indicated by STEPED and VUCA frameworks. These dynamics elevate the significance of agility and adeptness in change management to ensure organizational alignment and adaptability (Ulrich et al., 2017, 178–179).

In their role as Paradox Navigators, HR professionals are tasked with maintaining a clear trajectory for the organization in line with its vision. The challenge lies in effecting short-term adjustments while adhering to long-term objectives. Ideally, there exists a robust correlation among short-term, mid-term, and long-term goals, bolstered by strong alignment. However, there must be ample flexibility not only to prioritize and pursue directional goals but also to embrace divergence, facilitating exploration of alternatives and fostering diversity (Ulrich et al., 2017, 185).

The pivotal function of the Paradox Navigator is paramount within the contemporary paradigm of business partnership due to its profound influence on antecedent business efficacy and its integrative dimension. Paradox navigation thus substantially augments value generation and the evolutionary capacity of value provision within the present circumstances and notably in prospective scenarios.

Ulrich et al. (2017, 189–190) delineate five procedural stages for addressing paradoxes to optimize value creation:

1. Clarify the poles of the paradox
2. Define best outcomes
3. See others' points of view
4. Find common ground
5. Take first steps (Ulrich et al., 2017, 194–195)

5.5 The Category of Strategic Enablers

5.5.1 The Culture and Change Champion

The subsequent section delineates the roles of Strategic Enablers. The initial role of Culture and Change Champions pertains to acting as a catalyst for cultural transformation and organizational change. The requisite proficiencies associated with this function wield significant influence over the efficacy of HR, consequently impacting value generation. Consequently, HR practitioners exert substantial influence over both individual and collective outcomes through this capacity. The nexus between culture and change underscored within this role vividly illustrates the intrinsic correlation between these constructs, emphasizing their symbiotic relationship. Modifications instituted within HR initiatives and protocols, encompassing realms such as performance evaluation, career trajectory planning, skills enhancement, and data administration, must harmonize closely with the prevailing organizational ethos.

Owing to the volatile nature of the contemporary corporate landscape and its ramifications for business operations alongside HR initiatives, adept change management assumes paramount importance for fostering value. Change initiatives necessitate meticulous consideration of organizational culture, given their propensity to impact norms, behaviors, and value systems. Hence, it is imperative to assess the repercussions of these initiatives on organizational culture, potentially necessitating adjustments to align with the evolving business milieu. Ulrich et al. delineate a four-tiered approach aimed at enhancing proficiency in the role of culture champion:

1. Think outside-in to define the right culture
2. Audit the extent to which there is a shared desired culture among the management team
3. Translate external promises of brand identity into internal actions
4. Raise cultural issues at key events

In the process of change, it is imperative for individuals to demonstrate proficiency in establishing credibility, adeptness in strategic positioning, and prowess in navigating paradoxes. Change is more likely to happen effectively if HR professionals …

1. are aware of yourself and others
2. are transparent
3. can zoom out and zoom in
4. are an agile learner
5. are willing to share credit and accept failure
6. are disciplined by having a change toolkit
7. can sequence change (Ulrich et al., 2017, 199–209)

5.5.2 The Human Capital Curator

In the role of Strategic Enablers, the secondary function pertains to human capital curation. This role has garnered increased significance, particularly amidst the emergence of the "War for Talent", wherein individual worth is subject to influence, thereby impacting organizational potential. Ulrich et al. accentuate the term "curator", stressing its relevance in amalgamating the emotional dimension of employee retention and contentment, alongside talent cultivation and the alignment of extant and forthcoming HR competencies vital for organizational triumph.

The role of the Human Capital Curator emerges as the foremost value-enhancing element for line managers. Additionally, possessing adept talent and adequate human capital robustly buttresses performance, thereby augmenting organizational potential. The scrutiny of human capital and its enhancement assumes pivotal importance in organizational triumph, underscoring its indispensability in HR methodologies, procedures, and framework.

Furthermore, leadership assumes considerable significance owing to the value leaders can engender in human capital cultivation. For HR practitioners, proficiency in human capital curation holds paramount importance, as it yields immediate and future benefits for the organization, fostering credibility and aiding in surmounting challenges stemming from talent scarcity. To excel as Human Capital Curators, HR must:

1. Master the science of talent
2. Discover uniqueness and should not assume others to be like them
3. Manage quality and equity at the same time
4. Design and deliver integrated human capital solutions and not only isolated practices (Ulrich et al., 2017, 209–215).

5.5.3 The Total Rewards Steward

The third and ultimate function of Strategic Enablers pertains to the role of the Total Rewards Steward. In this capacity, HR professionals are tasked with intensifying their consideration of the significance of rewards within the framework of HR practices. Rewards, alongside the compensation framework at large, exert an influence on both employee and organizational conduct. Despite the findings of Ulrich et al., indicating a marginal effect on personal effectiveness, stakeholder value, and business outcomes, this role warrants attention as rewards and the compensation system serve as indicators of priority and can impact employee retention and satisfaction, particularly amidst the escalating "War for Talent." To enhance proficiency as Total Rewards Stewards, Ulrich et al. propose:

1. Worrying less about being a compensation expert and more about understanding basic compensation principles
2. Keep compensation messages clear and understandable
3. Listen to compensation experts
4. Use rewards to reinforce, not create, change
5. Help employees find meaning and purpose from their work. (Ulrich et al., 2017, 215–222)

5.6 The Category of Foundational Enablers

5.6.1 The Compliance Manager

The ultimate category delineated is the Foundational Enablers, representing fundamental elements essential for operational efficacy. It is evident that adept HR practitioners are tasked with overseeing both strategic and foundational dimensions. Within this paradigm, the foremost position is occupied by the Compliance Manager, whose primary responsibility involves ensuring adherence to established regulations and standards. Compliance assumes significant importance in organizational functionality owing to its profound implications on long-term outcomes. Adherence to policies and regulations is indispensable for the smooth execution of operational procedures. HR professionals are mandated to foster synergy among regulatory compliance, business performance, educational initiatives, and labor reservoirs. Facilitating regulatory innovation and striving for transparency are indispensable auxiliary components to be seamlessly integrated. Ulrich et al. advocate a specific set of guidelines for HR professionals assuming this pivotal role:

1. Learn current and anticipate future regulation
2. Do regulation forums with business leaders and employees
3. Act quickly and fairly when inappropriate behavior occurs
4. Be a role model (Ulrich et al., 2017 223–231)

5.6.2 The Analytics Designer and Interpreter

In the capacity of an Analytics Designer and Interpreter, enhancing information management poses a significant challenge in catalyzing positive business outcomes, with HR's potential contribution to value delivery being a focal point. Within this capacity, it becomes imperative to scrutinize the influence of HR professionals on organizational efficacy and business performance. Additionally, there arises a necessity to delineate a clear emphasis on business outcomes and subsequently discern which analytical pursuits merit attention in uncovering impactful investments. Through meticulous data acquisition, HR professionals can construct an HR scorecard, attain actionable insights, pinpoint effective HR interventions, and evaluate their consequential business ramifications. This comprehensive approach allows HR professionals to delineate and establish benchmarks for business impact assessment. For making improvements in the role of an Analytics Designer and Integrator, HR must …

1. create a line of sight between business challenges and HR investments
2. learn the basics of research methodology and statistics
3. see patterns in data that tell a story

Utilizing this framework, HR professionals possess the capacity to construct a formidable stance and exert influence during deliberations and eventual determinations (Ulrich et al., 2017, 232–240).

5.6.3 The Technology and Media Integrator

The third and conclusive function within the Foundational Enablers category pertains to the role of Technology and Media Integrator. Within this capacity, HR practitioners are tasked with assessing the evolution of technological advancements and media platforms, and their consequential effects on both business operations and HR methodologies. Of particular significance is the adept handling of technology and media interfaces, especially when engaging with clientele, operational supervisors, and stakeholders. The escalating pace of technological advancement, coupled with the pivotal role of media in areas such as employer branding, directly influences organizational efficacy and talent acquisition potential. To enhance proficiency and expertise in the capacity of technology and media integration, Ulrich et al. propose:

1. Recognize and learn the essential skills for technology and social media
2. Remember that technology and social media skills without the softer skills that apply the technology insights will remain inert
3. Access emerging technology and social media tools
4. Know the public target audiences for your social media messages
5. Create a personal brand that you would like to be known for and experiment with social media sites to promote that brand (Ulrich et al., 2017, 241–249)

5.7 HR Capacity Significance and HR Development Relevance

Individual competences significantly influence organizational value creation, as underscored by Ulrich et al. However, they assert a more potent impact emanates from the contributions of the HR department, thus amplifying organizational significance. Consequently, Ulrich et al. coined the term "victory through organization" in their book title. Furthermore, they incorporated the "War for Talent" into the title, recognizing its substantial ramifications for business leaders, HR professionals, and the developmental prospects of HR departments and organizations at large.

In this context, HR departments must enhance their capacity to develop and manage information effectively, culminating in the creation of integrated HR solutions tailored to present and future organizational challenges. Competence in the role of a Paradox Navigator is paramount due to the disparate temporal perspectives and objectives inherent within organizations. Hence, this role occupies a central position within the current Business Partner model.

Supporting roles such as the Credible Activist and the Strategic Positioner facilitate access to business deliberations and decisions, bolstering influence through the presentation of developmental proposals focused on value creation. The amalgamation of these nine roles aims to foster and fortify organizational capabilities, pivotal for business prosperity.

Consequently, HR professionals, particularly HR departments, should prioritize quality enhancement, skill elevation, and exemplification of leadership qualities. This entails effective information management, fostering collaboration, and establishing connections with other departments, not merely for inclusion in discussions but to genuinely contribute substantial value to the business (Ulrich et al., 2017, 254–263).

6 The Application of the Business Partnering Model and Its Challenges

The emergence of the Business Partner model instigated a profound transformation in the methodology of HR management. Initially, the model emphasized the imperative for HR management to validate its existence and articulated the imperative to evolve to attain relevance within organizational frameworks. HR management necessitates a departure from its historical role confined to administrative duties and challenges, thus transcending its classification as a cost determinant necessitating minimization. Rather, the HR department and Business Partners should pivot towards value addition and prioritize a results-driven approach across their operations, practices, programs, activities, and strategy. The advent of the Business Partner model catalyzed a significant shift in the developmental objectives, vision, mission, purpose, and goals of HR management. The pervasive adoption of the Business Partner model within organizations can primarily be attributed to its capacity to accentuate value creation and result orientation, alongside alignment with organizational strategy. This adoption stemmed not only from the model's potential for professional development among HR practitioners and management but also from the aspiration of HR management and professionals to demonstrate their contribution to organizational success through value delivery. By embracing the realization of the Business Partner model, HR professionals are empowered to rationalize investments in HR management within organizations, thus contributing to value creation.

The initial conceptualization of Business Partnering delineated the duties and obligations of Business Partners across four distinct roles. This segmentation into the roles of Administrative Expert, Employee Champion, Change Agent, and Strategic Partner effectively demarcated the tasks, responsibilities, accountability, and objectives of HR professionals. The categorization of HR professionals' work into process-centric versus people-centric orientations, as well as operational versus strategic focuses, accounted for both short-term and long-term objectives, emphasizing the significance of processes and HR. This delineation provided HR professionals with a clear framework for their work, outlining the challenges, requisites, and demands they face.

The model and its objectives offered a precise foundation for reshaping HR practices. An essential challenge for Business Partners lies in comprehending the developmental process, its underlying rationales, and the ensuing changes. They must integrate these novelties into their work, acquire requisite skills, discern the ramifications of these changes, and understand their interconnectedness. Additionally, they must ensure result-oriented approaches and value delivery to enhance their current situation, adapt and oversee their own skills development and strategy, bolster the acknowledgment of customer value creation, and orchestrate and advance the transformation process.

HR professionals are tasked with analyzing evolving factors and their potential impact on present and future work. Despite an organization's vision and mission delineating its developmental trajectory, managing evolving goals and achieving them pose significant challenges for value creation and results orientation due to their continual flux, necessitating frequent adjustments. Besides adapting goals, HR professionals must harmonize short-term and long-term value creation and development to establish credibility for justifying necessary investments in HR competencies to further professionalize Business Partnering.

Line managers and organizational management are inclined to invest in Business Partnering and the HR department only when they perceive benefits. Therefore, communicating delivered value to stakeholders becomes pivotal. To bolster their potential, HR professionals must devise and pursue a vision, mission, and goals for their development, evaluate Business Partner roles, and assess their skills and competencies across the nine current Business Partnering roles. Recent assessments by Ulrich indicate a considerable enhancement in skill levels across most roles, a development acknowledged by line managers.

The recognition that HR issues have evolved into business issues is conducive to Business Partners' development. Line managers increasingly view HR topics as vital, leading to greater integration and consultation with HR professionals. However, this integration also presents challenges, as it raises expectations for HR professionals, necessitating continuous efforts to maintain customer satisfaction and foster their own development. A significant challenge in greater integration into decision-making processes is the need for HR professionals to possess deeper business context knowledge. Furthermore, they must discern internal and external factors necessitating adjustments to HR activities, processes, programs, and strategies, proactively identifying crucial aspects impacting goal realization potential.

A primary challenge faced by HR professionals in implementing Business Partnering is the need to collaborate with line managers and persuade them that addressing HR challenges is not solely the responsibility of HR professionals. Many HR programs and activities entail shared accountability and responsibility between HR professionals and line managers, necessitating line managers to also assume HR tasks and responsibilities. Furthermore, in addition to acknowledging shared accountability with HR professionals, both line managers and organizational management must recognize the need for their own development, as well as that of HR professionals, requiring investments in talent. Collaboration between line managers and HR professionals is essential for enhancing value creation, and both parties must recognize the necessity for closer cooperation to achieve organizational success.

The aforementioned imperative for development also highlights the need for HR professionals to have a deeper understanding of their roles, associated challenges, obligations, and their interconnectedness. They must fully embrace the objectives and purpose of Business Partnering and actively pursue developmental pathways. Central to advancing Business Partnering are organizational success, result orientation, and value creation. Despite positive trends in the perceived competencies of Business Partnering roles, HR professionals cannot afford to diminish their focus on further skill and competency development, remaining vigilant about future developments.

Line managers closely scrutinize the competencies and skills of HR professionals, particularly in relation to delivering results. Perceived competencies and skills are tightly linked to the ability of HR professionals to provide timely solutions to new challenges, ideally in a proactive manner. Failure to do so may lead to a rapid decline in the current high skill level of HR professionals. Therefore, HR professionals are advised to stay abreast of megatrends impacting HR work and organizational dynamics. Among these trends, the "War for Talent," as integrated by Ulrich in his final book, holds significant sway, with its effects reverberating across organizations, HR functions, and the collaboration between HR professionals and line managers.

While the scarcity of talent poses significant challenges for HR professionals, it also presents a significant opportunity for the evolution of Business Partnering. Each of the nine Business Partner roles necessitates a reconsideration of development requirements and evolving competencies crucial for success. Given the scarcity of talent in terms of both quantity and quality, greater emphasis must be placed on HR development and the identification of leverage points. As discussed later, a key challenge for HR professionals lies in aligning HR development initiatives with each Business Partner role to ensure value creation and a tight alignment between organizational strategy and HR objectives.

Before delving into the ramifications of talent scarcity on HR development and Business Partnering, it is imperative to underscore its significance.

7 The Implications of the "War for Talent" on HR Development and Business Partnering

7.1 Talent Shortage and Demographic Shift

The primary deficiency in talent can be attributed predominantly to two factors. Firstly, the dwindling pool of available individuals in the labor market is a consequence of demographic shifts. Secondly, alterations in attitudes and expectations compared to preceding generations of workers impact the availability of employees. The subsequent discussion will elucidate these factors and their ramifications for organizations.

The labor market is confronting formidable challenges in the current and forthcoming decades owing to demographic transitions. The gradual departure of the "Baby Boomer" cohort from the labor force coincides with the ingress of smaller cohorts, notably Generation Z, into the workforce. Consequently, there is an overarching diminution in the labor supply, coupled with a curtailed medium-term growth outlook for the economy. This exacerbates the scarcity of adept workers. While skill shortages have persisted in certain countries, particularly within specific industries and occupational strata, for numerous decades, demographic shifts are exacerbating these shortages, extending their reach from previously affected sectors to encompass a broader spectrum of industries and occupational categories. A discernible trend emerges wherein the erstwhile niche existence of skill shortages gradually expands, encompassing additional industries and occupational segments, gradually evolving into a pervasive dearth of skills across many nations. Thus, demographic changes wield considerable influence over the labor supply across protracted periods and play a pivotal role in shaping the future trajectory of the labor market (Obst, 2023, 13–14).

The shortfall in skilled labor and its ensuing ramifications are anticipated to culminate in a reduction of labor force capacity. Specifically, the challenges encountered by organizations in reconfiguring their workforce post-financial downturn underscore the complexities stemming from the scarcity of skilled labor. The expansion prospects of enterprises, potentially attainable, are hindered by the dearth of adept HR. In numerous nations, there exists a heightened engagement in the labor force, leading to a diminished unemployment rate. Within this sphere, the capacities of the labor market are frequently maximized in various instances. Nonetheless, an augmentation in weekly work hours remains a viable avenue for elongating labor duration. Nevertheless, enterprises are met with the obstacle of adapting to evolving employee attitudes and perceptions, a subject to be expounded upon subsequently (Obst, 2023, 15).

Owing to demographic patterns and employment trends, a diminishing labor pool is anticipated across many nations. For national economies, this portends a substantial constraint on growth potential due to a scarcity of skilled labor. For enterprises, this translates into an insufficiency in realizing their complete potential, with their operations and developmental opportunities curtailed by the inadequacy of skilled laborers. Hence, proficient and ample skilled HR will emerge as the pivotal determinants of success for enterprises. Collaborations in business, particularly within the realm of HR development, will accrue heightened significance in the forthcoming era and assume greater indispensability for enterprise success. The more acute the quantitative and qualitative scarcity of skilled labor, the greater the constraint on a company's developmental potential. Skilled laborers and HR development will thus transform into constraining factors for enterprises, as organizational objectives and strategies increasingly necessitate alignment with the capabilities achievable through the workforce. This implies that HR development becomes a decisive element in the enterprise's evolution for Business Partners and the entire HR management (Obst, 2023, 15–17).

The progression and repercussions of the expanding deficit of skilled labor within companies induce an augmented imperative to enlist individuals lacking the requisite qualifications and experiences upon recruitment. This engenders an additional hurdle in the domain of HR development for companies, particularly for Business Partners. Through strategic HR development, they must ensure prompt filling of extant gaps by employees, thereby augmenting productivity and broadening deployment potentials. Business Partners must ascertain that investments in HR development and HR are efficiently and purposively crafted. This necessitates thorough engagement with HR development and deliberate implementation across the nine individual roles of Business Partnering (Obst, 2023, 17–18).

In addition to augmenting efficiency and competencies in HR development, Business Partners must ensure adequate financial resources are allocated by the company, substantiated by credible results and positive organizational outcomes. Line managers must be persuaded that investments in HR development yield returns. Moreover, Business Partners must convince line managers of their shared responsibility in HR development and its execution. This entails mutual accountability in rendering HR development attractive to current employees and potential recruits, thereby bolstering both employee retention and the company's attractiveness as an employer (Obst, 2023, 18–21).

Companies, line managers, and Business Partners must recognize that the scarcity of skilled workers leads to the inability to fill all vacant positions, even with less suitable HR. The attractiveness of a company inversely correlates with the number of unfilled positions, making employer attractiveness pivotal in a labor market increasingly marked by a scarcity of skilled workers. The assertion "The war for talent is over – talent has won!" aptly characterizes the labor market dynamics.

In forthcoming times, companies will need to intensify efforts to enhance employer attractiveness, refine working conditions, and augment wages to ensure both attraction and retention of HR, mitigating migration to other companies. Companies are faced with novel challenges in the labor market, compounded by the escalating demand for adaptability in employee competencies and skills. Adaptability, agility, and flexibility have become indispensable traits that dictate the prosperity or downfall of numerous companies. Insufficient adaptation to new circumstances, particularly in HR development, jeopardizes production objectives, potential growth, and customer satisfaction, thus imperiling the competitiveness and survival of companies (Lay & Niebling, 2023, 24-25).

The digitalization of processes poses a formidable challenge for companies and their Business Partners, necessitating the cultivation of corresponding competencies among employees and the formulation of a transformation strategy. Nevertheless, digitalization also presents an opportunity to address the shortage of skilled workers. The successful digitalization of processes and the ensuing transformation hinge greatly on the competencies, development of competencies, and adaptability of skilled professionals. The importance of Business Partners, collaboration between Business Partners and line managers, and especially competency in HR development are underscored once more in this context (Stettes, 2023, 32-33).

7.2 The Necessity to Advance Productivity and Commitment

The optimization of labor productivity through the integration of digitized workflows and the effective cultivation of competencies via HR development is pivotal not only in diminishing requisite workforce allocation but also in aligning with escalating wage pressures. Within the delineated labor market context, heightened competition for skilled labor empowers employees to command notably elevated remuneration. Sustaining competitiveness mandates concerted efforts from companies, particularly from line managers and Business Partners, towards substantial amelioration of both labor productivity and work standards via HR development (Stettes, 2023, 34-35).

For corporations, line managers, and Business Partners, the imperative arises from profound transitional processes necessitating adept management. Business Partners and line managers are specially tasked in this developmental exigency, as employees must be empowered to meet this adaptive demand, emphasizing the fostering of willingness and acceptance. Alongside indispensable entrepreneurial adaptability in the transition phase, employee engagement assumes paramount importance. Ensuring this entails a rigorous commitment from Business Partners, notably in elucidating the need for change, employing transparent strategies, accommodating employee needs, involving them in the transition process, and foremost, ensuring substantial and efficacious investments in both their and line managers' ongoing education (Stettes, 2023, 35-36).

7.3 The Challenges with the Generations Y and Z and Their Values and Attitudes

In conjunction with demographic patterns, which currently manifest as an inability of labor market entrants to counterbalance exits, companies face an additional hurdle due to the evolving values of Generation Y and Z. The substantial rationale behind the value evolution in Generation Y and Z can be discerned within their socialization milieu.

Generation Z has matured within a Western societal epoch distinguished by affluence, technological progress, diverse commodities, and seemingly boundless avenues for consumption. Educational prospects have reached unprecedented heights, with parents typically nurturing their offspring in a needs-oriented and relational manner. The omnipresence of smartphones engenders a rapid-paced and boundary-erasing mentality fixated on instant gratification.

Socialization within this delineated milieu engenders contrasting perceptions, dispositions, and principles in comparison to preceding cohorts. Generation Z harbors aspirations for heightened engagement and sway within the professional sphere, introducing novel dilemmas for enterprises. Adaptation to discerning the requisites of the younger demographic and implementing commensurate measures is imperative for businesses (Einrahmhof-Florian, 2022, 45–48).

A pivotal determinant for Generation Z is the perceived allure of prospective employers. This encompasses the benefits that potential employees associate with affiliating with a specific organization. Perceived employer attractiveness is paramount for the attraction and retention of HR. Key facets of this concept comprise favorable working conditions, equitable remuneration, an enticing job description, opportunities for skill enhancement, as well as autonomy and decision-making prerogatives (Gemann, 2023, 74–75).

An influential factor impacting Generation Z and Generation Y is the advocacy for achieving work-life balance by corporations. This is feasible through the implementation of adaptable working environments and acknowledgment of varied life trajectories. There is an impetus on companies and their leadership to reassess conventional career paradigms, fostering diversity in professional journeys and introducing novel paths of leadership. Strategies like part-time employment, telecommuting, and assistance with caregiving obligations aim to streamline the integration of work and personal life. Corporate wellness initiatives, particularly those targeting stress mitigation, are considered pivotal for the psychological well-being of Millennials (Klaffke, 2022, 101–102).

In tandem with the pursuit of work-life equilibrium, both Generation Z and Y exhibit a notable inclination towards finding purposeful employment. Coveted vocations are typified by their capacity to effect change, advance sustainability, uphold social accountability, and safeguard the environment. The emphasis lies not solely on altering the world but on engaging in meaningful and diverse responsibilities that foster enjoyment through collaboration and knowledge exchange. Generation Z esteems innovative and creative work methodologies, facilitated by digital infrastructure and connectivity (Einrahmhof-Florian, 2022, 50).

The younger demographic increasingly seeks significance and endeavors for a detailed comprehension of their duties. Unidimensional leadership approaches, which fail to contextualize tasks within a holistic framework, engender demotivation. It is advisable for leaders to invest greater effort in elucidating the contributions of tasks to the overarching system and delineating sustainable impacts for the corporation, society, and personal advancement. Ideally, tasks should be more closely aligned with employees' interests to foster their growth and the cultivation of valuable networks. Often, a paradigmatic shift is warranted, tailoring tasks more intimately to employees' inclinations. Leaders should articulate the significance of additional commitment, such as overtime, particularly for the younger cohort. Employee self-development opportunities should be underscored, with autonomous work and avenues for personal evolution being especially pertinent for young staff. Leaders should also aid in the quest for meaning, focusing on task-related domains. Employees should have the autonomy to assess if the company resonates with their lifestyle. However, it is acknowledged that certain spheres of responsibility, like administrative tasks or pivotal support for other organizational domains, may not foreground an excessive questioning of meaning within a functional organizational structure (Sass, 2023, 172–173).

The burgeoning cohort of the young generation heralds considerable potential for societal, work-cultural, and entrepreneurial advancement. Their adeptness with digital media catalyzes transformational processes, spawning novel arenas of application. By scrutinizing purpose and advocating for heightened individualized consideration of accomplishments, the young generation presents a challenge to established leaders. Consequently, there emerges a shift in leadership paradigms, with a discernible pivot towards nurturing individual potentials and fostering introspection on meaningfulness. Leaders are thus compelled to evince a holistic interest in their workforce, transcending organizational confines (Sass, 2023, 156).

Given the pronounced self-awareness characteristic of Generation Z and their penchant for immediate gratification of needs, addressing these facets becomes imperative. Discrepancies within the work milieu may engender uncertainty and attrition, as individuals from this cohort are unaccustomed to introspection. This necessitates leaders to shepherd Generation Z with lucid directives and manageable assignments to avert overwhelm. In tandem with the autonomy and meaningfulness ascribed to work, leaders grapple with the task of instating coherent structures and fostering a congenial work environment. A leadership paradigm amalgamating transactional and transformational elements, underscored by lucid objectives and individual appreciation, resonates aptly with Generation Z. Moreover, leaders should be cognizant of the heightened propensity for job turnover within Generation Z, driven partly by labor market dynamics and partly by diminished frustration tolerance, potential resilience deficits, and augmented awareness of personal resources (Germann, 2023, 71–72).

Owing to the evolving conditions, expectations, attitudes, and behaviors of Generations Z and Y, corporations and their leadership will increasingly necessitate holistic approaches that encompass the employee experience. Within this rubric, primacy should be accorded to facets such as education, leadership, collaboration, alongside HR development, remuneration, and work-life equilibrium, to leverage the full potential of the organization. The value chain in HR management warrants critical scrutiny and restructuring along the axis of the "employee journey" (Klaffke, 2022, 99).

Continuing education and professional development are increasingly vital due to the progressive attitudes and aspirations of Generation Z, compounded by the impacts of digitization, structural shifts, and the trend towards agile working. Generation Z, despite achieving higher educational credentials, necessitates guidance in lifelong learning endeavors. Supervisors are urged to devote more time to coaching and mentoring, while also furnishing more comprehensive elucidations concerning the significance and advantages of HR development initiatives (Klaffke, 2022, 100–101).

The facilitation of further education and professional development can be enabled by executives in collaboration with HR. This involves the orchestration of qualification measures and a judicious assignment of tasks that harmonizes with the individual objectives of the employees. Regular feedback and employee discussions afford the opportunity to discern the professional advancement of employees and address pertinent subjects in quarterly meetings (Einrahmhof-Florian, 2022, 50). Leading young employees is advised to delineate tasks and areas of responsibility as manageable sub-projects (Sass, 2023, 170–172).

To allure, retain, and engage Generation Y, a nuanced compensation structure is imperative. Alongside a competitive base salary, so-called fringe benefits assume a pivotal role. These encompass varied supplementary benefits such as mobility allowances, childcare subsidies, health programs, and tuition fee coverage. It is crucial to periodically review and adapt these supplementary benefits as necessary to accommodate the evolving needs of employees. The cafeteria model, which furnishes employees with a negotiated budget for fringe benefits, facilitates individual choices and fosters a diverse and employee-centric corporate culture (Klaffke, 2022, 102).

According to Herzberg's two-factor theory, which delineates motivators (e. g., recognition and advancement) and hygiene factors (e. g., compensation and working conditions), the judicious selection of motivators holds paramount importance for fostering job satisfaction among Generation Z. This significance stems from its profound influence on work motivation. Job satisfaction within Generation Z can be construed as synonymous with engaging and challenging tasks. In order to cultivate enduring job satisfaction, emphasis should be placed on promoting intrinsic motivators (Einrahmhof-Florian, 2022, 45–48). The pertinence of "soft factors" such as recognition and collaboration concerning job satisfaction is increasingly being acknowledged (Germann, 2023, 67–68).

To mitigate the dearth of skilled professionals, it is imperative to bolster monetary aspects, collaboration, and appreciation. Particularly within the realms of collegiality and appreciation, intervention is warranted. Inadequate compensation, limited opportunities for further education, and insufficient acknowledgment emerge as pivotal factors contributing to voluntary attrition from organizations (Sass, 2023, 170–172).

Corporations, their leadership, and Business Partners must contemplate incentives for fostering performance motivation among the younger demographic. Monetary incentives such as salary are perceived by youthful individuals as foundational, with non-monetary incentives, notably intrinsic motivation through meaningful tasks, a culture of feedback, and developmental prospects, assuming critical significance. The meaningfulness of the professional domain and the quest for significance take precedence. Executives must assume the role of developmental mentors to nurture the individual growth of employees. Additionally, it is underscored that the company's image, sustainable practices, professional acumen, and career pathways are pivotal in the attraction and retention of young talents (Sass, 2023, 161–166).

To offer young employees a clear orientation, notwithstanding the potential infeasibility of some of their requests within the operational framework (Sass, 2023, 170–172), it is imperative to consider the role of corporate culture in shaping a positive employee experience. As posited by Edgar Schein, corporate culture encompasses observable artifacts, publicly declared values, and underlying, tacit assumptions. Culture cannot be imposed but must be internalized by the workforce to cultivate corporate identity and bolster employee engagement. It is underscored that organizations should cultivate a culture inclusive of all age groups. Specifically targeting the younger cohort necessitates the establishment of a dynamic, adaptable, and open culture characterized by vigor, dynamism, and flexibility (Einrahmhof-Florian, 2022, 48).

Contrary to older cohorts, Generation Z demonstrates a reduced inclination to fully embrace corporate culture and hierarchy. Young employees tend to actively align organizational culture with their individual values early on. There exists a diminished propensity for employer loyalty, with employment choices heavily influenced by current life circumstances. The younger demographic places increased importance on managing temporal resources consciously and prioritizing experiential aspects of life. This inclination extends to executive communication, which should be direct and timely. Additionally, companies and their leaders must acknowledge that Generation Z no longer uniformly perceives role models but instead engages in a process of selectively adopting successful individuals from their personal circles (Sass, 2023, 153–156).

7.4 The Relevance of HR Development in Combination with Superior Business Partner Role Execution

The ramifications stemming from talent scarcity present significant hurdles for corporations, supervisors, and particularly Business Partners. In order to mitigate these ramifications and ensure sustained competitive advantage and organizational success, there exists a pressing necessity to emphasize HR development facets within the purview of Business Partners and their nine distinct roles. Given the current developmental landscape and anticipated future challenges, Business Partners are compelled to enhance their HR development competencies. This endeavor not only facilitates the progression of Business Partners in their transformational journey but also reinforces their standing as strategic and reputable allies for line managers.

The advancement of HR development and, consequently, the nurturing of the HR potential of an enterprise significantly contribute to sustaining its viability, particularly amid the backdrop of talent scarcity where HR considerations assume heightened importance. The extent of talent scarcity within an enterprise directly constrains its potential and strategic evolution owing to an insufficiency in both the qualitative and quantitative dimensions of talent. As talent scarcity emerges as a decisive limitation on organizational and business progression, HR development emerges as a pivotal strategic determinant. In order to engender value and prioritize results-driven outcomes, Business Partners must diligently integrate HR development competencies across all nine of their roles. Each role assumed by Business Partners necessitates a delineation of the corresponding HR development competencies, as elucidated in the subsequent discourse.

8   HR Development Competencies for HR Business Partners in the Latest Competency Model

As a result of inadequate talent availability and the resultant repercussions, the cultivation of HR emerges as a strategically imperative element for organizational success. The significance of Business Partners and their proficiencies, alongside their capacities and enhancement, surges as employees and thus HR, alongside human capital, evolve into pivotal assets for organizational advancement and progress (Ilic, 2024, 275–277). The duty and liability to furnish value through proficient and adept HR and their enhancement escalate. This presents Business Partners with a significant opportunity juxtaposed with a formidable challenge. In addressing the challenges and obligations of HR development for each of the nine roles, Business Partners must ultimately amalgamate them to optimize value provision. Subsequently, pertinent HR development domains are delineated for each of the three role classifications of Business Partners. The initial classification encompasses Foundational Enablers.

8.1   Technology and Media Integrator

The primary function entails serving as the Technology and Media Integrator. In this capacity, Business Partners are tasked with maintaining awareness of contemporary, ongoing, and prospective challenges and advancements in HR development facilitated by technological and media innovations. Over recent years, notable advancements have been observed in the domain of HR development within this sphere. Alongside conventional face-to-face instruction, novel modalities and structures of learning have gained traction and proven advantageous for HR development. Virtual learning, Blended Learning, personalized learning initiatives, the integration of artificial intelligence (AI) in learning processes, and the utilization of gamification represent the prevailing modes of contemporary learning environments.

8.1.1   Virtual Learning

Virtual Reality (VR) provides a controlled environment conducive to the enhancement of cognitive and motor skill acquisition. Through advanced measurement techniques, VR facilitates the reproducible capture of cognitive processes, including attention and memory. The immersive and stimulating nature of VR supports cognitive rehabilitation while augmenting social, psychological, and emotional outcomes. Additionally, VR environments positively influence physical, physiological, and psychological well-being.

Augmented Reality (AR) has demonstrated significant successes, particularly in the domain of personality development. Context-aware AR applications deliver just-in-time adaptive interventions tailored to the user's needs. The integration of VR and AR holds potential for innovative advancements in HR development, specifically by training employees on new tools and providing continuous support in their daily tasks through AR. This combined approach can lead to a safer and more error-free onboarding process (Vollendorf & Jansen, 2023, 100).

In HR selection and development, VR and AR are increasingly significant, particularly in the administration of situational judgement tests and realistic job previews. These technologies allow for an immersive experience of job roles and responsibilities. Utilizing VR in HR selection and development facilitates the identification of problem-solving skills as well as existing and deficient competencies. This approach enables a comprehensive assessment of competency levels and developmental needs. Regular repetition of tasks under consistent, adapted, or supplementary conditions permits the measurement of progress and the identification of additional HR development requirements, as well as potential strategies and approaches for improvement. For Business Partners, this necessitates an understanding of work environments and the requisite competency levels and developmental trajectories to create an optimal and growth-promoting environment using VR and AR. Furthermore, the subsequent individual development of competencies is influenced by the measurement capabilities of VR and AR. Depending on decisions made and existing competencies and skills, diverse yet realistic scenarios can be employed through VR and AR to explore and analyze the boundaries of these competencies and skills.

VR and AR provide significant opportunities to enhance knowledge transfer and facilitate the dissemination of specialized knowledge within HR development. Consequently, VR and AR are highly effective tools for fostering competency development. In the context of continuing education, these technologies serve as potent instruments for HR development (Vollendorf & Jansen, 2023, 101–104). The analysis of extensive datasets supports well-informed and individualized decision-making, which subsequently informs HR development strategies. Employing VR and AR allows for the creation of customized training programs within HR development. Furthermore, the use of data enables the review of critical decisions and their underlying rationale, leading to the development of alternative solutions. Evaluating previously conducted training sessions provides more accurate insights into the alignment between individual capabilities and job requirements (Vollendorf & Jansen, 2023, 106). The deployment and utilization of advanced application possibilities in HR development facilitate the realistic simulation of situations that are costly, logistically complex, or hazardous. This approach, in conjunction with its previously mentioned benefits, contributes to the reduction of both costs and effort. Additionally, it serves as an effective, practical, modern, and widely accepted method for teaching and learning.

Business Partners must engage deeply with the promising opportunities presented by the utilization of VR and AR to fully realize their potential. VR and AR are poised to significantly impact corporate talent promotion strategies (Vollendorf & Jansen, 2023, 109–111). The innovative approach to HR development also considers the participants' beliefs and habits, particularly when they belong to the typical target demographic. However, Business Partners, acting as Technology and Media Integrators, must recognize individual differences in participants' affinity for VR and AR. These differences critically influence motivation and the outcomes achieved in HR development programs.

Prior to implementing this methodology, Business Partners in the role of Technology and Media Integrators should engage in dialogue with the target audience and ideally conduct a target group analysis to assess the general applicability of VR and AR within the company. Additionally, it is essential, especially at the inception of this form of HR development, to demonstrate a commitment to support and educate regarding the format and objectives of this approach. This should be complemented by an assessment of potential participants' technological openness. When a critical attitude is anticipated, yet the use of VR and AR is highly promising, Business Partners as Technology and Media Integrators must develop effective communication strategies and thoroughly prepare potential participants for the new HR development paradigm (Peterke, 2021, 41).

8.1.2   Blended Learning

Blended Learning is an educational approach that integrates traditional face-to-face instruction with digital learning resources, enhancing the efficacy and versatility of the learning experience. The term "Blended Learning" refers to the amalgamation of various teaching and learning modalities, including in-person instruction, online instruction, self-directed study, and other educational methods. The implementation of Blended Learning addresses issues related to temporal presence and supports the individual and flexible developmental progress of learners. Additionally, it accommodates diverse learning speeds and preferences, optimizing time and cost efficiency and thus enhancing the effectiveness of HR development. Moreover, the consideration of individual circumstances and conditions fosters learner motivation. For Business Partners, the challenge in utilizing and designing Blended Learning lies in aligning company-specific conditions with the interests and expectations of participants to create targeted and effective HR development programs. One crucial aspect is the introduction or expansion of the Blended Learning approach within the organization. Business Partners must understand the attitudes, expectations, starting points, and requisite competencies necessary for the implementation or enhancement of Blended Learning.

In designing company-specific and development-specific frameworks, Business Partners can align their strategies with various models, although further modifications may be necessary for optimal corporate implementation. Empirical evidence indicates that models incorporating frequent transitions between face-to-face teaching and online content are less favored by participants compared to more comprehensive models, such as the rotation model, the self-blend model, the flex model, and the enriched-virtual model (Friedrich-Haßauer, 2023, 112).

The rotation model integrates multiple pedagogical approaches, including e-learning, mini-projects, and direct instruction. The transition between in-person sessions and online-supported learning materials is typically managed through self-directed scripts, online content augmented by chat forums, and concluding in-person sessions. The model's efficiency and effectiveness are contingent upon the quality of the delivered content and the participants' ability to engage with it independently. A well-balanced rotation among instructional modalities fosters continuous engagement with the material and supports individual knowledge acquisition. This engagement is often reflected in the successful development of competencies. Therefore, the rotation model is pivotal in enhancing the learning process's efficiency and effectiveness (Friedrich-Haßauer, 2023, 112–114). It is crucial for Business Partners to consider the competencies, learning capabilities, motivation, and autonomy of potential participants when implementing this model. Leveraging this understanding, Blended Learning can be introduced or expanded according to the company's specific prerequisites and conditions. Additionally, it is important to recognize that participants have varying needs for support and motivation, as well as requirements for exchanging information about learning content, posing questions to responsible individuals, and receiving feedback.

In the flex model, instructional content is disseminated through a combination of in-person sessions and online platforms. Participants are able to integrate the course flexibly into their daily routines, although the specific content and assessments remain predefined. HR development offers adaptable didactic guidelines. In-person sessions facilitate communication, address questions, and sustain high levels of motivation.

The primary distinction between the rotation model and the flex model is that, in the latter, study materials can be engaged with entirely at the learner's discretion, without a predetermined pace. Instructional sessions may occur in either virtual or physical environments. However, this flexibility could result in diminished motivation for some learners, as they may need explicit temporal guidelines. Therefore, it is crucial that prospective participants in HR development programs have a role in shaping the program's design.

The flex model in Blended Learning garners extensive acceptance due to its consideration of individual prerequisites, interests, learning velocities, and pre-existing knowledge levels. This multifaceted approach has the potential to economize substantial amounts of time in the development of individual HR, as familiar content may be omitted or briefly revisited for knowledge rejuvenation. Additionally, this model presents the opportunity to construct a goal-directed and efficient HR development regimen tailored to diverse starting points, all converging towards a common objective. Through the flexibilization of the development process, the individual overseeing competency development wields significant influence over learning outcomes and motivation. Positive elements such as an efficient and effective learning milieu, along with negative influencers like insufficient support and self-drive, may result in considerable fluctuations in competency progression (Friedrich-Haßauer, 2023, 114–116). Consequently, there exists a notable demand for Business Partners in the application of this model, particularly in the domains of motivation, self-sufficiency, and participant self-assessment.

In the self-blend model, individuals are empowered to independently amalgamate their educational materials from both physical and digitally supported sources. Unlike traditional Blended Learning frameworks, the determination of learning proportions rests within the autonomy of the individual. This affords adaptability and better acknowledges the learning preferences and favored methods of participants. However, there exists a risk that participants may opt for inaccurate or irrelevant content, thereby detrimentally affecting learning outcomes and assessment performance. The efficiency and efficacy, therefore, heavily rely on participants' proficiency and expertise in navigating digital learning environments (Friedrich-Haßauer, 2023, 116–117). Consequently, this approach is better suited for cohorts possessing a heightened self-awareness and understanding of the content, goals, and requisites of personalized HR development.

Business Partners acting as Technology and Media Integrators must prioritize the facilitation of autonomous selection of pertinent and efficacious content by participants engaged in HR development initiatives. Additionally, it is imperative to establish avenues for participants to access support and guidance for inquiries and recommendations concerning the pertinence of HR development components. Furthermore, there should exist a robust proficiency in assessment among individuals tasked with addressing queries and offering feedback, ensuring a comprehensive approach to competency evaluation.

In enhancing the value proposition within self-directed learning paradigms, it becomes imperative for corporate stakeholders to bolster self-reflective capacities among participants. This enables individuals to accurately gauge their comprehension of learning material, ascertain the necessity for assistance, and discern the appropriateness of engaging in conventional instructional sessions. Challenges frequently manifest within this framework due to a prevalent phenomenon wherein participants in HR development initiatives harbor a conviction regarding their comprehension and applicability of acquired knowledge, which often fails to align with their practical experiences in professional contexts.

The enriched-virtual model delineates from other Blended Learning frameworks through the amalgamation of online-supported learning phases alongside face-to-face instruction. Predominantly, internet-based materials are employed, supplemented by in-person sessions. The adaptability inherent in web-based content has the potential to influence learning engagement. Therefore, maintaining engagement necessitates the provision of compelling content. Overall, the efficacy and efficiency within the learning paradigm are heavily contingent upon individual dispositions and selected learning modalities. The pronounced emphasis on self-responsibility within the enriched-virtual model markedly impacts success, with the Business Partner serving as a significant determinant. Self-directed iterations require a high degree of self-responsibility during online-supported phases. Novice participants may experience adverse effects, whereas seasoned learners can bridge knowledge lacunae through online-supported resources. Within this Blended Learning construct, the incorporation of AI and its concomitant individualization of learning holds promise. The internet-based learning framework facilitates the analysis of individual competencies and learning progression, thereby accommodating variations in developmental velocities. Furthermore, the incorporation of repetitions is feasible if comprehension is inadequate, thereby ensuring meaningful advancement tailored to individual competencies, aptitudes, and learning trajectories.

The integrated focused rotation paradigm amalgamates e-learning, in-person pedagogy, and project-based activities. This comprehensive paradigm, exemplified in the provision of didactic guidance by instructors on a weekly basis, facilitates participant engagement in advanced learning endeavors. The assessment of efficacy and productivity is feasible through the utilization of metrics, as participants furnish feedback amenable to quantitative evaluation (Friedrich-Haßauer, 2023, 117–119).

In collaboration with line management, Business Partners must evaluate the merits of individual design alternatives and their amalgamation within the domain of Blended Learning to cater to participants' needs, encompassing their attitudes, skills, competencies, motivation, and learning preferences. Additionally, they should assess the strategic attainment of content in a purposeful, efficacious, and resourceful manner. This necessitates Business Partners to formulate and execute an optimal Blended Learning design, grounded on extant opportunities, program-specific nuances, and company-specific requisites, exigencies, and impediments. The program-specific and company-specific requisites, exigencies, and impediments necessitate scrutiny regarding the integration and facilitation of group work and collaborative learning, fostering idea exchange, discussions, and collective problem-solving (Foelsing & Schmitz, 2021, 233–235). Furthermore, the thematic content and application facet within the learning trajectory bear significance, prompting Business Partners to deliberate upon thematic content, instructional methodologies, and learning modalities conducive or indispensable for specific content domains. A prerequisite entails Business Partners' acquaintance with the learning content prelude to the development and refinement of HR development initiatives, synchronizing the planning process accordingly. Substantial backing can be derived from line management, ascribed to their anticipated high level of professional acumen (Gabathuler & Bajus, 2021, 179).

The consideration of technological prerequisites and competencies of prospective participants is paramount in Blended Learning methodologies, wherein learning platforms, webinars, social media tools, and virtual classrooms are harnessed. Absent adequate knowledge or substantial assistance in utilization, optimal outcomes remain elusive despite the caliber of the content within the HR development program. Furthermore, the temporal adaptability of prospective participants significantly influences the planning, conception, and execution phases. When dealing with participant cohorts marked by spatial and temporal constraints due to other pressing obligations, heightened attention must be directed towards leveraging temporal and spatial flexibility. However, if such adaptation impedes competency enhancement, compromises must be sought in the pursuit of efficacy and efficiency, benefiting both the HR development program and the Business Partner (Assies, Thiel & Stulle, 2021, 191).

Blended Learning, as an educational approach, furnishes a customized and bespoke learning milieu conducive to augmenting learning efficacy. The successful execution of this methodology mandates meticulous strategizing, transparent dissemination of information, and ongoing assessment to ascertain the attainment of learning benchmarks. Subsequent to evaluation, Business Partners, in collaboration with line management, are tasked with discerning pertinent insights and pinpointing avenues for enhancement for subsequent implementation (Blaha, 2021, 68–73).

8.1.3 Individual Learning

The prevailing educational paradigms fail to meet the exigencies posed by the rapidly evolving landscape of occupational endeavors. The assimilation of future skills emerges as an imperative corollary to ensure the incessant accrual of knowledge and proficiencies among HR. Future skills denote proficiencies and aptitudes that are progressively gaining significance in anticipation of the forthcoming exigencies of the labor market and societal dynamics. They encompass a myriad of competencies, including but not limited to, technological acumen, critical cogitation, adeptness in problem-solving, creative aptitude, emotional intelligence, intercultural adeptness, and proficiency in collaborative endeavors within interdisciplinary frameworks. Within the realm of HR development, future skills assume pivotal significance in preparing personnel for the evolving exigencies of professional settings and in fortifying the competitive prowess of enterprises. Through targeted initiatives encompassing training, continuous education, and developmental pathways, employees can acquire and refine these proficiencies, thereby adeptly adapting to mutations within their milieu and ingeniously addressing forthcoming challenges.

Conventional HR development strategies are no longer adequate; novel approaches and frameworks are imperative. Employees ought to be equipped to engage in autonomous knowledge acquisition, facilitating continuous, forward-thinking learning endeavors. The function of HR development ought to transition from merely furnishing seminars to assuming the role of a "learning coach," fostering individual progression and facilitating adaptable learning pathways. This transition is imperative, particularly in light of the escalating demand for personalized approaches. The paradigm of lifelong learning within professional settings necessitates a comprehensive reevaluation and restructuring. Paramount considerations and core proficiencies such as introspection, self-directed learning, cultivation of future skills, and intra-organizational networking must be accorded heightened emphasis (Winkler & Fink, 2022, 62–63). Business Partners confront a substantial hurdle as a consequence, primarily attributable to the imperative to facilitate personalized learning via appropriate pedagogical methodologies and ensure its efficacy.

The relentless advancement of automation, digital tools, and overall digitization is presenting formidable challenges that are fundamentally reshaping the tasks and workflows undertaken by employees. Given the multifaceted nature of these challenges and drawing upon the unique skill sets of individual employees, it is imperative for HR development to comprehend their distinct starting points and facilitate lifelong learning in a precise and tailored manner. Understanding and embracing change or evolution, along with maintaining a constructive outlook towards it, are pivotal in actively propelling HR development forward. Nonetheless, Business Partners functioning as Technology and Media Integrators must not solely concentrate on the individual level but also take into account the organizational dimension. This is particularly critical in customizing teaching-learning processes, as this is where the fundamental areas, pivotal topics, and thus the essence of HR development programs, including their objectives, are delineated.

Individual competence development relies heavily on the capacity for introspection, denoted as the aptitude for self-assessment, which stands as a pivotal competency. It is imperative for individuals to cultivate the skills necessary to evaluate their own progression and tempo, facilitating an active role in shaping their developmental trajectory and the assimilation of novel information. Soliciting feedback from within one's network serves to unveil blind spots in self-perception, fostering further growth. This dynamic also holds considerable significance concerning the assumption of accountability for one's own employability. Nonetheless, leaders and HR management must purposefully adopt a supportive stance. The conventional function of HR management solely as a supplier of seminar programs proves inadequate in ensuring contemporary, efficient, effective, and value-enhancing HR development, which must also accommodate the evolving values and objectives of employees. Business Partners are compelled to embrace novel approaches in HR development, assuming the role of learning facilitators to champion the individual, autonomous, and self-directed progression of employees (Winkler & Fink, 2022, 63–66).

Business Partners are required to substantially contribute by modifying their methodology to bolster self-accountability, facilitating the detection of cognitive lacunae and skill deficits at the individual level, thereby mitigating prevailing inadequacies. Collaboration between Business Partners and line management executives is essential to guarantee the integration of self-accountability institutionalization within HR development, thereby becoming a fundamental aspect of corporate operations (Winkler & Fink, 2022, 66).

Acknowledging the uniqueness of individuals in the enhancement of competencies, skills, and knowledge facilitates the voluntary and self-responsible engagement of employees in additional training opportunities. This phenomenon arises from their ability to advance at a personalized developmental rate and to discern progress through reflective processes, facilitated by individualized assistance from executives and Business Partners. Consequently, this tailored approach to HR development contributes significantly to employees' assurance of their ongoing employability (Frodl, 2023, 158–161).

A nurturing educational milieu serves as a facilitative environment for the cultivation of future skills over extended temporal horizons. Networking mechanisms contribute to the cultivation of learning alliances and the facilitation of knowledge dissemination. It falls upon employees, leaders, and Business Partners to cultivate and advocate for the requisite circumstances conducive to this endeavor. Moreover, imperative is a cognitive paradigm shift towards recognizing self-directed, perpetual learning as an intrinsic facet of occupational engagement. This imperative extends to encompass both employees, leaders, and Business Partners alike (Winkler & Fink, 2022, 81–82).

Technological progress presents myriad opportunities for Business Partners acting as Technology and Media Integrators to forge knowledge networks, fostering the exchange of competencies and substantially augmenting the value proposition of HR development. Essential to this endeavor is the establishment by Business Partners of HR development networks conducive to the exchange and refinement of competencies, experiences, and skills, thereby fostering a culture of learning and readiness for knowledge acquisition. Frequently, competency enhancements can also be attained through non-traditional forms of education, such as experiential learning. Alongside constructing the requisite infrastructure for this purpose, Business Partners shoulder the responsibility of ensuring the utilization of networking and fostering a high propensity for knowledge sharing (Romeike & Hager, 2020, 401–407).

8.1.4 Artificial Intelligence in Learning

The advancement of AI and the resultant opportunities are becoming increasingly significant in the realm of HR development. AI permits companies and Business Partners to implement innovative strategies to cultivate or enhance employee capabilities with greater efficiency and effectiveness. In the capacity of Technology and Media Integrators, Business Partners must rigorously investigate the potential and opportunities that AI presents, acknowledging its value-added contribution to HR development. Through AI, HR development processes can be rendered more efficient, targeted, and cost-effective, thereby substantially augmenting the company's value creation. The following are pertinent application areas of AI within HR development. AI facilitates the automation of repetitive and labor-intensive tasks in HR management. For instance, through the deployment of algorithms, administrative tasks such as managing training materials or organizing continuing education programs can be streamlined. This automation enables employees to concentrate on the more strategic and creative dimensions of HR development.

Through the analysis of data on employee performance, skills, and learning styles, AI can generate personalized learning plans, thereby enhancing the customization of HR development. Individualized employee development is facilitated by addressing their specific needs and competencies. Consequently, employees obtain access to targeted training and development programs that align with their unique requirements, considering their skill level, knowledge, and learning pace (Groß, 2023, 217–220).

AI can process vast datasets, enabling the early identification of employee potential and deficiencies. This facilitates the targeted nurturing of talent and the implementation of interventions to address weaknesses. Early detection of potential optimizes a company's human capital, aligning it with future career trajectories and necessary developmental steps. The utilization of AI-driven analytical tools enables more objective and precise evaluation of performance data. This enhances the fairness and transparency of performance assessments by reducing human bias. Consequently, employees receive constructive feedback grounded in accurate data, leading to improved motivation and performance.

AI allows for the application of predictive analytics to anticipate future HR needs. This supports proactive workforce planning, enabling companies to swiftly respond to changes. This includes both quantitative and qualitative workforce planning, closely tied to HR development. The optimized alignment of the workforce with future demands enhances long-term competitiveness and value creation.

It is evident that AI presents numerous opportunities to enhance efficiency, customization, and quality in HR development. The critical challenge for Business Partners acting as Technology and Media Integrators is to thoroughly engage with the advancing potential of AI, understanding its applications and success potentials. This requires comprehensive competencies in understanding employee operations and in developing HR programs or segments utilizing AI. Central to this is the individualization of learning, which enhances the effectiveness of HR development.

8.1.5 Gamification

Gamification is increasingly employed as a mechanism to augment motivation and engagement across various life contexts. Elements from video game design are integrated into non-game-related facets of life. Although predominantly observed in private settings, gamification is also gaining traction in HR development. It is particularly well-established in the realm of education and training, where playful methods have long been utilized. These gamified educational tools, referred to as serious games, are the subject of extensive research, with studies demonstrating their fundamental efficacy. Additionally, gamified applications are making strides in corporate communication, particularly within virtual environments and decentralized teams, where they serve to enhance user engagement and motivation (Korn et al., 2022, 43–44).

The core of gamification lies in augmenting intrinsic motivation, explicitly referring to self-determination theory, which bolsters three fundamental psychological needs: competence, autonomy, and social relatedness. Competence involves effective interaction, autonomy concerns freedom in task execution, and social relatedness pertains to the sense of belonging within a group. When designing gamification applications, it is crucial to address these needs to foster intrinsic motivation, especially in professional and educational settings (Korn et al., 2022, 45–46). Nonetheless, Business Partners acting as Technology and Media Integrators must ensure that gamification significantly enhances competence development rather than being perceived merely as entertainment. It is essential that the knowledge and skills acquired through gamification are recognized by participants and are practically applicable in their everyday work. Consequently, Business Partners must engage deeply with gamification to facilitate the acquisition of competencies, knowledge, experiences, and skills through game-based approaches.

The Flow theory posited by Csikszentmihalyi underscores the pleasure and total absorption experienced during activities. Within the flow state, individuals become deeply engrossed in an activity, disregarding external stimuli and temporal perception. This phenomenon hinges upon achieving equilibrium between the demands of an activity and an individual's skill set. Gamification strategies, particularly those involving real-time progress visualization, have the potential to facilitate the induction of the flow state. Nonetheless, it is crucial to acknowledge the finite nature of attentional resources. Therefore, the objective should not be to indefinitely sustain the flow state but rather to orchestrate a cyclical oscillation between phases of flow and phases characterized by perceived control, achieved through the manipulation of tasks varying in difficulty (Korn et al., 2022, 46–47). Practically, this entails integrating phases of practice and repetition into gamified environments, following established pedagogical methodologies, to solidify acquired knowledge, enhance application proficiency, and cultivate new skills.

In gamified ecosystems, the heterogeneity of user collectives serves as a pivotal factor, given that users' individual traits exert influence over their receptivity towards gamification components. The Big Five model, alternatively termed the OCEAN model, presents an empirically validated framework for categorizing personality archetypes predicated on dimensions encompassing openness, conscientiousness, extraversion, agreeableness, and neuroticism (OCEAN). Nonetheless, its application within corporate contexts may encounter impediments, particularly regarding traits like neuroticism that potentially engender exclusionary dynamics. One conceivable remedy involves the voluntary administration or anonymized implementation of assessments.

In the development of gamified applications, exhaustive examination of the target audience akin to the OCEAN test is not indispensably mandated. Simplified frameworks like Bartle's player typology proffer a commendable approximation of user cohorts. Bartle classifies players into four groups: achiever, socializer, killer, and explorer, each exhibiting distinct preferences concerning incentives, collaboration, competition, and exploration. While most individuals exhibit a dominant type, they also manifest characteristics of other player archetypes. To accommodate user diversity, identification of the prevailing player types within the target demographic is imperative, subsequently tailoring gamification components accordingly. Instruments such as the Bartle Test can aid in discerning player typologies and ensuring a user-centric experience (Korn et al., 2022, 47–49). Business Partners encounter the challenge of deeply engaging with the fundamental facets of gamification and gaming to strike a balance between user-centricity and content orientation, with the aim of crafting the content dimensions of the gamification process in a manner conducive to efficiently achieving developmental objectives.

In the nucleus of gamification process conception, emphasis should be placed not only on the execution of content, but also on the assessment of the importance of feedback mechanisms and rewards. Prominent components encompass points, badges, and leaderboards, with points and badges demonstrating notable efficacy while also exhibiting susceptibility to a level of diminishing returns. Leaderboards bolster competitive spirit and comparability amongst participants and evaluators in individual advancement endeavors, albeit concurrently fostering diminished exchange of competencies, experiences, and knowledge due to the competitive dynamics they engender.

The utilization of points is well-suited for educational contexts, yet it may induce stress in certain users. Levels present an alternative, particularly in iterative learning environments. Badges function as incentives for diverse accomplishments and can be structured hierarchically. Leaderboards exhibit rankings in a descending manner, though they may induce stress, underscoring the importance of positive design. Additional lives, akin to badges, can be granted to mitigate frustration.

Establishing a clear link to real-life scenarios, such as through monthly prizes, augments the motivational impact and provides an incentive for gamification elements. Visual representations of progress, avatars, and interactions with fellow players further emphasize minor achievements and cultivate a sense of belonging and social engagement. The capacity to personalize gamification elements caters to the autonomy and freedom of choice imperative for users.

Moreover, motivation can be significantly bolstered by integrating rewards not solely based on in-game progress but also considering their applicability in everyday professional settings. Such motivational incentives prompt participants to thoughtfully assess how and when to employ newly acquired skills and knowledge. Furthermore, this approach ensures that the transfer of skills to daily work tasks is acknowledged, thus showcasing tangible benefits for the company's success (Korn et al., 2022, 49–54).

Diverse methodologies and paradigms are available for the dissemination of educational material, encompassing E-Learning, Edutainment, (Digital) Game-Based

Learning, Gamification, as well as Agile Education and Lean Learning. E-Learning denotes the utilization of computer-based systems for educational purposes, drawing inspiration from agile methodologies originating from software engineering practices. Edutainment amalgamates educational content with entertainment elements within interactive multimedia learning environments. Game-Based Learning and Digital Game-Based Learning leverage gaming mechanisms for educational objectives, with Digital Game-Based Learning specifically focusing on electronic gaming mediums. Serious Games transcend conventional knowledge transfer by targeting educational competencies and skill enhancement.

Gamification constitutes a holistic paradigm that utilizes game components within non-game scenarios to amplify the involvement and drive of participants while effecting alterations in behavior towards educational objectives. Conversely, Serious Games manifest as complete gaming entities. The demographic scope for these digital modalities spans across all age cohorts, amalgamating instructional activities within gameplay to uphold an absorbing milieu and consequently perpetuate motivation. Nonetheless, the demarcations among distinct classifications remain nebulous, and contention persists concerning their definitional confines (Kodalle & Metz, 2022, 67–70).

In the application of gamification, Business Partners should extensively collaborate with line management leaders to assess the competencies, skills, preferences, and desires of the target audience. This collaboration is pivotal for optimizing efficacy and attaining desired outcomes. Simultaneously addressing individual needs, preferences, motivation, and engagement, the tailored design of gamification for the target audience can optimize the utilization of resources efficiently. Employees demonstrate heightened motivation and engagement when their personal objectives and interests are incorporated. The recognition of organizational support for their individual professional growth further augments employee motivation and retention rates. Additionally, customized training contributes to cost-effectiveness by consciously targeting essential skills. Despite prioritizing enjoyment, the design of gamification must align with employees' professional requisites, ensuring the seamless integration of acquired skills and knowledge into daily tasks, ultimately positively impacting organizational performance and long-term success.

In conjunction with the adaptation of HR development methodologies, gamification facilitates engagement with demographics historically less amenable to competency enhancement frameworks, such as those disinclined towards conventional text-centric training initiatives. This phenomenon may stem from factors beyond mere disinterest, encompassing challenges encountered in assimilating knowledge via traditional text-oriented HR development programs. Gamification accentuates a ludic paradigm in learning and advancement, thereby reshaping perceptions surrounding HR development and competency cultivation within diverse cohorts (Korn, Schulz & Hagley, 2022, 54–61).

8.1.6 Chances and Challenges of Business Partners in the Role of Technology and Media Integrator

As Technology and Media Integrators, Business Partners encounter numerous opportunities to influence HR development owing to technological progress. The primary task for Business Partners lies in recognizing these advancements and their advantages, while maintaining continuous vigilance over them. Collaborating with line management executives, Business Partners can strategize on optimizing HR development alignment with organizational goals, thus enhancing its value contribution. Furthermore, they can enhance their capability to cultivate necessary competencies more accurately and efficiently. Targeted utilization of emerging technologies can address existing competency gaps effectively. Proficiency in analysis and deriving appropriate insights becomes imperative for Business Partners, especially in roles such as Analytics Designers and Interpreters, to fulfill HR development requirements (Holtbrügge, 2022, 293–301).

8.2 Analytics Designer and Interpreter

The second role within the Foundational Enablers category is that of the Analytics Designer and Interpreter. In this capacity, the formulation of concepts pertinent to HR development is facilitated through the examination and assessment of data. Business Partners and executives are tasked with comprehending the strategic goals of the enterprise and contributing to the formulation of an HR development framework that is efficient, effective, and targeted, thereby ensuring the availability and utilization of appropriate competencies in both quantity and quality, at the opportune juncture and location (Wienkamp, 2021, 108–110).

8.2.1 Data Analysis and Identification of Skill Demand

During periods of skill scarcity, this presents a unique challenge as the caliber and quantity of skilled workforce available can impede a company's potential. HR development, being a strategic asset for an organization, must thus be refined to enhance value generation and broaden the scope of opportunities, consequently influencing the strategic trajectory of the enterprise. Emphasis should therefore be laid on crafting a bespoke comprehensive or partial framework, delineating clear objectives, appropriate measures, and processing modalities (Kobi, 2021, 375–380). These frameworks must initially be devised by Business Partners in collaboration with executive line management, and continuously reassessed to effect timely and promising adjustments. Particularly in a demanding and dynamically evolving milieu, this presents a challenge and pivotal responsibility for Business Partners as the necessity for adaptations becomes more frequent under such circumstances. Furthermore, complications emerge in the analysis and assessment of data amidst evolving challenges. Instances may arise where the evaluation of HR development falters due to unmet objectives stemming from alterations during a change process. This might be construed as inadequate by line management and corporate leadership, thereby diminishing the efficacy of HR development. To forestall a deterioration in collaboration, close cooperation premised on data analysis and deviations becomes imperative, necessitating a collective evaluation by Business Partners in the capacity of Analytics Designers and Interpreters alongside line management and corporate leadership at the earliest signs of deviation, enabling prompt response and adjustment (Jensen, 2022, 163–168).

An efficient HR development process necessitates a thorough and systematic evaluation of requirements to effectively enhance both individual and collective competencies of HR and achieve corporate objectives, alongside executing corporate strategy. The assessment of needs in HR development involves the systematic identification, analysis, and assessment of existing and prospective skill and competency gaps within the company's workforce. It aims to discern both individual and organizational development needs and formulate specific actions for competency enhancement.

The initial phase entails scrutinizing the company's strategic direction. Aligning HR development initiatives with the strategic objectives of the company ensures that individual employee development contributes to the overarching goals of the organization. Various tools such as employee dialogues, performance evaluations, surveys, and other assessment methods are utilized to identify existing skills and qualifications. Discrepancies between current and required competencies are pinpointed as qualification gaps. To preempt future demands, an exhaustive analysis of industry-specific trends, technological advancements, and evolving market dynamics becomes imperative. This facilitates the timely recognition of emerging needs for novel competencies and their integration into HR development practices (Jensen, 2022, 184–185).

Based on identified needs, distinct development objectives are articulated for individual employees and teams, acknowledging both immediate and enduring perspectives, and aligning with individual competencies and corporate objectives. Through meticulous needs assessment, resources are allocated towards fostering competencies pivotal for business prosperity, facilitating efficient allocation of financial resources and HR. Engaging employees in the developmental process while considering their unique needs enhances motivation and fosters stronger identification with the company, thus enhancing employee retention and mitigating the risk of skill shortages (Schreyögg & Koch, 2020, 686–691).

Incorporating present and future HR development needs ensures the company's adaptive capability to respond to evolving circumstances. Continuously upskilling employees aids the company's success in dynamic markets. In the capacity of Analytics Designers and Interpreters, leveraging data for analysis and evaluation facilitates continual enhancement through the derivation of suitable approaches, thus embodying a self-referential role. The rapid progression of enterprises necessitates an annual strategic elucidation of HR development requirements, subject to periodic reassessment and modification contingent upon fluctuations in the business milieu. The configuration, whether structured as an annual regimen or routine recalibration of priorities, holds secondary importance. HR development consistently assimilates inputs to adapt and evaluate emerging needs within the framework of corporate transformations. The interrogation of how these changes engender challenges for employee competencies and credentials constitutes the focal point. HR development must empower the organization to address both immediate exigencies and enduring challenges (Sagradov & Müller, 2022, 67–71).

In conjunction with the contextual processing of alterations, HR development ought to embody foundational insights for prospective orientation, at minimum, once annually. This encompasses adaptations, re-prioritizations, and realignments. Such procedures may manifest through workshops or interviews. Nonetheless, HR development personnel should routinely engage in internal deliberations regarding the influence of evolving tasks and demands from the business line and whether their positioning remains adequate (Peterke, 2021, 207). This methodology endeavors to avert an excessively situational outlook and response. Despite the imperative of reacting to transient trends and challenges, the utilization of data, its analysis, and evaluation must be recurrently employed to address the macroscopic perspective and apprehend strategic and enduring trends and ramifications.

8.2.2 Data-Driven Long-Term Strategic Orientation in HR Development

To ensure the robustness of HR development amidst dynamic changes and external influences, it is imperative to establish a foundational framework that delineates key principles and provides directional guidance, thereby setting a trajectory for development commensurate with its depth. Within this framework and its foundational principles, the involvement and accountability of Business Partners must be enshrined, given their pivotal role and responsibility in executing and adapting requisite strategies. Additionally, owing to their heightened awareness of environmental shifts, Business Partners are adept at furnishing crucial insights into how such changes impact the necessitated proficiencies, experiences, and knowledge domains, thereby impelling adjustments in HR development paradigms. Consequently, this necessitates a nuanced framework capable of encapsulating the multifaceted nature of the issue, while concurrently integrating various facets of HR management to amalgamate short-term reactive measures with those of a medium- to long-term outlook (Weber & Feistel, 2019, 190–194).

The function of the Analytics Designer and Interpreter encompasses the refinement of this fundamental notion through the application of experiential knowledge, empirical evidence, their assessment, and the scrutiny of the impacts and probabilities of their occurrences. This process aims to establish an optimal equilibrium between short-term responsiveness, long-term trajectory, and the frequency of requisite adaptations, thereby necessitating adequate adaptability and resilience. It is imperative to account for the temporal dimension, as adaptability tends to be more conspicuous concerning immediate or recent influential factors compared to those projected further into the future. This necessitates discernment in recognizing that line management not only holds partial accountability for HR development but also assumes a substantial role in its analysis and interpretation. Moreover, line management must grasp that the cultivation of competencies is a time-intensive endeavor entailing costs, where long-term triumphs may engender short-term challenges and potential setbacks in HR development. Often, line management inclines towards overemphasizing present challenges while overlooking HR development due to the acute nature of other issues demanding attention. This tendency is frequently rooted in the relegation of HR development activities to a secondary position due to temporal constraints, pressures for immediate success, and the pursuit of predefined objectives. However, this practice runs counter to a strategic orientation and therefore undermines the strategic cultivation of competencies. Consequently, the challenges confronting line management are poised to exacerbate in the future owing to the inadequate attention accorded to HR development. The scarcity of skilled personnel significantly contributes to this predicament, as existing HR resources are already stretched thin in coping with prevailing challenges and tasks, thus limiting the capacity for additional assignments and projects. In light of data analysis, Business Partners assuming the role of Analytics Designers and Interpreters must therefore delineate with greater precision the imperative for HR development initiatives and their objectives to yield returns for the company, individual departments, and teams, even at the expense of larger short-term gains (Schüll, 2020, 1–2).

Built upon this anchoring within the fundamental concept, it is imperative to actively promote it to both line management and the workforce. Subsequent to this, thorough evaluation of the implementation is necessary, with adjustments to the concept warranted if the outcomes fall short of expectations (Peterke, 2021, 205–207). The modification of HR development programs holds paramount significance, constituting a pivotal responsibility within the role of the Analytics Designer and Interpreter, particularly when the initially established objectives remain unmet. Failure to promptly discern the necessity for adaptation, informed by data analytics and the structure of HR development, including its programs and processes, can yield severe ramifications for both the organization and its workforce. The need for adaptation, rooted in practical application, draws upon diverse scientific methodologies and frameworks derived from organizational psychology and development, alongside empirical insights within HR development. The efficacy of HR development initiatives hinges significantly upon their capacity to adjust to evolving circumstances and demands. The dynamics inherent in contemporary work environments necessitate perpetual adaptation of skills, competencies, experiences, and knowledge, owing to fluctuations in market conditions and technological advancements, thereby necessitating corresponding adjustments in organizational frameworks. Should the stipulated objectives of HR development and the desired enhancement in effectiveness remain unattained, the central objective of HR development programs is unmet, thereby unveiling a misalignment between program content and the actual requisites of the organization.

Business Partners, acting as Analytics Designers and Interpreters, possess the capacity to ascertain, via data analysis and evaluation, the insufficiency of adaptability to evolving work conditions and the associated changes in competencies and competency requirements. Nonetheless, the failure to meet developmental objectives may also emanate from alternative sources. It is conceivable that leaders in line management demonstrate deficient engagement, interest, and unsupportive incentive structures. This phenomenon manifests, for instance, when metrics and associated financial and non-financial incentives inadequately align with the demands and complexities of HR development. Another contributor to unmet developmental goals may reside in Business Partners' misjudgments concerning the quality and efficacy of HR development programs, methodologies, and strategies. For each of these potential rationales, causes necessitate analysis, deliberation, and subsequent formulation of improvement methodologies. Moreover, emphasis should be placed on the competencies requisite for bolstering goal attainment and adaptability, thereby mitigating the probability of future goal lapses (Wienkamp, 2021, 154–158).

Development objectives not attained via HR development initiatives may precipitate severe repercussions for employee motivation, organizational efficacy, and ultimately, competitive advantage. Inadequate adaptability within HR development schemes can foster employee frustration and discontentment, owing to insufficient attention to their unique developmental requisites. Consequently, this phenomenon may precipitate a downturn in employee involvement and efficiency. These facets, in turn, substantially impact the execution of corporate objectives and strategic advancement. It is evident that Business Partners, operating as Analytics Architects and Interpreters, wield considerable sway over numerous pertinent domains of HR administration. They are poised to exert a substantial influence on the evolution of diverse domains through retrospective and predictive data analysis and assessment (Thommen et al., 2023, 513–515).

8.2.3 Data-Driven Integration of HR Development within Organizational Learning and Development

The need for modifying HR development initiatives can also be elucidated through the lens of "organizational learning," which posits that organizations must undergo learning processes and adaptations to achieve success. Identifying unmet goals presents an opportunity to glean insights from errors and subsequently refine the programs. Responding to setbacks through adjustments and enhancements not only facilitates individual learning but also fosters organizational learning (Schwengber, 2024, 15–24). Analysis of causes and effects enables Business Partners and line management to comprehend the repercussions, prompting reflection on shared responsibility and impact on competitiveness and value generation.

Furthermore, in such scenarios, collaboration and shared accountability are reinforced, contingent upon both parties eschewing blame and instead embracing cooperative enhancement endeavors.

During the conceptualization phase and the examination of anomalous outcomes, attention from Business Partners and line management is imperative towards the architecture of HR development programs, encompassing their substance and modalities, with the aim of ensuring efficient alignment and practical applicability of the contents. In numerous instances, a prevalent tendency or hazard persists within HR development, wherein the contents of such programs become excessively disjointed from practical utilization, leading to suboptimal resource allocation and investment, thereby fostering inefficiencies within HR development endeavors. A concerted effort between Business Partners and line management, particularly in fostering symbiotic collaboration, serves to mitigate this risk while augmenting the practical relevance thereof. This endeavor chiefly entails meticulous analysis and targeted adjustment of the constituents, configuration, framework, and substance of HR development programs, thereby ensuring heightened practical relevance or a more pronounced emphasis on effectuating the acquired proficiencies. It is paramount to acknowledge that discrete constituents within HR development programs comprise merely a fraction of the overarching system, with particular emphasis on the interconnections among these constituents, serving as pivotal focal points for enhancements.

In the realm of data analysis and assessment, the focal aspect concerns the initial facet of the function of Business Partners, denoted as Analytics Design. It is imperative that this phase be orchestrated to comprehensively account for the interdependencies and holistic view within the data analysis framework.

The subsequent diagram delineates a structured procedure commencing with the elucidation of requirements and corresponding objectives, followed by progressive developmental stages leading up to the appraisal of the HR development process elucidated earlier, alongside requisite adjustment modalities.

In practical implementation, many methodologies within the domain of HR development often exhibit limitations by focusing solely on isolated facets. Such limitations commonly stem from overlooking a comprehensive framework. However, a holistic managerial viewpoint is imperative for gauging organizational efficacy based on its human capital. To accomplish this, Business Partners and line management must collaboratively devise a self-assessment tool that espouses a comprehensive strategy toward strategic HR management, thereby fostering practical knowledge management and HR development. This endeavor must ensure that the strategic significance of HR development lies in fortifying competitive advantages and ensuing value generation through the intellectual prowess and performance efficacy of employees. A pivotal aspect herein lies in prioritizing the enhancement of human capital, a notion underscored by Business Partners and line management. Given the significance of HR development and the concomitant augmentation of human capital, an evaluation of approaches and configurations of architectural elements influencing HR outcomes, substantiated by quantifiable

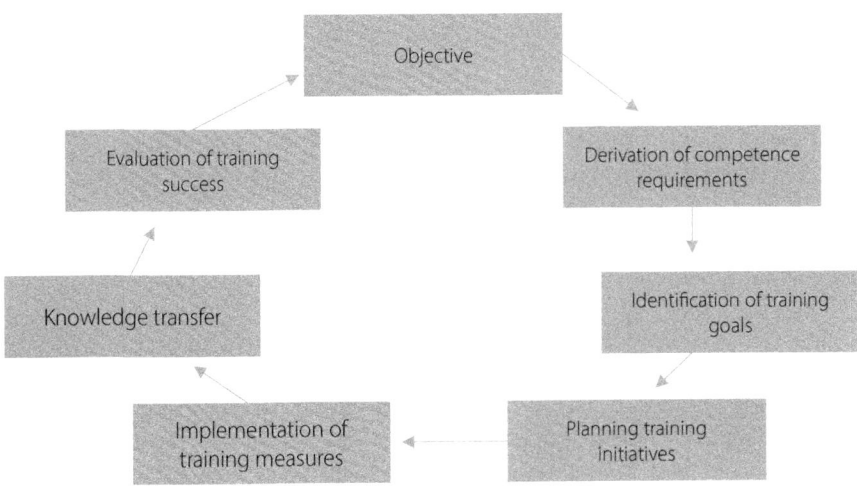

Fig. 8-1: Process of Educational Controlling (Blaha, 2021, 69)

attributes, becomes imperative to illustrate HR development's contribution to success and to discern necessary adaptations and their ramifications. Of particular importance is the scrutiny of HR management elements, encompassing systems, processes, resources, and capabilities, in terms of both outcomes and design. The findings of such scrutiny reverberate across HR development, appraising not only the employees directly but also managerial influencers, including the role of HR development. These ramifications should be seamlessly integrated into data analysis for meta-level enhancements.

In the examination of HR development schemes and their constituents, due regard should be accorded to leadership practice and management practice. Emphasis should be laid on the efficacy of managerial endeavors in augmenting the human capital of the organization through deliberate, efficient, and productive processes. Aspects encompassing communication, performance feedback, trust-building efforts, and the manifestation of the organization's fundamental values should be incorporated by Business Partners and line management. These thematic domains exert influence on the outcomes attained, thereby impacting the efficacy of HR development. Consequently, these accompanying elements necessitate collective consideration by Business Partners and line management. Should opportunities for enhancement or adverse effects be discerned within this framework, Business Partners and line management must collaboratively exert influence on corporate governance to effect alterations conducive to HR development enhancement. In the imperative course of persuasion, Business Partners and line management ought to concentrate on elucidating the desired improvements and rationale behind their desirability, expounding why the ensuing positive repercussions warrant adjustments and the consequent costs of the change management process. The probability of recognizing the necessity and advantages of the adjustment process amplifies when Business Partners and line management can expound not only on the desired concept and correlated structures of the HR development process comprehensively but also substantiate these with qualitative and quantitative indicators (Ilic, 2024, 283–287).

8.2.4 Data Analysis in HR Development for Enhancing Performance

The supplementary focus on performance enhancements and associated outcomes is beneficial. It is imperative to underscore the significance of augmenting value-added contributions through talent development and retention, encompassing knowledge, competencies, and skills, alongside their targeted application and utilization in the workplace, thereby resulting in heightened company performance. This approach enables Business Partners and line management to demonstrate their profound engagement with the company's learning capacity and the cultivation of human capital, fostering the company's overall capacity for learning, adaptation, and continuous improvement. The close collaboration between Business Partners and line management fosters knowledge exchange, thereby enhancing mutual comprehension. In addition to scrutinizing the HR development system and its associated programs and structures, this collaboration cultivates a culture of cooperation, consolidating existing endeavors, abilities, knowledge, and ideas across organizational boundaries. Ultimately, this synergistic effort fortifies developmental capacity and mutual understanding, accentuating shared responsibility and bolstering cooperation in adaptation (Peterke, 2021, 212).

The role of the Analytics Designer and Interpreter encompasses the consideration of participants' expectations and perceptions, alongside the content, methodology, and didactic implementation in HR development programs. This multifaceted approach is essential for crafting efficacious HR development initiatives.

The imperative for this stems from various factors. Firstly, the necessity to account for individual needs and objectives arises. Each employee possesses distinct professional aspirations, competencies, and requirements. By integrating expectations and perceptions, HR development programs can be personalized to accommodate the unique demands and preferences of employees.

Secondly, the consideration of these factors can heighten motivation and engagement. Employees feel valued when they perceive that their expectations and perceptions are being acknowledged in HR development efforts, thereby fostering increased motivation. Alignment of programs with personal objectives bolsters engagement, thereby amplifying the efficacy of training endeavors. Moreover, it fortifies the willingness of employees to participate in training initiatives.

Thirdly, optimizing resource utilization is facilitated. Prioritizing individual expectations enables the more effective allocation of resources. Instead of offering generic training, targeted interventions can be deployed to address specific competencies and requirements of employees. This optimization enhances the efficacy of training initiatives.

Fourthly, the heightened identification of employees with developmental domains is facilitated. Taking into account expectations aids in pinpointing employees' developmental domains with greater precision. This facilitates the formulation of precise programs and training initiatives aimed at fortifying these domains, thereby enhancing the efficacy of HR development.

Fifthly, the consideration of expectations and perceptions among prospective participants fosters a favorable organizational milieu. A corporation that earnestly regards employees' expectations and perceptions cultivates a positive organizational milieu. This engenders a sense of worth and backing among employees, resulting in augmented job contentment and retention, alongside heightened enthusiasm for and engagement in training opportunities.

Sixthly, the adaptation of offerings to evolving needs holds significance. Employees' expectations and perceptions may evolve over time. Sustained dialogue empowers the corporation to adjust to these shifts and ensure the ongoing relevance and efficacy of HR development initiatives.

Seventhly, on a comprehensive scale, the consideration of expectations and perceptions can yield superior outcomes in HR development. By integrating individual expectations, the probability of attaining predetermined objectives is heightened. Employees exhibit greater motivation and involvement when their personal aspirations align with the company's aims.

In conclusion, the integration of individuals' expectations and perceptions is pivotal in crafting personalized and targeted development programs that not only cater to employees' specific requirements but also bolster the effectiveness and success of these endeavors (Winkler & Fink, 2022, 81–82).

8.2.5 Analyses of Employee Expectations for Performance Improvement

In order to synchronize with the expectations, perceptions, and aspirations of the employees, it is imperative to conduct an initial analysis thereof. These elements exhibit a broad spectrum and frequently hinge upon individual requisites, vocational objectives, and the prevailing organizational hierarchy. A significant number of employees aspire to professional growth and promotional prospects, anticipating that HR development initiatives will furnish them with the requisite competencies and credentials to realize their career aspirations. These employees seek initiatives aimed at augmenting their vocational proficiencies and capabilities. Motivations and interests in this domain can manifest diversely and be uniquely molded. Common inclinations toward enhancing competencies and skills may entail streamlining work processes to enhance efficiency and velocity, integrating novel technologies, adapting to evolving circumstances, broadening existing expertise, such as preparatory measures for subsequent career advancements, or acquiring proficiency in emerging domains to bolster employability. Frequently, personal evolution is intertwined with the enhancement of professional competencies. Employees yearn for initiatives that fortify their social, communicative, and interpersonal aptitudes (Winkler & Fink, 2022, 68–69).

In the realm of daily occupational activities, numerous employees encounter limited occasions for introspection regarding their daily operational procedures and customary practices. Consequently, there exists a minimal probability for contemplating one's own objectives, ambitions, anticipations, and avenues for advancement. Frequently, it proves challenging to allocate time for critically scrutinizing personal interests and individual expectations. A considerable number of employees actively seek initiatives that afford opportunities for introspection and self-evaluation, aspiring to identify their inherent strengths and weaknesses, and endeavoring to enhance their personal and vocational growth. In the capacity of an Analytics Designer and Interpreter, the focus extends to capturing and assessing the unique circumstances of employees, thereby comprehending their predicaments and formulating improvement strategies predicated upon such insights (Sander et al., 2023, 255–260).

Employees anticipate the consideration of flexibility in the implementation of HR development programs by those tasked with their design. The integration of HR development programs into daily work routines and their concurrent operation are essential. Often, employees are engrossed in their daily tasks and must navigate through spontaneous alterations and challenges. Consequently, HR development programs need to exhibit flexibility to minimize additional stress, enabling the completion of ongoing tasks. Employees value programs that conform to their individual needs and schedules. The adaptability of the learning process and the accessibility of resources play pivotal roles in sustaining motivation and ensuring the efficiency of learning endeavors. It's noteworthy that employees harbor diverse preferences concerning the timing and location of learning, which significantly impacts the outcome of HR development programs. Business Partners, functioning as Analytics Designers and Interpreters, bear the responsibility of crafting HR development programs grounded in data and its evaluation. This ensures the adequate consideration of the aforementioned aspects, while not forsaking the content goals, and mitigating the risk of prolonged HR development periods (Gabathuler & Bajus, 2021, 161–167).

Employees have multifaceted motivations for pursuing further education, encompassing both substantive and personal incentives. Among these, they harbor expectations concerning the recognition of their involvement, alongside the concomitant rewards or potential advancement opportunities. Within HR development initiatives, employees actively seek acknowledgment for their contributions and accomplishments, which, whether in monetary form or through professional validation, can serve as additional stimuli. Nonetheless, such programs are not solely perceived as a means to an end; there exists a prevalent anticipation that the newly acquired competencies, skills, and knowledge will find practical application within the regular work milieu. An emergent trend among employees involves a heightened consideration for diversity and inclusivity within HR development schemes. There is a growing insistence that these programs should ensure equitable opportunities for all, irrespective of gender, background, or other distinguishing factors.

Employees establish a nexus between explicit objectives and anticipations when engaging with further training initiatives, grounded in a deep comprehension of their individual requirements. To tailor HR development endeavors to the specific needs of employees, proactive communication regarding goals, expectations, and aspirations becomes imperative. Such discourse not only sustains participant motivation but also forestalls potential disillusionment. Both employees and HR development practitioners must meticulously and transparently delineate the program's content, objectives, learning modalities, flexibility, and practical relevance. This precision not only influences motivation but also impacts the pace of learning and the resultant outcomes. From the outset, it is imperative to address feedback and evaluation mechanisms within HR development programs. Such measures wield significant influence on employee motivation while ensuring tangible progress in skill acquisition. These feedback mechanisms not only foster personal growth but also underscore the value of organizational commitment to employees. Moreover, they facilitate the identification of opportunities for process enhancement (Häring, Grandpierre & Mynarek, 2023, 18–21).

Consideration must also be given to the incorporation of sustainability principles in HR development initiatives. Employees prioritize the sustainability and enduring positive impacts of such programs on their career trajectories. Additionally, the expedient utilization and integration of new competencies, skills, and knowledge into daily tasks are pertinent to them. For the organization, this immediacy fosters learning and motivation, thereby ensuring prompt returns on investments in HR development. Furthermore, the alignment of learning endeavors with direct application guarantees timely dividends from HR development investments.

Companies should heed these considerations to craft HR development programs that align with employee needs and expectations, thereby fostering individual growth and positively impacting the organization as a whole.

8.2.6 Data-Driven Selection and Development of Coaches and Mentors

In the capacity of Analytics Designers and Interpreters, those tasked with responsibility must acknowledge the criticality of the selection of coaches and mentors in HR development for the success of the developmental trajectory. Coaches and mentors serve as pivotal figures in providing support to employees in their professional evolution and wield substantial influence over the overall efficacy of HR development endeavors. The rationales and factors exerting influence are manifold and expansive, encompassing domains necessitating diverse competencies from Business Partners.

Primarily, attention must be directed towards the individual requisites of the participants. Each employee harbors unique strengths, weaknesses, aspirations, and areas necessitating enhancement. An adept coach or mentor should demonstrate proficiency in comprehending and addressing the distinct requirements of each employee. Opting for coaches and mentors endowed with this acumen ensures bespoke and efficacious HR development initiatives.

The professional prowess of the coach or mentor assumes paramount significance. A coach or mentor of high caliber ought to possess robust knowledge and practical experience in the pertinent industry and business domains. The selection of professionals equipped with relevant expertise guarantees that employees receive practical and industry-specific counsel and direction. Furthermore, the evaluation of competence and the potential advantages derived from the coach's or mentor's expertise hold substantial sway over motivation and receptivity to learning.

Coaches and mentors necessitate robust communicative aptitudes within their professional repertoire. Effective dissemination of information is paramount for the efficacious outcome of coaching and mentoring alliances. The adeptness to furnish lucid directives, attentively absorb information, and proffer constructive criticism constitutes indispensable attributes. The curation of coaches and mentors with adept communication proficiencies engenders an atmosphere of openness and trust between the coach or mentor and the employee, thus fortifying their partnership.

Empathy and emotional intelligence emerge as salient facets within the domain of coaches or mentors. The trajectory of HR development often precipitates emotional quandaries. Coaches and mentors must exhibit empathic discernment and grasp the emotional exigencies of their charges. The capacity to resonate with employees cultivates a supportive milieu conducive to personal and vocational growth.

The selection of coaches or mentors should also hinge upon their proficiency in monitoring and assessing progress. Coaches ought to possess the acumen to quantify advancements, reassess initial objectives, and effectuate modifications as warranted. This regimen ensures the efficacy and precision of HR development initiatives. Additionally, it facilitates the identification of hurdles in HR development and the provision of targeted assistance. This holds particular pertinence in mitigating technical obstacles and grappling with intricate content-related facets. Business Partners, in their capacity as Analytics Designer and Interpreter, shoulder the onus of ensuring the seamless assessment of competencies, dispositions, and professional as well as social aptitude, thereby deriving pertinent deductions regarding the developmental requisites of individual coaches and mentors. This paradigm can significantly amplify the efficacy of HR development through its cascading impact.

Integral to HR development programs is the conveyance of the company ethos and its concomitant values and objectives. A congruence between the coach or mentor and the organizational ethos augments the assimilation of HR development within the overarching corporate strategy. Hence, HR development proffers a high degree of consonance with the company's overarching vision. The meticulous curation of coaches and mentors exerts a substantial influence on the efficacy of HR development initiatives. Precise selection procedures guarantee that the guidance provided resonates with the specific requirements of employees, fostering enduring professional advancement within the organization (Helmold, 2022, 119–124).

In addition to the aforementioned aspects, the relational dynamics between the coach or mentor and the guided individual also exert a notable influence within the HR development program. Often, these dynamics wield substantial impact on the program's efficacy. The underlying rationales for this phenomenon are delineated below.

Firstly, trust and openness constitute pivotal elements within the coach or mentor-guided individual relationship. An affirmative relational plane cultivates trust and openness between the coach and the guided individual, pivotal for the latter's receptivity towards personal developmental endeavors and willingness to disclose to the coach.

Secondly, an optimal relational milieu facilitates efficacious communication. The coach's ability to furnish lucid and supportive communication aids the guided individual in discerning their strengths, weaknesses, and areas necessitating development.

Thirdly, a favorable relational framework propels the motivation and involvement of the guided individual in the HR development initiative. The coach assumes a pivotal role in fostering a supportive atmosphere conducive to personal advancement.

Fourthly, an advantageous relational setting enables tailored responses to individual requirements. Given the uniqueness of each individual, a robust relationship empowers the coach to better cater to the guided individual's idiosyncratic needs and personality traits. This, in turn, facilitates customized coaching methodologies and strategies, thereby influencing the guided individual's developmental trajectory.

Fifthly, a commendable relational standing facilitates the constructive resolution of conflicts inherent in any developmental process. Through such adept navigation, impediments and challenges are more readily surmountable, thereby ensuring continued developmental advancement.

Sixthly, within the relational domain, it is imperative to incorporate cultural sensitivity considerations. Particularly in instances where collaborators hail from disparate cultural backgrounds, the Business Partner must exhibit cultural acumen and reverence for diversity to foster a constructive rapport.

Seventhly, ethical considerations and integrity also hold significance. These factors wield considerable influence over the relational dynamic between the Business Partner and the mentee, profoundly contributing to the establishment and sustenance of trust. Such trust, in turn, markedly impacts collaboration, thereby shaping the enhancement of competencies and skills.

Accounting for these socio-cultural factors in the coach selection process is paramount for facilitating effective HR development. It ensures that the relational dimension between the Business Partner and the mentee fosters an environment conducive to developmental endeavors.

8.2.7 Key Performance Indicators in HR Development Effectiveness Evaluation and Improvement

The primary function of the Analytics Designer and Interpreter role is the continual evaluation of HR development programs, along with the assessment of HR development approaches and strategies. This evaluation is crucial for gaining insight into the outcomes of HR development efforts and for facilitating a continuous process of improvement and adaptation. Consequently, the establishment of operational educational controlling processes is imperative. To ensure effective and efficient implementation of HR development programs within the company, it is essential to measure the degree of goal attainment. This principle is rooted in the understanding that only that which is quantified can be effectively managed. Analytics Designers and Interpreters must possess the ability to identify and articulate competencies and skills, as well as comprehend the evolving competency requirements for specific tasks over time. Collaboration with line management is vital, alongside critical self-assessment of one's own competencies in this domain. Should Business Partners, in their role as Analytics Designers and Interpreters, detect competency gaps, the initial step involves advancing their own competency development in close collaboration with line management. In this capacity, Business Partners must engage critically and reflectively with a diverse range of topics, acknowledging the breadth of the subject matter. This entails proactive consideration of future developments, timely intervention in steering processes, goal-setting based on normative and strategic deliberations, continual assessment of current progress against desired objectives, and prompt initiation of appropriate corrective actions. Experience in HR controlling is indispensable for shaping the continuing education process and for exploring methodologies to evaluate even intangible, challenging-to-measure factors. Additionally, relevant Key Performance Indicators (KPIs) from the training and development domain can be incorporated to facilitate communication and discussion (Blaha, 2021, 67).

Central to the formulation and application of KPIs within the context of HR development are several fundamental aspects. Firstly, paramount is the criterion of measurability concerning performance and progress. KPIs furnish an objective framework for the quantification of performance and progress in HR development endeavors, thereby facilitating the assessment of training effectiveness, developmental initiatives, and related activities.

Secondly, the utilization of KPIs endeavors to facilitate enhancements in efficiency. By harnessing KPIs, the processes inherent in HR development can be subject to more comprehensive monitoring and analysis, thereby enabling the identification of inefficiencies and the subsequent implementation of measures aimed at bolstering efficiency.

Thirdly, the purpose of KPIs is to contribute to the cultivation of strategic congruence. KPIs empower enterprises to more effectively synchronize their HR development undertakings with strategic imperatives. Through the delineation of key competencies and the assessment of HR development's contribution toward the attainment of corporate objectives, strategic alignment becomes attainable.

Fourthly, KPIs function to ensure that needs analyses are underpinned by empirical data and facilitate profound insights. By virtue of KPI analysis, the demand for specific competencies or skill sets within an organization can be discerned, thus facilitating the targeted formulation of training programs to address extant gaps.

Fifthly, strategically deployed, KPIs can foster employee motivation and retention. Their application within HR development can engender heightened employee motivation through the establishment of clear objectives and criteria for success. Moreover, this fosters employee retention by fostering a sense of support for professional advancement among employees.

Sixthly, KPIs can optimize the allocation of resources. Through the analysis of KPIs, resources, including financial resources and employee time, can be more judiciously utilized. Strategic investment in the cultivation of key competencies can culminate in the optimal utilization of resources over the long term.

Seventhly, KPIs serve as the foundation for benchmarking endeavors. They afford enterprises the opportunity to juxtapose their performance against industry standards or best practices, thereby facilitating the identification of potential areas for enhancement and nurturing a culture of continuous development.

Eighthly, the utilization of KPIs fosters agility and adaptability. By incorporating KPIs into HR development practices, enterprises can cultivate a more agile and adaptable approach. Regular monitoring of KPIs empowers enterprises to swiftly respond to shifts in industry dynamics, market conditions, or corporate objectives, thereby enabling the adjustment of developmental strategies accordingly.

In summation, the integration of KPIs into HR development endeavors is pivotal for ensuring effective, strategic, and competency-driven alignment. They furnish the requisite transparency for evaluating performance, identifying deficiencies, and propelling continuous improvements.

The depicted table delineates pivotal determinants of efficiency and effectiveness in measurement, alongside their corresponding circumstances and hurdles. These factors serve as facilitators for the formulation and implementation of KPIs, while also aiding in the enhancement HR development initiatives, and should be regarded as instructive tools.

The former portrayal of the process commences from the conventional scenario of formulating HR strategies. An alternative methodology becomes imperative when the dearth of proficient workforce becomes so conspicuous that it profoundly impacts the alignment of strategic objectives and advancement to a degree where an extensive disparity emerges in the requisite proficiencies and abilities that cannot be mitigated by HR development within a foreseeable timeframe. Upon identification of such a circumstance through needs assessment, Business Partners, line management, and corporate leadership must collectively negotiate to realign the company's strategic objectives with the capacities of HR development. This departure from the standard protocol and the emphasis on prevailing proficiencies and abilities in terms of both quality and quantity, coupled with the corresponding adjustment of strategic objectives, facilitates the maximization of value-added contributions. Additionally, it ensures the absence of significant deviation from existing proficiencies and abilities vis-à-vis the company's goals.

Tab. 6: Factors of Efficiency and Effectiveness Measurement, Factors of Framework Conditions and Challenges (Friedrich-Haßauer, 2023, 94)

Factors of efficiency and effectiveness measurements	Factors of the framework conditions and challenges
Efficiency: • Assessment of the resources and capabilities of the learning system • Preparation of educational contend and quality • Ease of use	Efficiency: • Independence, time flexibility • Design and structure of content • Self-explanatory, simplicity • Speed of feedback
Effectiveness: • Performance, learning outcome • Use of the learning environment • System design, content output of the learning environment, relative effectiveness, self-efficacy • Contribution to learning, satisfaction, subjective overall evaluation through learners • Organization, behavior and reaction to learning content, degree of pedagogical effectiveness	Effectiveness: • Learning success • Local flexibility (and its usage) • Content fit (completeness / test questions) • Benefits of knowledge acquisition • External control (quality of didactic instructions)

Under such circumstances, the utmost priority must be accorded to enhancing the efficacy of HR development systems and programs. This enhancement is indispensable for augmenting both the company's strategic objectives and its value-added contribution. Investments in HR development systems and programs should be approached with a focus on return on investment (ROI) to substantiate the value contributed by these investments. This approach also serves to rationalize and ultimately sustain potentially substantial investments in HR development. For line management and corporate leadership, this culminates in the acknowledgment of the strategic importance of HR development and the realization that HR development and its associated systems are constraining factors in strategic corporate advancement (Kobi, 2021, 373–380).

8.3 Compliance Manager

Within the domain of Foundational Enablers, the Compliance Manager emerges as the third and paramount function of Business Partners. This classification denotes a crucial role in guaranteeing adherence to predetermined regulations, protocols, and standards within initiatives, activities, and strategic frameworks of HR development. The significance of guidelines, standards, and objectives in HR development programs, as well as in HR development control, finds justification across various dimensions. These components contribute to ensuring the efficacy, efficiency, and sustainability of HR development endeavors.

8.3.1 Compliance Management and the Use of Standards

In the domain of guidelines, strategic alignment, compliance, and needs analysis hold relevance. Strategic alignment involves the establishment of guidelines in the form of strategic objectives that delineate the trajectory for HR development. These objectives should be closely intertwined with corporate goals to ensure that HR development bolsters the overarching strategy. Consequently, in their role as Compliance Managers, Business Partners must ensure the presence of alignment and its justification. It is imperative to verify that guidelines and standards comply with legal and regulatory requisites, while also aligning with agreements and corporate culture. Moreover, ethical and societal dimensions ought to be factored into compliance assessments.

The examination of HR development requirements, HR development schemes, and their execution falls under the purview of compliance. As Compliance Managers, Business Partners are tasked with scrutinizing the directives concerning the identification of skill gaps and developmental necessities arising from strategic goals. A precise delineation of directives facilitates the formulation of precise programs customized to the specific demands of the enterprise. It is imperative to ensure that organizational values, corporate culture, as well as norms and anticipations are deliberated upon and complied with. This holds particularly true for the execution of HR development programs by the accountable parties.

Within this framework, the intimate association and correlation with standards become evident. A pivotal facet of compliance pertains to quality assurance. Standards within HR development initiatives ensure a certain level of quality and uniformity in execution. This guarantees that employees acquire akin qualifications and proficiencies, irrespective of the development program they partake in and the leader, coach, or mentor overseeing them. A central challenge in this domain is for Business Partners to prioritize compliance with societal, ethical, and value-driven requisites in their capacity as Compliance Managers and to recognize their adherence as significant. It is also crucial for Business Partners to espouse these principles and requisites and consistently underscore their importance.

Regular reviews of benchmarks are essential for the Compliance Manager's role. This practice facilitates the comparison of HR development strategies with industry standards, fostering competitiveness within the organization. Moreover, it enables the identification and adoption of best practices. Utilizing benchmarks ensures a comprehensive analysis of alignment with requirements, expectations, attitudes, values, and organizational culture. Significant deviations from these benchmarks, whether positive or negative, necessitate root cause analysis to identify reasons and implement appropriate adjustments. Depending on the circumstances, the objective may involve achieving desired goals or deriving insights from underperformance to strive for superior outcomes. Evaluation of standards is closely intertwined with this process. Standards serve as the foundation for evaluating HR development initiatives. By establishing criteria, the effectiveness of programs becomes quantifiable, providing a robust framework for future development endeavors and facilitating alignment analysis.

In the role of the Compliance Manager, three primary objectives are pursued. Firstly, there is a focus on enhancing performance in accordance with established directives and standards. Clear objective definitions are pivotal in this pursuit, enabling the improvement of employee performance through the development of specific competencies, skills, and behaviors aligned with workplace requirements. The Compliance Manager primarily evaluates the adequacy of performance descriptions and competency profiles, alongside analyzing adherence to established standards.

In periods characterized by skilled labor shortages, the significance of the Compliance Manager's function escalates concerning talent management within the organizational framework. Within HR development initiatives, the delineation of objectives serves to facilitate the discernment and cultivation of aptitudes. Through the establishment of unambiguous targets for high-potential individuals, particularly in pivotal roles, the organization fosters the sustained advancement of pivotal workforce. Within the purview of the Compliance Manager's responsibilities, it becomes imperative to ascertain the appropriateness and efficacy of these objectives, alongside evaluating the methodologies, techniques, and strategies deployed to ascertain their efficacy in yielding the desired outcomes.

8.3.2 Compliance and the Use of Metrics and Procedures

The scarcity of proficient laborers intertwines closely with the dilemma of employee retention within the purview of the Compliance Manager. Analogous to the previously delineated talent management quandary, HR strategies necessitate articulation with the aim of fostering employee retention by accentuating avenues for professional growth and career trajectories. This endeavor serves to uphold the retention of adept workforce within the organizational framework. Within the domain of the Compliance Manager, paramount attention is directed towards scrutinizing the feasibility of realizing these objectives in practical terms. Hence, their responsibility encompasses assessing the utilization and execution of developmental prospects to ascertain their efficacy and extent.

For Compliance Managers specializing in HR development, controlling aspects frequently assume precedence. In this capacity, Business Partners are tasked with quantifying the efficacy of HR development initiatives utilizing predefined metrics. They are obligated to ascertain goal attainment and effect modifications as warranted. Varied outcomes necessitate analysis, with emphasis placed on adherence to prescribed protocols and standards governing accountable parties. Regular validation is imperative to assess ongoing relevance or the potential for adjustments yielding superior outcomes. Boundaries are demarcated by attitudes, beliefs, values, ethical considerations, and organizational culture.

Efficiency in guideline and goal execution by responsible party's mandates scrutiny in the Compliance Manager's purview. The allocation of resources and the efficacy of HR development endeavors necessitate evaluation. This is paramount to prioritize adherence to directives and objectives within operational endeavors. In their capacity as Compliance Managers within HR development, analyses must be conducted to facilitate post-feedback provision, potentially prompting corrective action in cases of substantial goal or guideline deviations. Continuous scrutiny of HR development initiatives is thus mandated. By scrutinizing outcomes and feedback, programs can be refined and better aligned with evolving corporate requisites.

Efficiency in this context also entails the imperative for Compliance Managers to operate in a manner that is both goal-directed and resource-efficient while conducting their analyses and evaluations. Each specific aspect should be thoroughly examined without unnecessary excess, thereby establishing a robust foundation for determining the presence of deviations from established objectives, standards, and guidelines, as well as their underlying causes. Through the establishment of an adaptation process, strategies can be formulated to mitigate these discrepancies, potentially leading to significant enhancements. In a broader sense, the presence of clear directives, standards, and objectives within HR development initiatives contributes significantly to fostering a structured, objective-driven, and enduring progression of both employees and the organization as a whole. The process of controlling serves to finalize this endeavor by ensuring the attainment of set objectives and the efficacy of implemented measures, while also maintaining close alignment with the organization's objectives, beliefs, attitudes, values, norms, and corporate culture.

The principal challenge faced by the Compliance Manager lies in the transference of acquired competencies, skills, and knowledge into the operational domain via HR development procedures and their subsequent application. Collaboration with line management is essential for ensuring that the content of HR development initiatives corresponds to the requisite competencies and is effectively communicated. Furthermore, it is imperative to establish a direct application framework in practice, facilitating the immediate utilization of new competencies, thereby enhancing the learning process and motivation.

Nevertheless, it is crucial for Business Partners and line management to acknowledge that the efficacy of training measures is contingent upon the participants' engagement. Ultimately, it is the employee who determines which components are integrated into daily operational routines. Consequently, a collaborative reflection with supervisors or within the team post-training is advisable to establish the nexus between training content and individual work contexts. Assisting the supervisor in the transfer process and establishing the requisite framework conditions constitute responsibilities of the Compliance Manager and line management to mitigate ineffective HR development interventions. The absence of adequate transfer support poses a risk of failure or yields minimal benefits in HR development initiatives.

In order to rationalize investments in HR development initiatives and enhance their value-added contribution, Business Partners, acting as Compliance Managers, must conduct evaluations in this domain. Not only the possession of requisite competencies, skills, and knowledge is pivotal, but also their application in day-to-day operations. The application of competencies, skills, and knowledge differentiates and enhances value creation. Consequently, the evaluation process is retrospective, examining past interventions and their outcomes, while also being prospective, allowing for adjustments and setting new objectives. These objectives pertain to both the structure of HR development initiatives and the advancement of competencies, skills, and knowledge among individual participants.

8.3.3 Assessing and Improvement Methods of HR Development Programs

According to Kirkpatrick, the assessment of HR development interventions comprises four phases (Blaha, 2021, 70–71). In the initial stage, attention is directed towards the satisfaction of participants subsequent to a training intervention. This assessment is conducted using methodologies such as questionnaires and encompasses dimensions such as fulfillment of expectations, instructor competence, and practical applicability. Affirmative responses imply effective training structuring, while negative feedback signals areas necessitating enhancement. Consequently, it is imperative that Business Partners, in their capacity as Compliance Managers, meticulously scrutinize the feedback utilizing predetermined guidelines, norms, and benchmarks, extracting accurate inferences from it. The significance of this feedback emanates not only from the participants' expectations, perceptions, and attitudes that necessitate fulfillment, as previously mentioned, but also from their acute assessment of the adequacy of planning, development, and execution.

In Stage 2, the evaluation of learning success is contingent upon the training objective. Compliance Managers and line management are tasked with elucidating the methods by which the assimilated knowledge and its practical application can be gauged. Quantifying knowledge acquisition can readily be achieved through standardized tests, whereas the assessment of soft skills, transferability, and the logical integration of knowledge necessitates more qualitative methodologies. The utilization of control groups is viable across various domains for monitoring advancements in competence development. However, it is imperative for Business Partners and line management to recognize that such measurements offer only a momentary insight. Particularly concerning knowledge content, there exists no assurance of its enduring presence unless routinely applied in real-world scenarios. The protracted effects and anticipated accomplishments of HR development programs often elude precise measurement or representation. This challenge arises not solely from the periodic application of newly acquired knowledge but also from the intricate attribution of competencies, skills, and knowledge to specific components of HR development initiatives. Frequently, novel competencies, skills, and knowledge emerge from their amalgamation with pre-existing ones and from external influences such as interpersonal communication with colleagues or supervisors. Nevertheless, Compliance Managers in HR development should endeavor to articulate, delineate, and evaluate discernible gains in competency levels. This endeavor assumes particular significance in subsequent stages of the model.

Stage 3 is primarily dedicated to the culmination of transfer success, placing significant emphasis on the practical application of acquired knowledge within the operational setting. Assessment procedures entail a combination of deliberations, executive surveys, and direct observations. Both Compliance Managers and line management need to recognize that the efficacy of HR development initiatives, contingent upon their nature and substance, alongside the participant's daily responsibilities, can manifest varied impacts on parameters like quality, costs, time efficiency, and productivity, as well as the feasibility and intensity of evaluation efforts. When the evaluation primarily centers on quantitative metrics of work performance, such as throughput rates per hour with predefined quality benchmarks, the process is relatively straightforward compared to tasks involving creative undertakings. Business Partners, in collaboration with line management, are encouraged to explore suitable evaluation methodologies, understanding that achieving comprehensive attribution is inherently challenging due to the attribution problem.

In Stage 4 of Kirkpatrick's model, the evaluation pertains to the influence of HR development initiatives on organizational efficacy. This phase necessitates distinct competencies, proficiencies, and expertise from Business Partners acting in the capacity of Compliance Managers. Beyond Stage 3, they must discern and assess intricate interrelations within the enterprise, a task compounded by the multifaceted nature of modern business operations. This complexity is particularly pronounced in agile enterprises, where knowledge dissemination, experiential sharing, and task execution are project-centric.

An exhaustive evaluation at this stage would entail scrutinizing the application of knowledge in specific domains and attributing it to HR development interventions. Moreover, there are additional hurdles as novel insights and methodologies often emerge from project deliberations or collaborative endeavors with peers, necessitating continuous refinement of assessment protocols. In addition to the challenge of attribution, the efficacy of solutions also demands scrutiny. Particularly in domains where processes are primarily assessed qualitatively, the complexity of evaluation is further amplified. It becomes evident that quantifying organizational efficacy under specified conditions, while considering all potential causal linkages, demands considerable resources, often outweighing the benefits. Consequently, Stage 4 typically lacks a meaningful cost-benefit ratio in most scenarios (Blaha, 2021, 72–73).

Phillips extends Kirkpatrick's model to enhance the evaluation of training measures, particularly emphasizing considerations for assessing the effectiveness of such measures. Central to his approach is the quantification of investment success, as indicated by ROI. This concept is recognized as a cornerstone of business practice, widely accepted and now applied within the realm of HR development. Training initiatives and HR development initiatives, more broadly, are conceptualized as investments yielding future returns. The feasibility of measuring ROI varies depending on the nature of the training content. The duration of the impact of training measures is subject to uncertainties, including the degradation of acquired skills and knowledge over time, along with the persistence of entrenched behavioral patterns. Additionally, Phillips critiques Kirkpatrick's evaluation stages, suggesting that they may not necessarily occur sequentially. He contends that an HR development intervention, notwithstanding participants' self-assessments indicating low efficacy, can still yield positive outcomes in terms of skill enhancement, behavioral change, and organizational success (Blaha, 2021, 73–74).

An alternative method for assessing HR development initiatives and interventions involves the application of the Learning Scorecard, which is rooted in Kaplan and Norton's Balanced Scorecard (BSC). This methodology converts organizational mission and strategy into quantifiable goals and measures. The BSC encompasses four dimensions – financial, customer, internal business processes, and learning and development –, each of which is duly considered. By integrating non-financial indicators, particularly within the learning and development dimension, the BSC extends corporate objectives beyond mere financial parameters. Educational management strategies delineate pertinent goals within these dimensions, complete with specified benchmarks and activities for ongoing progress evaluation. The customer dimension centers on participants engaged in educational initiatives, while the financial dimension emphasizes profitability, the process dimension concentrates on operational efficiency, and the resource dimension evaluates available resources within educational administration (Blaha, 2021, 78).

In both methodologies, it is imperative that the outcomes of training undergo consistent measurement and reporting to maintain a sustained emphasis on competency development. Periodic evaluation and adjustment of competency levels offer a transparent assessment of deficient competencies among individual employees or employee cohorts relative to established standards. This process also illuminates areas requiring intervention. Furthermore, it enables the identification of potential avenues for strategic alignment within the company. This concept is depicted in the subsequent figure.

8.3 Compliance Manager

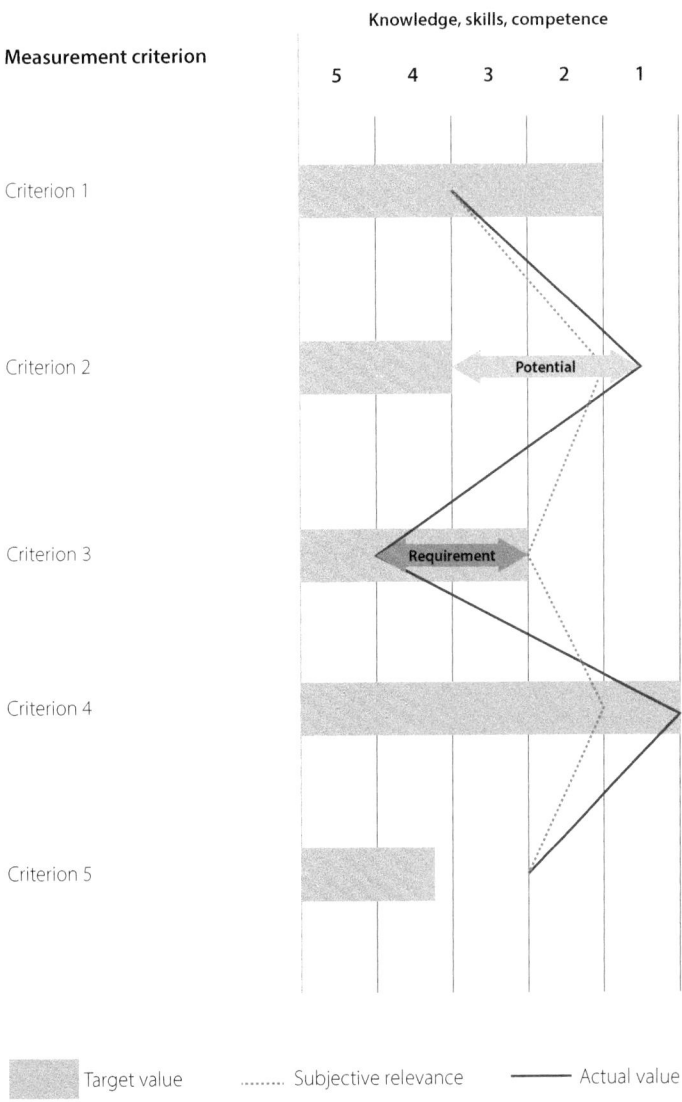

Fig. 8-2: Measurement Criterion (Blaha, 2021, 81)

Potential deviations from the centrally defined target values may stem from various sources, such as misjudgment of pertinent competencies by management or the HR department. However, these discrepancies invariably signify a necessity for intervention. Thus, routine assessment and modification of this training methodology are imperative to ensure that competency enhancement aligns with corporate objectives (Blaha, 2021, 80). A prerequisite for discerning the necessity for intervention and adjustment is the possession of a well-elaborated systematic comprehension by Business Partners, enabling them to conduct analyses to evaluate the current status and progression. Besides expertise in the realm of analysis, Business Partners necessitate operational knowledge to forge intimate connections.

Drawing from the framework delineated by Kirkpatrick, discrepancies in training endeavors can be identified, subsequently remediated through fitting measures. At stage 1, it is imperative to acknowledge that mere high satisfaction does not suffice as an indicator of training efficacy. The primary objective lies in the acquisition of implementation competency, with positive feedback serving as a supportive, albeit non-compulsory factor.

Stage 2 underscores that the crux of implementation competency lies in the genuine learning of participants. Discrepancies may arise from inappropriate methodologies, instructors, environments, or deficient motivation. The self-motivation of participants and the capacity of HR development to nurture it assume pivotal roles.

Stage 3 presents potential discrepancies stemming from insufficient learning in stage 2 or impediments to behavioral alterations. Despite possessing the requisite competencies, participants might abstain from implementation due to diverse reasons. In such cases, organizational impediments must be eradicated or target competencies adjusted accordingly.

In stage 4, deviations emanate from preceding stages. If the requisite skills and knowledge have been imparted but the anticipated impact on business outcomes remains elusive, the derivation of competency needs from corporate objectives might be inadequate or fail to meet cost-benefit considerations.

The subsequent diagram elucidates the deviations observed in training initiatives, elucidating that the higher the stage of deviation, the more probable it is that an earlier error transpired in the HR development process (Blaha, 2021, 80–82).

Business Partners acting as Compliance Managers and line management must acknowledge the evolving challenges and requisites of the commercial milieu. In this context, HR development initiatives necessitate continual fine-tuning.

Technological advancement stands as the foremost influential factor. The swift progression of novel technologies impacts myriad sectors. Companies must ensure their workforce is adept with cutting-edge technologies and methodologies to sustain competitiveness. Consequently, HR development schemes need periodic revisions to encompass training on the latest technological advancements.

The subsequent pivotal factor is the escalating trend of globalization. Corporations increasingly operate within a global framework. This necessitates employees to cultivate intercultural proficiencies and acclimate to the exigencies of international commerce. Hence, HR development programs must incorporate global perspectives and aptitudes.

The third salient factor is demographic shifts. The demographic composition of the labor force is undergoing transformation. There is a surge in the influx of millennials and Generation Z cohorts into the workforce, while senior employees retire. HR development programs must accommodate the disparate requirements and learning modalities of diverse age cohorts.

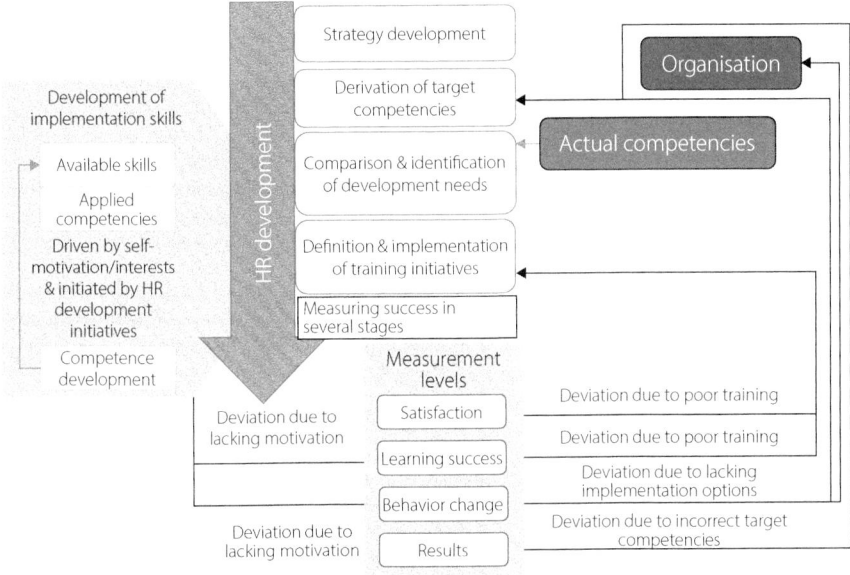

Fig. 8-3: Causes of Deviations in Competence Measurement (Blaha, 2021, 83)

The fourth consequential determinant lies in the escalating pace of business model evolution. Market dynamics, customer demands, and sundry factors are catalysts for this transformation. Corporations are tasked with ensuring that their workforce possesses the requisite competencies to seamlessly adapt to these novel business paradigms.

The fifth notable influencer pertains to the burgeoning deficit of adept laborers. There exists a conspicuous scarcity of proficient professionals across numerous and progressively varied sectors. Enterprises must foster a culture of ongoing education and skill acquisition among their staff to address the burgeoning demand for specialized talents. Compliance Managers are entrusted with ensuring the adequacy of incentives and the alignment of potential participants' interests, particularly in light of demographic shifts and the diverse array of stakeholders.

The sixth significant determinant revolves around the evolving landscape of work structures. The proliferation of remote work, flexible scheduling, and digital platforms is reshaping conventional labor practices. HR development initiatives must adapt to these emerging work modalities and equip employees with the requisite competencies to thrive in the contemporary workplace.

Within the purview of compliance management, Business Partners wield considerable influence in advancing the company's long-term prosperity. By tailoring HR development programs in accordance with strategic objectives and adhering to organizational ethos, attitudes, and corporate culture, they play a pivotal role in shaping the workforce's trajectory.

An effective compliance management system within HR development is instrumental in bolstering performance metrics. This is achieved through targeted training initiatives, which enable employees to augment their skill sets, consequently elevating the collective performance of the team. Furthermore, such interventions serve to enhance the innovation potential within the organization. Employees equipped with contemporary skills and knowledge are better positioned to generate innovative concepts and propel the company's progression. Moreover, proficient compliance management within HR development serves as a catalyst for employee retention. Firms that invest in the professional growth of their workforce tend to foster greater loyalty among employees, thus retaining top talent and solidifying their allegiance to the organization. This, in turn, fortifies the company's competitive stance.

Continuous adaptation to fluctuating market dynamics is paramount for enhancing or sustaining competitiveness within the industry. Hence, adherence to robust compliance measures facilitates this agility, enabling the company to remain responsive to market exigencies. In essence, the role of a Compliance Manager within HR development extends beyond mere oversight of program design and implementation; it strategically aligns with the evolving corporate landscape, thereby underpinning long-term success and value generation.

8.4 Culture and Change Champion

The second category to be discussed is Strategic Enablers. The first role of Business Partners in this category is the Culture and Change Champion. In their capacity as Culture and Change Champions, Business Partners are tasked with elevating the perceived relevance of HR development within the organizational framework. The exigencies stemming from skills scarcities and the swiftly evolving competency prerequisites mandate immediate action in this regard. Business Partners, assuming the mantle of Culture and Change Champions, must advocate to line management the imperative for active involvement in HR development, emphasizing its significance not only for HR management but also for their own roles. Line management must grasp that HR development constitutes a pivotal locus for intervention to secure both present and, notably, future organizational success. To foster a deeper integration of HR development into the corporate culture and effectuate a corresponding attitudinal shift within line management, Business Partners, functioning as Culture and Change Champions, must foremost underscore the favorable ramifications of HR development, particularly accentuating opportunities for value generation and enduring success. This necessitates that Business Partners possess a commensurate operational acumen to discern interdependencies within the organization and grasp their resultant implications.

8.4.1 The Integration of HR Development into Organizational Culture

HR development endeavors to bridge skill disparities, often attendant to skills scarcities, thereby ensuring that employees possess the requisite proficiencies and knowledge to meet labor market exigencies. Effective HR development facilitates targeted investments in employee training and the cultivation of requisite competencies. In their capacity as Culture and Change Champions, Business Partners necessitate competencies, knowledge, experience, and anticipations regarding the business milieu and its potential transformations vis-à-vis the realm of change. Only upon this foundation can the imperative for change be discerned, and appropriate determinations made concerning HR development, encompassing its initiatives, objectives, and substance.

In value creation, besides targeted development and skilled worker acquisition, the retention of talent emerges as a pivotal aspect. Within a competitive milieu, the preservation of a proficient workforce escalates in significance. Precision in HR development, catering to individual employee requisites and offering developmental opportunities, facilitates long-term talent retention within the company. This is intrinsically linked to the company's allure as an employer. Enterprises exhibiting robust HR development strategies are perceived as desirable places of employment. The provision of avenues for continuous development and professional advancement stands as a significant determinant in workplace selection. A meticulously crafted HR development blueprint contributes to positioning the company as forward-thinking and investment-friendly within the labor market.

Strategic and efficacious investments in HR development typically culminate in heightened innovation prowess. Subsequently, this fosters a favorable employer image, thus bolstering the retention of skilled labor and the attraction of talent. A company's adaptability and innovation capacity hinge crucially upon the competencies of its workforce. Through targeted HR development initiatives, employees can be empowered to ideate and implement innovative solutions, consequently enhancing the company's competitive edge.

Sophisticated HR development efforts aid in attaining flexibility and agility, qualities especially indispensable for line management and novel leadership paradigms. Given the perpetually evolving job market, companies must possess the capacity to promptly adapt to these transformations. Well-orchestrated HR development endeavors enable companies to equip their employees for emerging demands, thereby enhancing organizational flexibility and agility.

Ultimately, HR development substantially contributes to knowledge retention within the company and its transmission to younger cohorts. This assumes heightened relevance in companies confronted with both skill shortages and significant demographic challenges stemming from the mass retirement of employees. Business Partners play a pivotal role in ingraining HR development more deeply into the corporate fabric by addressing the aforementioned aspects, thereby fostering positive growth in terms of agility, innovation prowess, competitiveness, and employer attractiveness.

The imperative lies with line management to be collectively persuaded of the imperative nature of enhanced HR development, essential for proactively mitigating skilled labor scarcities, amplifying employee efficacy, and safeguarding the prospective viability of the enterprise. Business Partners, in their capacity as Cultural and Change Champions, within HR development, must not only bolster their pertinence to line management but also elucidate the relevance of the adjacent domain of HR marketing to the prosperity of line management and the corporation. Targeted HR marketing endeavors, robust employer branding initiatives, and the inception of an internal talent reservoir collectively augment the potential for value creation and foster the formation or expansion of a competitive edge.

By judiciously amalgamating HR development and HR marketing, Business Partners can contribute to the enhancement of employee competencies and the maximal exploitation of extant potentials. Furthermore, through intimate collaboration with line management, Business Partners, acting as Cultural and Change Champions, can conceive strategies, approaches, and interventions conducive to sustainable career trajectories and prospect-laden career schematics. This is especially pertinent when a symbiotic relationship is established with HR development schemes. To ensure enduring success and optimal value addition within the organization, a deliberate nexus with succession planning is imperative. Research within the domain of talent management evinces that enterprises furnishing effective career advancement prospects are adept at enticing and retaining adept professionals. This phenomenon stems from employees feeling esteemed owing to transparent career schematics and discerning avenues for their professional advancement.

Career paths and HR development programs, when sustainable and carefully crafted, directly correlate with strategic corporate progression. Within the realm of strategic planning research, emphasis is placed on the imperative nature of harmonizing a company's enduring objectives with the individual career aspirations of its workforce. Precision in career and succession planning ensures a consistent influx of adept professionals into leadership roles, individuals who comprehend and can further the organization's aims. HR development, coupled with associated HR marketing, career planning, and succession planning, alongside fitting HR development initiatives, stand as indispensable elements for effective knowledge management and competence enhancement. Particularly within a milieu increasingly reliant on application competencies rooted in knowledge, a company's success hinges largely on the expertise and growth potential of its workforce. Systematic HR development, competence augmentation, and career mapping facilitate the targeted cultivation of essential proficiencies for forthcoming challenges. A tight integration with succession planning guarantees the swift filling of pivotal roles with capable personnel, thereby ensuring operational continuity. A prerequisite of utmost importance is that Business Partners possess advanced knowledge in these domains and wield application competence to forge productive ties with company-specific demands. Innovation management studies underscore that adept career and succession planning empower a company to promptly adapt to shifts in market dynamics or organizational structure. Proficiently trained personnel are poised to embrace novel challenges and engineer innovative resolutions. This significantly augments competitiveness and consequently, value generation.

8.4.2 Cooperation of Business Partners and Line Managers to Advance HR Development Marketing

Linking HR development with HR marketing, career planning, and succession planning presents an additional advantage in fostering employees' motivation and engagement, a phenomenon consistently substantiated by psychological research. Transparent career planning communicates to employees that their endeavors and accomplishments are acknowledged, providing a pathway for advancement toward their career objectives, thereby cultivating a motivated and engaged workforce. Strategic amalgamation of these domains enables companies to mitigate risks during employee or executive transitions. Nurturing talent strategically via HR development initiatives and appropriate programs catalyzes growth post-identification, incentivizing further skill refinement and advancement. Consequently, this facilitates adept preparation for future demands across existing or alternative roles.

Strategic HR development is intrinsically linked to upholding corporate values and culture. By deeply ingraining these facets within strategic HR development and succession planning, companies ensure continuity of principles and objectives among employees, especially in leadership roles, in alignment with their predecessors. Ultimately, strategic succession planning within strategic HR development represents a proactive approach ensuring the availability of adept employees and leaders to confront challenges, capitalize on opportunities, and secure enduring success. Nevertheless, the efficacy of this strategy hinges upon HR development being firmly ingrained in organizational culture, particularly among Business Partners serving as Culture and Change Champions, as well as within line management. This integration must initially occur within Business Partners before permeating through persuasion to line management and corporate leadership.

The integration of HR development into corporate culture stands as a pivotal determinant for a company's enduring success. Business Partners are tasked with accentuating the significance of HR development within the shared values, norms, beliefs, and practices upheld by line management and corporate leadership, assuming the mantle of Culture and Change Champions. Within this framework, HR development wields the power to influence employee conduct and shape the corporate identity in response to pertinent challenges. HR development can seamlessly integrate into collaborative processes, decision-making procedures, and innovation frameworks, thereby fostering its deeper integration into corporate culture and facilitating sustainable transformations. Strategic incorporation of HR development, encompassing continuous employee advancement and empowerment, is deemed an intrinsic element of corporate operations within such a cultural milieu.

The anchorage of HR development in corporate culture necessitates the cultivation and institutionalization of a conducive learning ethos within the organization. This entails fostering receptiveness to novel ideas, a commitment to ongoing growth, and collective accountability for workforce development. Business Partners bear the responsibility of propelling this evolution, particularly to augment value creation and confront contemporary and future challenges. A fundamental prerequisite entails Business Partners persuading line management of the imperative nature of HR development and its attendant positive repercussions. Beyond their own roles and contributions, Business Partners must recognize line management's pivotal role in executing the company's strategy, including HR development initiatives. Efforts are required to instill this understanding within line management, who must champion and endorse the relevance of HR development while aligning individual employee competencies with strategic objectives. To achieve this alignment, line management, in collaboration with Business Partners, must proffer tailored developmental pathways. In tandem with enhanced collaboration between the two entities, there is a pressing need for the further advancement of leadership competencies within line management, particularly within the sphere of HR development. Augmenting HR development competencies within line management is especially desirable due to the requisite adaptability, which profoundly influences competitiveness and thereby, value generation.

Within an ever-evolving business milieu, the cultivation of agility and subsequent alignment with the requisite competencies within the workforce, both qualitatively and quantitatively, assumes heightened significance. This exertion notably impacts competitiveness. A more robust incorporation of HR development into the fabric of corporate culture, buttressed by Business Partners in their capacity as Culture and Change Champions and endorsed collaboratively by line management, facilitates a strategic alignment of the company and a continuous enhancement of HR development – a pivotal element for success, competitiveness, and value creation. Within this framework, Business Partners must persuade line management executives of the necessity to adapt to an evolved role, accompanied by a shift in the requisite competencies, skills, and methodologies.

Leadership must be approached and comprehended through a distinct lens by line management executives, as modern leadership paradigms such as agile leadership, complementary leadership, and digital leadership are imperative. Consequently, leaders themselves necessitate HR development programs, the significance of which they must initially grasp. This constitutes a pivotal contributing factor to augmenting modern leadership efficacy and, consequently, enhancing value addition, as well as fostering the HR development, satisfaction, and retention of those under their stewardship.

8.4.3 Empowering Change: Agile Leadership and HR Development for Business Success

The envisioned progression entails a transformative procedure that necessitates initiation and propulsion by Business Partners, with line management assuming a pivotal function. Business Partners are mandated to excel as Culture and Change Champions, directing the substance and configuration of the change process. Meanwhile, line management assumes the decisive mantle in executing the change process, being directly accountable for steering and supervising the operational stratum. In their capacity as Culture and Change Champions, Business Partners must not only focus on conceptualization but also actively participate in implementation alongside line management, ensuring the adaptation of organizational structures and processes, coupled with a deeper integration of HR development within the corporate culture.

Change management competencies serve as indispensable instruments in ensuring the successful assimilation and endorsement of changes by employees. The execution, and subsequently the triumphant realization, necessitate Business Partners and line management to possess and adeptly utilize the requisite skills for navigating change management processes. Given the significance of fortifying the integration of HR development within the corporate fabric and the concomitant imperative to forestall the failure of the change process, a comprehensive scrutiny of change management competencies, skills, and prior achievements should precede. Within the delineated change framework, considerable emphasis must be laid on concentrating, amalgamating, and cultivating agile competencies. The dynamic evolution of the business landscape, employee anticipations, the imperatives for leaders to concentrate on strategic dimensions, and the overarching competitiveness and value-added contributions all mandate the possession of agile competencies. Research corroborates the significance of agile competencies and methodologies for HR development, yet it also underscores the necessity for fulfilling specific prerequisites and stipulations to effectuate the transition from conventional to agile HR development. Assessing extant processes and configurations is not only imperative for the enterprise but also within the purview of HR development. Business Partners, in their capacity as Culture and Change Champions, and line management must prioritize surmounting entrenched hierarchical and structural paradigms in favor of fostering adaptable frameworks that facilitate prompt and pertinent responses to contemporary exigencies, thereby ingraining HR development more deeply within the corporate culture.

In the planning phase, there must be adequate consideration given to dynamic elements, facilitating the replacement of long-term plans and fixed decisions with short planning cycles and feedback loops. This approach fosters agility in HR development and reinforces employees' self-organization and accountability. To attain this objective, the establishment of an agile corporate culture is imperative, characterized by appreciation, feedback mechanisms, trust, and tolerance for errors. This necessitates a shift in leadership style towards agile leadership, fostering equitable engagement with employees and greater involvement in decision-making processes. To facilitate this transition, HR developers, Business Partners in the role of Culture and Change Champions, and line management must cultivate agile competencies to effectively steer the transformation and change management processes. These competencies encompass continual learning, rapid adaptability, and innovative problem-solving. Effective communication skills are also crucial for the successful implementation of interdisciplinary exchange and collaboration processes (Assies, Thiel & Stulle, 2021, 203–204).

The investigation findings demonstrate that the agile proficiencies of the examined HR developers are generally appraised as robust. This observation is notably pronounced in the domain of agile "People Skills," encompassing accountability, adaptability, collaboration, and outcome orientation. Nevertheless, there exists an opportunity for enhancement in agile "Business Skills," primarily concerning methodologies and digital proficiencies. In light of the swift technological progressions and the escalating demand for competence cultivation within the workforce, it is imperative for HR developers to allocate more resources towards augmenting these business skills. This endeavor is imperative not solely to sustain relevance as a collaborative partner for employees and executives but also as strategic allies of the enterprise.

In the realm of agile methodologies in HR development, a disjunction is observed between the acknowledgment of their significance and their practical implementation. Despite HR developers recognizing the importance of agile methodologies, their incorporation into practice remains infrequent. While certain departments already harness creativity and innovation methodologies, they frequently languish unused. Given that agile methodologies harbor considerable potential for HR development and the entire organizational framework, it is advisable for HR developers to increasingly integrate them into their internal processes and throughout the organization. In particular, Business Partners and line management assume pivotal roles in establishing conducive environments and elucidating the benefits for employees.

It is imperative for Business Partners assuming the role of Culture and Change Champions to engage in more closely intertwined collaboration with line management. This collaboration forms the cornerstone upon which HR development can be customized to cater to individual requirements, thereby fostering optimal value generation for both employees and the organization. Within this framework, Business Partners and line management must maintain acute awareness that the effective implementation of agility stands as a pivotal determinant in amplifying the significance and efficacy of HR development within the corporate milieu. This implementation significantly bolsters business triumph and fortifies overall competitiveness (Assies, Thiel & Stulle, 2021, 204–205).

Within the context of value creation orientation and competitive prowess, the evolution toward agile HR development and the requisite leadership demeanor must increasingly prioritize performance management. This prioritization aims to align with the triumph of the enterprise, teams, and individual personnel. The primary objective is no longer confined to the cultivation of employee potentials but rather to enable and catalyze performance. Performance is not merely restricted to the attainment of outcomes but is construed as contextually adept successful conduct founded upon competencies and their cultivation and application. These competencies, particularly those of a technical-methodological, social, and personal nature, facilitate effective action amidst uncertain circumstances. Such circumstances arise with greater frequency owing to the delineated evolution of the business ecosystem, the exigency for agility, and the amplification of decision-making autonomy and responsibility cascaded from managers to employees.

In the realm of performance orientation, it is imperative for Business Partners to recognize their role as Culture and Change Champions, as well as line management's responsibility, wherein performance is evidenced through task-related action outcomes, monetary gains, social contributions, ecological impacts, and adherence to company values and culture. The foundation of performance lies in self-organizational dispositions facilitating effective action amidst uncertain conditions. Technical-methodological, social, and personal competencies are pivotal and correlate with contextual determinants.

Business Partners encounter the challenge of comprehending the significance and extent, along with the objectives, of non-monetary advancements encompassing ethical conduct, social perspectives, and personal competencies, including their envisioned and potential value addition. Particularly within the domain of non-monetary factors, persuading line management and corporate leadership regarding their importance becomes imperative for driving enhancements and enhancing awareness of these aspects.

Through job-integrated learning, social learning, and personal development, Business Partners and line management can optimize performance. Job-integrated learning harnesses individual and collective experiential knowledge to augment performance, while social learning nurtures competency development aligned with performance objectives and cultivates informal knowledge exchange. HR development caters to the requisites of agile enterprises, focusing on honing competencies and fostering stimuli for individual professional growth.

Performance-oriented HR development underscores the importance of employees and their competence requirements tied to performance within the workplace. During the implementation phase, the challenges and opportunities posed by digitization, demographic shifts, and evolving values must be duly considered (Armutat, 2021, 466–467). Business Partners must initially grasp these factors comprehensively in their capacity as Culture and Change Champions, then devise a strategy aimed at maximizing performance, and subsequently collaborate with line management to implement it effectively.

8.4.4 Enhancing Corporate Culture: The Crucial Role of Performance-Oriented HR Development and Social Learning Strategies

Business Partners and line management need to acknowledge that the performance orientation within HR development in the corporate culture necessitates adjustments in learning process design to augment performance. Structures are imperative to foster cooperative behavior and learning processes emphasizing experience exchange and implicit knowledge. Business Partners and line management should possess familiarity with various forms of learning processes and possess sufficient application competencies. Social learning encompasses self-organized learning processes where individuals network to address common tasks and enhance competencies through practical experiences. The methods of social learning exhibit variability based on exchange partners and media characteristics, encompassing personal encounters and virtual exchanges. Personal encounters can be leveraged through methodologies like job-shadowing, job-pairing, peer feedback, and experiential mentoring. Interactions of individuals within groups also offer opportunities, including multiplier models, retrospectives, and debriefings. Virtual exchange via chats, communities of practice, and online employee academies facilitates knowledge exchange. The concept of Working-Out-Loud serves as a relevant approach in fostering a culture of learning and exchange by connecting relationship networks and personal development goals. Despite the extant understanding regarding the potentials and opportunities afforded by these methodologies, regrettably, their widespread dissemination in practice remains infrequent (Armutat, 2021, 468–471). Business Partners are required to augment the adoption of these methodologies within enterprises owing to their significant potential and the concomitant enhancements in HR development. These methodologies are instrumental in reinforcing and facilitating lifelong learning endeavors.

The function of performance-oriented HR development encompasses the diagnosis and regular evaluation of employees' competencies and potentials across various career trajectories. This approach aligns with the company's performance culture, underscoring its significance. Career-related personality development adheres to a resource-oriented HR cycle, highlighting the central tenet of "performance". The orientation towards this paradigm shapes diagnostics, assessments, and developmental interventions (Armutat, 2021, 474–475).

Business Partners, in their roles as Culture and Change Champions and line management, must recognize that the performance orientation of HR development fundamentally alters the landscape. It becomes pivotal to the business agenda, acting as a catalyst for performance and supporting learning processes within workflows. Moreover, it functions as a designer of work systems, introducing structures that enhance both learning and performance in organizational development. A cohesive strategic alignment among Business Partners and line management, operating as Culture and Change Champions, is crucial for crafting a business-focused HR strategy. The performance-oriented perspective holds particular promise for HR development amid digital transformation, especially as the demand for self-organized and creative action intensifies in Industry 4.0 and Work 4.0 contexts (Armutat, 2021, 475–476).

In addition to the previous content-based approach to integrating HR development more deeply into corporate culture, Business Partners in the roles of Culture and Change Champions and line management should incorporate adjustments to the incentive system. Beyond the intrinsic motivation stemming from recognizing HR development's necessity for company success, value addition, and competitiveness, an extrinsic incentive framework is also established (Wegerich, 2015, 15).

For the strategic advancement of the outlined transformational process, Business Partners, acting as Culture and Change Champions alongside line management, must engage in close collaboration at the organizational level, particularly within the domain of organizational development. Jointly, these cohorts shoulder a collective responsibility for formulating initiatives aimed at enhancing decision-making, collaboration, implementation, and innovation capabilities within an organization. Emphasizing the augmentation of problem-solving and innovation proficiencies, along with endeavors directed at enhancing structures and processes to bolster efficiency, holds paramount significance.

In the context of the described transformational journey, participants must conscientiously deliberate on measures that elucidate actions and their ramifications, fostering comprehension of the comprehensive context of the value chain within the enterprise. This methodological approach enables the desired organizational changes, ensures resources are allocated in line with objectives, and firmly integrates new cognitive and operational requirements into the organizational culture. Hence, Business Partners necessitate adept communication skills, strategically employing them in interactions with line management, corporate leadership, and employees, thereby contributing to the cultivation and internalization of a new learning ethos and the heightened role of HR development at this echelon.

In their capacity as Culture and Change Champions, along with line management, Business Partners must contemplate the milieu in which the envisaged change is slated for implementation. Empirical evidence underscores the efficacy of a systemic approach to HR development and organizational advancement, which entails incorporating the perspectives of all stakeholders. Furthermore, this approach endeavors to apprehend intricate interdependencies and causality, eschewing siloed viewpoints, thereby fostering collective learning processes and an analytical-planning paradigm (Wegerich, 2015, 15–17).

This strategic approach plays a pivotal role in synchronizing the congruence of HR development and organizational development, grounded on a holistic comprehension. It prioritizes corporate objectives, competitiveness, and the maximization of value creation, thereby aligning with Ulrich's fundamental objectives. Apart from the requisite involvement of Business Partners and line management, substantial endorsement from senior management is advantageous. It is ideal for

Business Partners and line management to collectively advocate for proactive backing and direction from the organization's top echelons, ensuring not just participation but active endorsement of the desired transformation (Assies, Thiel & Stulle, 2021, 203–204).

8.5 Human Capital Curator

Within the domain of Strategic Enablers, the second role is the domain of the Human Capital Curator. This title signifies a concentration for Business Partners and line managers on the cultivation and evaluation of human capital, specifically aimed at addressing both current and future human capital demands. Furthermore, a close integration between human capital management and curation in alignment with organizational strategy is essential.

8.5.1 Elevating Business Partners: The Imperative Role of Human Capital Curators in Strategy and Success

In numerous enterprises, a scenario unfolds wherein senior management plays a pivotal role in determining the importance of human capital. Significant influencing factors encompass the business rationale of the enterprise, ideologies, principles, and the implicit strategic methodology. Recognition of the imperative nature of intensive human capital management is notably contingent upon the sector and the accessibility of adept personnel. The persistent deficit of skilled laborers prompts many enterprises to increasingly perceive the relevance of this matter in corporate governance. For Business Partners, the skills deficit serves as a catalyst in advancing human capital management within the enterprise, especially when the significance of human capital for business triumph is prominently emphasized. Nonetheless, in numerous instances, Business Partners must undertake persuasion efforts and illustrate how heightened human capital management can contribute to the value generation of the enterprise and amplify its value proposition. To this end, it is imperative for Business Partners to possess or cultivate adept competencies in the realm of human capital management.

Business partners must enhance their prominence in the capacity of Human Capital Curators since, regrettably, they often play an insignificant role in the sphere of human capital management processes within enterprises. The rationales for this frequently lie in the perception of senior management that the HR function remains passive or fails to contribute adequately to the discourse. This could stem from a deficiency in the perception of a cohesive HR strategy and the absence of decision-relevant data from the HR department (Lebrenz, 2020, 141–142). Nonetheless, the evolution of the skills deficit and the associated escalating strategic significance of HR necessitate Business Partners to substantially augment their role as Human Capital Curators.

The initial step for Business Partners assuming the role of Human Capital Curators entails the analysis of requisite human capital for strategy execution and its significance in strategy formulation. This necessitates Business Partners possessing a profound comprehension of processes, procedures, routines, as well as competencies, skills, and experiences essential for the task, requiring close collaboration and interdisciplinary exchange with line management. From this basis, Business Partners in the capacity of Human Capital Curators can evaluate whether extant human capital serves as a foundation for future strategy or is perceived merely as a passive asset. Following an assessment of the current scenario, the objective should focus on shaping the involvement of human capital in strategy formulation to garner enhanced recognition and consideration, aiming at securing a competitive edge through adept human capital management (Lebrenz, 2020, 140–141). Business Partners, acting as Human Capital Curators, can adopt various methodologies toward this end, as delineated below.

8.5.2 The Role of Human Capital Curators in Achieving Competitive Advantage

The first option involves the application of the Market-Based View (MBV), which entails deriving HR strategy from corporate or business unit strategy. Business Partners, acting as Human Capital Curators, ascertain the quantitative and qualitative requirements of employees, including specific qualifications, competencies, and experiences. Subsequently, HR management is tasked with ensuring the availability of this human capital through suitable developmental programs at the required time. However, this necessitates an initial gap analysis to compare existing competencies, experiences, and knowledge with future demands. Moreover, Human Capital Curators must evaluate the feasibility of developing the required human capital or the challenges involved in acquiring it. This approach posits that organizational structure should align with corporate strategy. In the context of MBV, this principle extends to HR management, which must also align with the strategy. Here, human capital assumes a passive role in the strategy formulation process. However, this does not diminish its significance, as it can still be pivotal in a market-based approach. Nonetheless, Human Capital Curators must recognize that, in the MBV, existing human capital does not serve as the foundation for strategy development, unlike other approaches (Lebrenz, 2020, 142).

Given the persistent adherence of numerous enterprises to traditional paradigms, Business Partners, acting as Human Capital Curators, must initially embrace and propagate human capital management rooted in this framework. Successful navigation of this entails articulating the company's challenges within this context, effectively communicating them to both line management and corporate leadership, thereby enhancing awareness and understanding of human capital management and its contributory value. Consequently, this augments the likelihood of the integration of considerations regarding skill shortages, HR development, and overall human capital management into the company's strategic formulation.

The resources encompassing HR management, HR development, and human capital management thereby attain significance, particularly in light of their alignment with the company's objectives and their impact on value creation and contribution through heightened involvement in strategy formulation. Consequently, this amplifies the importance of the Business Partner role in the capacity of Human Capital Curators, subsequently bolstering their influence. It becomes evident that Business Partners, in their role as Human Capital Curators, can transcend market-centric perspectives and adopt more proactive approaches (Lebrenz, 2020, 142).

The scarcity of skilled labor and its evolution, coupled with its ramifications for value generation and the developmental trajectory of enterprises, underscores the growing significance of human capital as a resource. This resource assumes a critical role in the cultivation of novel business models and adaptability to evolving market dynamics. Within most innovation and adaptation processes, proficient HR holds pivotal importance, serving as key agents in shaping and executing new business models. It is apparent that the strategic deployment of specific HR within an organization is paramount for success and warrants explicit consideration within human capital management (Lebrenz, 2020, 142–143).

The Resource-Based View (RBV) stands in opposition to passive perceptions of human capital, positing that specific resources within a company can yield enduring competitive advantages. Unlike the MBV, RBV directs attention internally, highlighting the importance of core competencies and contending that successful enterprises consciously leverage them. Core competencies possess value, are challenging to replicate, and can be transferred. RBV underscores the strategic significance of resources and capabilities, stressing the necessity for continual rejuvenation. Human capital's role is deemed pivotal to corporate strategy, notwithstanding challenges many firms face in harnessing it as a competitive edge. Despite the growing significance of human capital, established processes and investments often trail behind other business domains (Lebrenz, 2020, 143–147).

Business Partners, assuming the mantle of Human Capital Curators, can apply RBV while concurrently integrating it with strategic HR management, contingent upon achieving the aforementioned advancements. However, successful execution necessitates Business Partners in the role of Human Capital Curators to possess or cultivate a profound comprehension of RBV, its methodologies, and objectives. In instances where such comprehension is lacking among Business Partners, they must first enhance their proficiency in this realm to realize the stated objectives. Essentially, Business Partners must initially invest in their own human capital and be furnished with requisite resources to do so. A precondition for this is their capacity to persuade management regarding the pertinence and advantageous outcomes, as well as the multiplier effect.

Within the RBV, resources are construed as company-specific and enduring, serving as the bedrock for competitive advantages. Consequently, this approach

8.5 Human Capital Curator

lays the groundwork for requisite adaptations and alterations arising from shifting market dynamics and talent scarcities. Business Partners must recognize that the significance of resources within the RBV may fluctuate and evolve, but those contributing to sustainable competitive advantage invariably take precedence due to their non-replicability (Schwarz, 2010, 57–59).

Business Partners should recognize their role as Human Capital Curators when employing the RBV, acknowledging the difficulty in transferring firm-specific resources. Success in aligning the HR of the company with the strategy in cooperation with line management often leads to a competitive edge. This edge becomes enduring when the resource possesses characteristics such as value, rarity, uniqueness, imperfect imitability, and non-substitutability. Conversely, the heterogeneity and immobility of resources are crucial prerequisites for transient competitive advantages, which, nonetheless, can evolve into sustainable competitive advantages for the reasons expounded below. The subsequent diagram delineates a potential developmental trajectory (Schwarz, 2010, 59–61).

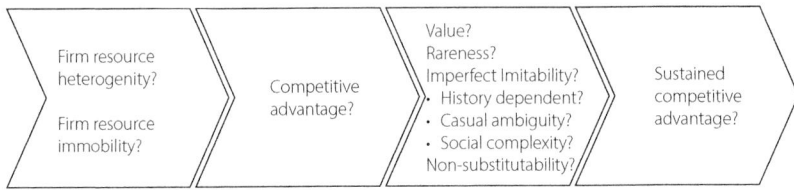

Fig. 8-4: Potential Development Process Concerning Competitive Advantage (Schwarz, 2010, 60)

8.5.3 Leveraging Unique Human Capital for Sustainable Competitive Advantage

The strategic significance of HR development within the RBV becomes particularly prominent when sustainable competitive advantage is derived from a transient competitive opportunity. This advantage is due to the heterogeneity and immobility of HR, characterized by high value contribution, scarcity, limited imitability, and non-substitutability (Schwarz, 2010, 62). In periods marked by increasing skill shortages, the role of the Human Capital Curator becomes critical in developing unique HR. While this development fundamentally relies on HR recruitment and retention, it is significantly influenced by HR development. This importance is justified by the necessity to align HR development with company-specific requirements and its substantial incentive effect on many (potential) employees. Uniqueness is further enhanced by working conditions and the company's inimitable approach to its employees. The formulation of corporate culture, employer branding, compensation systems, bonus structures, and leadership principles also contribute to this uniqueness (Schwarz, 2010, 64). A crucial prerequisite is that Business Partners possess a comprehensive understanding and the ability to evaluate operational activities, as well as the capability to establish a direct link to strategic objectives.

HR, as a strategic lever and source of value creation, gain significance in the domain of imitability due to the limited availability of suitably skilled HR. Qualified employees are pivotal to company productivity by acquiring resources, formulating strategies, and executing them in core processes. These specific elements of the value creation process are challenging for competitors to replicate. However, Business Partners, acting as Human Capital Curators, must not view the contribution of HR sources to transforming corporate processes into competitive advantages as static. This transformation is influenced by workforce structure, HR policies, turnover, health status, qualifications, and collaboration. Consequently, continuous investment in retaining and developing organizational members is essential, along with an adaptation process to ensure the provision of the necessary quantitative and qualitative resources for long-term benefits (Schwarz, 2010, 64–65).

8.5.4 Leveraging Human Capital: The Key to Sustainable Competitive Advantage Through Unique HR Processes

Business Partners must recognize, in their role as Human Capital Curators, that the imitability of HR is constrained by historically developed corporate structures and the integration of knowledge and experiences into products and services. This constraint can provide an advantage in developing a sustainable competitive edge if the proper foundations are established, but it can also pose a disadvantage if not. It must be acknowledged that HR are challenging to imitate due to their influence on historical development, causal ambiguity, and social complexity. Implementing successful HR policies from competitors is difficult because they operate in distinct environments. Therefore, Business Partners must recognize that firm-specific HR processes can yield different outcomes, necessitating the development and implementation of company-specific processes (Schwarz, 2010, 65–66). Thus, Business Partners in the role of Human Capital Curators must not only possess a deep understanding of their own company's processes and structures but also consider the broader business environment and direct competitors to pursue, develop, and sustain competitive advantages. In this context, Business Partners must initially evaluate the conditions necessary for maintaining a sustainable competitive advantage in their capacity as Human Capital Curators. A comprehensive analysis of the previously identified barriers – namely non-imitability, causal ambiguity, and social complexity – underscores the importance of path dependency in developmental trajectories.

Causal ambiguity denotes the situation wherein firms may not fully understand the underlying reasons why specific practices or resources contribute to their success. This opacity creates a "black box" phenomenon, complicating efforts by competitors to replicate the success factor. Conversely, the firm itself may face challenges in transferring these success factors to other products or services, necessitating that Business Partners, acting as Human Capital Curators, undertake rigorous analysis, develop innovative approaches, and provide nuanced interpretations.

Social complexity pertains to the intricate collaboration among employees within the organization. The management of knowledge – particularly tacit knowledge – and the propensity for knowledge sharing and collaboration significantly affect social complexity, thereby influencing the design and efficacy of HR development programs. Furthermore, social complexity serves as a foundation for establishing human capital as a sustainable competitive advantage through the enhancement of social capital and organizational capital.

Path dependence posits that decisions, once enacted, incur reversal costs, and specific opportunities manifest only at particular junctures. For instance, initial strategic decisions can constrain future options for companies. Consequently, Business Partners must recognize that initial decisions significantly influence future trajectories and opportunities for change, incurring costs and limiting deviations from the established path. Before making decisions, particularly strategic ones, Business Partners should evaluate the implications for path dependence and reassess the intended decision's viability from this perspective.

In the realm of substitutability, Business Partners serving as Human Capital Curators must distinguish between various activities and their impacts on competitive advantage and value creation. Substituting technical devices for less cognitively demanding tasks is more achievable. However, such technical substitution rarely fosters sustainable competitive advantage and is easily replicated by other companies. Conversely, for skilled tasks, the assumption is that knowledge is not readily replaceable due to its quality, composition, and company-specific working conditions, thereby facilitating a sustainable competitive advantage (Schwarz, 2010, 65). Hence, Business Partners must prioritize this aspect of substitutability to secure a sustainable competitive advantage. Emphasis should be placed on HR development, given the centrality of qualitative factors.

Furthermore, it is imperative for Business Partners to comprehend the company's operational processes to effectively classify necessary skills, competencies, experiences, and knowledge, and to develop strategies that enhance efficiency through HR development. This understanding is predicated on the belief that highly qualified employees contribute to a sustainable competitive advantage for companies by providing high value through their engagement and performance. The performance disparities among average, good, and exceptional employees are particularly pronounced in areas requiring specialized knowledge, skills, and experiences (Lebrenz, 2020, 149–151). Although well-qualified employees command significantly higher remuneration, companies face challenges with this demographic. These employees are cognizant of their market value and may depart if their performance is not suitably rewarded or if offered a significantly higher salary elsewhere. This retention challenge, or appropriability, poses a threat to companies (Lebrenz, 2020, 149–151). When crafting a competitive advantage based primarily on competencies, skills, and experiences, as well as targeted HR development, Business Partners must remain cognizant that even outstanding employees cannot indefinitely shield the company from competitive pressures, thereby endangering any existing competitive advantage (Lebrenz, 2020, 149–151).

8.5.5 Strategic Human Capital Management: Navigating the "War for Talent" through Dynamic Capabilities and Evidence-Based HR Strategies

The intensifying "War for Talent" is a direct consequence of the expanding skills shortage and the concomitant reduction in workforce potential. Business Partners must recognize that not all organizations can succeed in this competitive talent landscape. Nevertheless, the guiding principle for Business Partners, acting as Human Capital Curators, should be to cultivate superior employees compared to their competitors. Achieving a long-term competitive advantage does not necessarily hinge on offering substantial financial incentives or maintaining a highly attractive employer brand; it can also be realized through other aspects of organizational design (Lebrenz, 2020, 149–151).

Previous discussions on the MBV and the RBV underscore that Business Partners, in their role as Human Capital Curators, must adopt a more strategic approach and focus on the internal potential of the company. This is particularly crucial given the increasing complexity and dynamism of the business environment, where it is essential to identify and forecast internally relevant strategic success factors. Business Partners encounter the challenge that the tools for implementing a resource-based HR development are inadequately empirically supported, necessitating the development of company-specific approaches.

The dynamic capabilities approach, which evolved from the RBV, offers a potential solution to this challenge. This approach emphasizes an organization's capacity to adapt to a changing business environment through organizational learning processes. The objective is to measure the value of employees, forecast the company's HR needs, and develop efficient, resource-oriented strategic HR management and HR development. In light of the expanding skills shortage and its implications, the RBV and dynamic capabilities approach highlight the need to consider changes in the availability of qualitative and quantitative HR. The insights derived should inform evidence-based HR strategies and development strategies that can establish a sustainable competitive advantage (Schwarz, 2010, 66–69).

The foundation of this concept lies within Human Capital Management, a discipline centered on quantifying the significance of human capital in relation to corporate valuation. This holds pivotal importance in the governance and manipulation of human systems within organizational frameworks. Such a focus facilitates the alignment between HR and corporate structures, thereby optimizing the value addition and potential of the workforce, ultimately enhancing the organization's success. Sustaining this optimization necessitates recurrent assessments, presentations, and evaluations of the economic worth of a company's human capital, encompassing measurements of productivity as a fundamental performance metric (Schwarz, 2010, 69–72). Within the realm of human capital evaluation and progression, Business Partners acting as Human Capital Curators are tasked with ensuring the prioritization of HR as a strategically indispensable asset. To achieve this, they must gauge input, change, and outcome parameters, expressing the value of human capital in monetary terms. This method supports internal strategizing, decision-making processes, and oversight, showcasing the value added through HR development. Moreover, it transparently elucidates the rationale behind HR development investments and the resultant value contributions. Such an approach thereby aids in fortifying the company's value addition and creation potential, bolstering the role and impact of Business Partners, and forms an integral facet of purpose-driven strategic corporate governance (Schwarz, 2010, 73–75).

8.5.6 Harnessing Social and Organizational Capital for Business Success

In the realm of human capital management for Business Partners occupying the role of Human Capital Curators, a fundamental challenge lies in their adept comprehension of potential influencing factors and their capacity to effectively utilize and assess them. Social capital and organizational capital, distinct from human capital management, warrant consideration in the implementation of strategies pertaining to human capital management. Human capital primarily concerns the aptitude for collaborative endeavors and the facilitation of processes, while social capital centers on an individual's interpersonal relationships and organizational capital on the frameworks and practices facilitating collaboration within the organizational context. This differentiation underscores that organizational capital transcends dependence on individual contributors, contrasting with social capital, which diminishes upon the departure of a particular individual. Fostering social capital entails nurturing connections within and beyond the organizational boundaries, intentionally fostering environments conducive to impromptu interactions and knowledge exchange to bolster its cultivation. Within the sphere of HR development, Business Partners must ensure the cultivation of social capital to effectively disseminate acquired knowledge and competencies throughout the organization. This involves purposefully engaging individuals who stand to benefit from such exchanges, thereby enhancing the value proposition of HR management.

Business Partners in the capacity of Human Capital Curators ought to particularly prioritize the self-reinforcing process of network formation. The accrual of valuable contacts correlates with heightened interest in integration within this network. Employee attributes, notably networking prowess, play a pivotal role, with individuals proficient in connecting diverse entities within the organization dubbed "relational stars." The assessment of a company's social capital poses a considerable challenge, a difficulty shared by its Business Partners. This challenge extends to the evaluation of human capital and its administration, underscoring the importance of recognizing and leveraging social capital for human capital enhancement through effective management. Social network analysis emerges as a valuable tool in this pursuit, capable of uncovering latent group dynamics and collaborative efforts not readily apparent in the organizational hierarchy. Business Partners must acknowledge the significance of this approach, mindful of the requisite investment and the need to strike a balance between costs and benefits (Lebrenz, 2020, 151–154).

Beyond social capital, organizational capital assumes a pivotal role in human capital management, particularly in the purview of the Human Capital Curator. Company processes and routines serve not only to uphold existing frameworks but also to shape the mechanisms of organizational learning and adaptability. These processes, cultivated over time, constitute the cultural repository of the organization. Organizational capital, an integral facet of human capital management, presents challenges in replication, thereby establishing itself as a sustainable competitive advantage, particularly in specialized processes. Its value emanates from the synergistic interactions among diverse stakeholders, rendering it elusive yet invaluable, especially when harmonized with social capital by Business Partners operating as Human Capital Curators.

In contrast to social capital, organizational capital is less contingent on individual employees, deriving its efficacy from the collective interactions within the organization. Consequently, its value is more intricate to ascertain or transplant, affording the company a prolonged competitive edge. In terms of appropriability, social capital and organizational capital exhibit disparities. Social capital enables employees to assert claim over surplus value generated, while the risk is diminished in organizational capital due to the complexity in attributing performance to individuals. It is apparent that social and organizational capital are intricately linked yet delineate distinct dimensions. The pivotal contrast lies in social capital being vested in the employee, whereas organizational capital is vested in the company. Enterprises endeavoring to cultivate new organizational capital encounter obstacles, particularly in implementing agile methodologies necessitating a transformation in existing organizational capital.

Business Partners must immerse themselves in the role of Human Capital Curators concerning the significance and ramifications of social and organizational capital, pivotal constituents of the company's intangible HR. Many enterprises face the risk of inadequate allocation of time and resources toward fostering social and organizational capital. Specifically, Business Partners bear responsibility as Human Capital Curators to facilitate a robust understanding of the issue among line management and corporate leadership, fostering enhanced value contribution through collaboration, thereby bolstering corporate success. Furthermore, Business Partners, in their intermediary capacity, are accountable for fostering the cultivation and expansion of social and organizational capital through the refinement and adaptation of processes enhancing the organization's competencies and, consequently, its value contribution. A discernible nexus between the roles of Human Capital Curators and Culture and Change Champions emerges, notably concerning corporate culture, a point of differentiation in competition, thereby influencing value contribution (Lebrenz, 2020, 155–158).

The comprehensive and efficient integration of social capital and organizational capital considerations facilitates the establishment of a strategic assessment framework for human capital. Within this framework, Business Partners are pivotal in advancing strategic human capital management, thereby underscoring its importance, and significantly contributing to value generation and the optimal utilization of HR. This becomes particularly pertinent in a milieu characterized by shortages in skilled labor. Strategic evaluation of human capital aids in discerning the present capabilities and future requisites of the company, ensuring the attraction, long-term retention, and deployment of appropriate talents to maximize value and foster development at the levels of social and organizational capital.

In addition to cross-functional analysis of social and organizational capital, this analytical approach enables the identification of employees' strengths and weaknesses, facilitating targeted design and implementation of training and development initiatives. This, in turn, enhances employee performance and productivity. Furthermore, the formation of teams based on skills, competencies, and experiences fosters innovation and HR development, thereby augmenting human capital. Combining this approach with a precise assessment of human capital allows for the identification of potential risks associated with dependence on specific skills or individuals, enabling the formulation of plans for risk mitigation, continuity, and strategic alignment of HR development with the company's objectives.

8.5.7 Usage of the Balanced-Scorecard and Its Enterprise Alignment

Integrated analysis of employee performance, efficiency, resource utilization, and potential adjustments within an optimization process contributes to cost efficiency and value enhancement through the streamlining of processes, procedures, and structures. Business Partners, in their role as Human Capital Curators, must recognize the pivotal role of human capital in shaping and sustaining corporate culture. Strategic evaluation ensures that the company's values and culture are reinforced through recruitment and employee development, thereby enhancing value, flexibility, and adaptability. Moreover, a close nexus emerges between this role and that of Culture and Change Champions.

The methods delineated suggest that Business Partners are integral components of Strategic HR Management, amalgamating HR practices, strategies, routines, and processes with the overarching strategic objectives of the organization. In this process, human capital and its administration are intentionally synchronized with the strategic goals or opportunities of the enterprise. Particularly in enterprises encountering a pronounced scarcity of adept personnel, it becomes plausible to incorporate human capital management into the strategic trajectory, thereby considering the developmental prospects of human capital. This integration aids in minimizing deviations from strategies and their execution as much as feasible. This holds paramount significance, especially in firms whose value generation heavily relies on knowledge-based and application-based determinants of success. The impact of learning processes and the dissemination of knowledge and skills swiftly becomes strategically imperative in such circumstances. Consequently, a systematically enhanced competency management approach should be strategically employed, taking into account competencies, qualifications, and experiences, to ensure the alignment of requisite competencies with the corporate strategy. One avenue for this is the utilization of a BSC within the domain of human capital management and its evolution. This strategic instrument can articulate its intentions by delineating concrete objectives through metric-based targets. By employing the BSC, Business Partners, in their capacity as Human Capital Curators, can guarantee that employee development is intricately linked to strategic endeavors by instituting quantifiable benchmarks for skills and qualifications (Peterke, 2021, 89–93).

The utilization of a BSC facilitates the establishment of a nexus with organizational learning. This framework enables the integration of pivotal facets such as HR development, social capital, and organizational capital into the BSC structure, thereby bolstering strategically directed and systematically harnessed learning processes. Consequently, there ensues a heightened propensity for employees to continuously enhance their competencies and adeptly respond to evolving demands, thereby augmenting their value-added contribution.

Incorporating Human Capital Management into the framework of a BSC also plays a pivotal role in fostering employees' perception of their work as aligned with the strategic objectives of the organization. Empirical research underscores heightened levels of engagement in such contexts, attributed to HR development initiatives aiding employees in delineating their roles within the broader organizational milieu. This, in turn, nurtures motivation and commitment towards strategy implementation.

8.5.8 Unveiling the Strategic Imperatives of Human Capital Curators: Maximizing ROI in Business Partnerships

Operating as Human Capital Curators, Business Partners are tasked with adeptly applying the ROI methodology to gauge the financial efficacy of human capital management investments and ascertain their value proposition. Furthermore, the ROI approach facilitates prognostication of future profitability and value augmentation, thereby rationalizing investment decisions, resource allocation, and resource requisites. The crux of employing the ROI methodology in human capital management, alongside its concomitant social and organizational capitals, lies in identifying quantifiable metrics and subjecting them to financial evaluation. The challenge is exacerbated by the qualitative nature inherent in human capital, social capital, and organizational capital, compounded by intricacies and associated ramifications that defy facile measurement and precise quantification.

However, Business Partners, acting as Human Capital Curators, should allocate justified temporal and financial resources towards achieving a pragmatic evaluation, with a primary emphasis on long-term perspectives. This approach underscores the cultivation of a learning organization and the adaptability of the workforce, particularly crucial amidst burgeoning skill deficits. Such facets wield substantial influence on perpetuating competitive advantage and augmenting value contribution over time via strategic deployment of HR development measures, programs, and strategies (Treier, 2019, 255–265).

Utilization of benchmarks becomes imperative for recurrent assessment of HR development and human capital management performance, facilitating timely identification of improvement avenues and adaptation imperatives. Persistent utilization and maintenance of established indicators are necessary to ensure comparability. Leveraging this groundwork, decisions can be rendered more robustly, while the quantification of contributions to value creation and corporate success becomes more readily attainable.

Assessing the performance of Business Partners poses a challenge due to the complexity of factors such as innovation potential, which are inherently difficult to quantitatively gauge and qualitatively evaluate. Furthermore, the importance of the capacity to conceive and introduce innovative solutions into the market is on the rise. Companies endowed with highly esteemed HR and effective human capital management mechanisms are typically more adept at implementing innovative strategies and adapting promptly to evolving market dynamics, thereby capitalizing on emerging opportunities. The ability to manage intricate tasks efficiently is presumed to be closely linked to robust human capital management practices and comprehensive HR development initiatives. Consequently, for Business Partners occupying the role of Human Capital Curators, ensuring a thorough assessment of human capital within the organization is pivotal. This necessitates adequate resource allocation and the possession of requisite competencies, alongside the ability to showcase the value-added contributions. Given the inherent intricacies, comprehensive evaluations often occur retrospectively. However, accumulating experience, coupled with enhanced application and a deepened comprehension of the interplay between social and organizational capital, progressively enables a more accurate prognosis of human capital and its evolutionary trajectory.

In summary, the role of the Human Capital Curator is central to the generation of value within an organization, serving as a pivotal driver of success. The systematic evaluation and continuous enhancement of human capital emerge as critical imperatives for sustaining long-term competitiveness in an ever-evolving and demanding business landscape (Ludwig, 2024, 38–43).

8.6 Total Rewards Steward

Within the realm of Strategic Enablers, the third position is inhabited by the Total Rewards Steward, where financial and non-financial incentives constitute pivotal factors influencing talent attraction and retention dynamics. Incentive mechanisms play a crucial role in fostering and perpetuating engagement with HR development initiatives and endeavors. Owing to the influential nature of these variables, Business Partners are entrusted with ensuring a high level of alignment between HR development strategies and employee reward systems.

8.6.1 Navigating the Complexities of Compensation Design: Challenges and Strategies for Total Rewards Stewards

Compensation emerges as a pertinent subject that impacts every employee, not solely during career transitions but also during routine activities such as annual salary evaluations. The formulation of compensation strategies yields far-reaching and enduring consequences as it endeavors to support the attainment of corporate objectives. Nonetheless, adverse effects on a company's economic performance emerge when organizational structures and remuneration systems diverge in their aims, leading to conflicting employee behaviors. Consequently, Business Partners assuming the mantle of Total Rewards Stewards must ensure a close correlation between organizational structures, operational objectives, and the company's remuneration framework. Amidst this milieu, Business Partners encounter multifaceted challenges, encompassing the determination of bonus structures, execution of salary adjustments or classifications, transparent dissemination of compensation decisions, and establishment of wage differentials across hierarchical tiers and disparate roles, while considering the magnitude of leadership responsibilities. In this context, the scope of authority, hierarchical stratification, and integration within the organizational framework become pertinent considerations.

Leaders at various hierarchical levels are engaged in the conceptualization and development of compensation frameworks within an organizational setting. A proficient execution of this task is significantly enhanced by a comprehensive understanding of the structural dynamics of compensation. Queries pertaining to the selection of suitable compensation models, their impact on motivational paradigms within the pertinent environment, and the feasibility of achieving equitable remuneration are pivotal.

It is imperative to meticulously consider the multifaceted aspects of compensation design (Halene, 2022, 515–516). Business Partners are tasked with acquiring profound expertise in this domain and adeptly applying it to the unique circumstances of their organization. Establishing intimate linkages and ensuring transparent integration of motivational elements, incentivization mechanisms, and structural configuration are imperative prerequisites. Business Partners must possess operational acumen and appreciate the value propositions of discrete domains within their purview to strike an optimal equilibrium between base salaries and performance-based bonuses vis-à-vis value generation.

In addition to the equity aspect inherent in wage frameworks, which is subject to varying degrees of acknowledgment and acceptance among stakeholders, motivation assumes pivotal significance owing to its susceptibility to the configuration of remuneration schemes. Intrinsic motivation, rooted in personal aspirations, convictions, attitudes, and values, is predominantly influenced by internal motivational factors. Conversely, extrinsic motivation, largely modulated by the wage structure, plays a pivotal role. Organizations deploy financial incentives through remuneration systems, and indirectly through tangible rewards like promotions, which inherently carry financial implications, to shape the behavior, productivity, and demeanor of employees. Business Partners must exhibit acute cognizance of the interplay between the incentive mechanisms embedded within wage frameworks, the modality of motivation, and the resultant impacts within their role as custodians of Total Rewards.

The phenomenon known as the crowding-out effect arises when extrinsic rewards or regulatory mechanisms diminish the inherent motivation initially associated with an activity. Specifically, the implementation of performance-based compensation, contingent upon individual performance metrics, can result in diminished effort if the task originally held intrinsic appeal and the compensation is perceived as exerting control. This effect is particularly salient among senior leaders and can be elucidated through the lens of self-determination theory, which posits that perceived control undermines autonomy. Conversely, the reinforcement effect manifests when specific incentives, encompassing both intrinsic and extrinsic factors, bolster the innate motivation toward an activity. Factors such as participation opportunities, procedural equity, and market-aligned remuneration can serve as positive incentives, fortifying intrinsic motivation. Notably, performance-based incentives can even augment intrinsic motivation in cases where it was previously absent, with the anticipation of prosocial conduct within the organizational milieu further reinforcing this effect.

The impact of performance-based remuneration on task performance exhibits nuanced dynamics. While it may enhance performance in straightforward, repetitive tasks, it tends to attenuate performance in tasks characterized by novelty and creativity. Moreover, goal-based bonuses, predicated on employees meeting predetermined targets, may inadvertently impede organizational goal attainment by fostering manipulation and incomplete goal achievement. Nevertheless, it is imperative to acknowledge that while a critical assessment of the motivational ramifications of individual incentives is warranted, the significance of compensation to employees should not be understated. Despite occasional assertions in surveys suggesting diminished importance of salary, empirical evidence underscores its enduring influence on motivation (Halene, 2022, 516–517).

Business Partners and company management must acknowledge that salaries and bonuses exert significant control over behavior, incentives, and motivation, while also directly influencing corporate culture and HR management. Additionally, they generate secondary effects, such as employee interactions and customer relations, thus indirectly impacting customer relationships. Procedural justice in compensation pertains to the decision-making process in distribution. Research indicates that procedural justice holds more weight in organizations than distributive justice, emphasizing the importance of the decision-making process in determining compensation. Criteria ensuring procedural justice encompass consistency across individuals and time, impartiality and absence of bias in decision-makers, precise adherence to procedural rules, avenues for rectifying judgments, consideration of the needs and opinions of all affected parties, and alignment with ethical principles.

8.6.2 Striking a Balance: Navigating Procedural Justice in Compensation Systems for Optimal Organizational Dynamic

The social and communicative aspect of procedural justice underscores the need for accurate, timely, and honest explanations, coupled with respectful interactions with involved parties. Employees engage in justice monitoring to alleviate uncertainties, especially during events like new hires, wage adjustments, or contract modifications. A well-defined and transparently communicated compensation system mitigates uncertainties. Overall, it's clear that compensation systems must address both distributive and procedural justice. Moreover, considering the impact of individual design elements on motivation is crucial, particularly in a dynamic and intricate labor market. Hence, organizations must address diverse justice claims as social systems (Halene, 2022, 518).

Business Partners within this context are required to engage in a comprehensive understanding of the social framework, attitudes, perceptions, and anticipations of personnel across various hierarchical tiers, while also assimilating performance-related factors crucial for collective workforce comprehension. Challenges frequently emerge in achieving a nuanced equilibrium with the company's strategic trajectory, particularly in the recruitment and retention of strategically pertinent and pivotal HR. The foundational salary, commensurate with position requisites, typically constitutes the predominant segment of the overall remuneration, serving as the foundational element for computing supplementary salary constituents. These requisites are ascertained through either summative or analytical evaluations. Summative evaluations are conducted for akin roles, whereas analytical assessments encompass diverse requisites. Attributes such as professional acumen, self-competency, and social proficiency are assigned weights, with each role assessed accordingly. The outcomes of this appraisal dictate salary allocations.

Enterprises possess latitude in determining and prioritizing attributes. For instance, accentuating social proficiency can augment its importance in remuneration. Employee adaptability can be fostered by delineating versatility as a characteristic, thus bolstering organizational alignment.

8.6.3 Crafting Equitable Compensation: The Complex Role of Total Rewards Stewards in Job Evaluation and Incentive Structures

Job evaluation entails labor-intensive procedures necessitating a lucid and comprehensible systematic methodology. Business Partners, acting as Total Rewards Stewards, must contribute not solely their professional acumen to crafting a compensation framework, but also their comprehension of substantive elements, duties, accountabilities, and intricacies to ensure perceived equity. Given the hurdles, it is advisable for Business Partners to engage line management executives, employee representatives, and corporate leadership. Existing protocols often prove convoluted for laypersons to grasp and simplistic. It is imperative to acknowledge that employees frequently employ dissimilar common benchmarks in categorizing roles and positions compared to management. For numerous employees within a company, the rationale behind inconsistencies in job evaluation procedures across management tiers remains opaque. This could precipitate deliberations concerning executive salaries and the disparity between the highest and lowest wages within an organization (Halene, 2022, 519–520). In this context, the mandate of Business Partners extends beyond merely ensuring consistent evaluation across all levels and roles within the company, encompassing the establishment of transparency and explicit evaluation criteria, alongside their dissemination.

The implementation of incentive structures predicated on goal attainment fosters a company's alignment toward objectives. Within this framework, the Equity Theory underscores the imperative of factoring in performance differentials in remuneration to uphold a perceived equitable ratio of contribution to reward. Compensation tied to performance hinges on employee assessments encompassing diverse criteria like productivity, conduct, and progress. These assessments yield a persistent performance component integrated into monthly salaries, reflecting variances between outstanding and average performance. Such performance-linked remuneration schemes also facilitate synchronization with competency enhancement, thereby fostering positive performance outcomes. The pinnacle extent of this performance augmentation is contingent upon the still inadequately explored performance variances among employees occupying identical roles (Halene, 2022, 519–521).

During periods of skilled labor scarcities, HR management considerations assume primacy within entrepreneurial agendas, encompassing salary structures and their formulation. An appealing compensation framework is devised to heighten employer allure, engender employee attraction, and retention. This engenders a causal progression: enticing compensation motivates employees, augments performance reserves, and culminates in heightened work fulfillment.

The objectives of compensation systems evolve across the three stages of the employment continuum. In the nascent phase, compensation assumes pivotal significance for employer allure. Subsequently, compensation inculcates endeavors to sustain or elevate performance, often through variable elements. The denouement of the employment relationship marks the third phase, where compensation may harbor a retention dimension. Business Partners are thus confronted with the challenge of factoring in workforce composition alongside market dynamics when devising and revising salary and incentive frameworks.

8.6.4 Balancing Generational Expectations: Crafting Effective Compensation Systems for Today's Workforce

The demographic transition influences the expectations of distinct generations within the organizational milieu. Prospective wage systems must harmonize objectives with employee anticipations. Of growing significance are Generations Y and Z, esteeming autonomy, purposeful labor, adept leadership, work-life balance, individualism, flexibility, equitable compensation, adaptable workplaces and schedules, alongside purposiveness (Fritz & Schneider, 2016, 340–343).

Traditional social benefits are undergoing scrutiny in contemporary discourse. Loyalty to the company appears diminished among newer generations, who demonstrate a propensity for frequent job transitions. The inclination towards networking and active participation fosters superior team management and a heightened emphasis on collaborative projects. Despite intergenerational disparities, all cohorts exhibit a common pursuit of recognition and acknowledgment, often manifested in performance-based remuneration schemes. Business Partners confront the formidable task of comprehending the values, objectives, aspirations, and anticipations of Generations Y, Z, and Alpha when formulating remuneration frameworks, including wages, bonuses, and structures, particularly with regard to the potential afforded by work-life balance. Notably, younger demographics exhibit a propensity to weigh salary against work-life balance, showing a distinct preference for a condensed workweek, which retains allure even in the absence of additional compensation. In light of the burgeoning scarcity of skilled labor and the imperative of continual adaptation to evolving market dynamics, encompassing the enhancement of employees' competencies, knowledge, and experience, the consideration of HR development assumes pivotal significance in the delineation of remuneration systems (Rittershaus, 2024, 161–170).

Within the compensation paradigm, there arises the imperative not only to integrate performance-based bonuses commensurate with contemporary accomplishments but also to incorporate financial incentives designed to augment individual competencies, knowledge, experience, and skills, thereby mitigating an overreliance on short-term performance metrics. Consequently, the compensation framework must also encompass the future development of competencies, knowledge, skills, learning trajectories, and potential growth, as advocated by Business Partners assuming the role of Total Rewards Stewards, to ensure a compelling yet equitable stimulus for HR development initiatives and programs.

The compensation architecture should embed competency development, leveraging models of competency management and career development theory. To foster career progression and competency enhancement among the workforce, deliberate efforts should be made to instill competencies, skills, knowledge, and application proficiencies among leaders, incentivizing them to champion HR development endeavors among their teams, recognizing the reciprocal benefits therein. Should incentives be exclusively tethered to current performance metrics, such as revenues, leaders may be inclined to overlook HR development initiatives in favor of immediate financial gains.

Evidently, a performance-centric salary and bonus structure catalyze leadership development and afford a substantial degree of consideration for HR development when coupled with clearly defined objectives and performance metrics. Such frameworks incentivize leaders to integrate HR development seamlessly into their leadership approach, thereby bolstering the medium- and long-term prosperity of the organization. The adoption of models such as the Path-Goal Theory and Transformational Leadership Theory can serve to fortify leadership acumen and facilitate the integration of HR development imperatives. A goal-oriented remuneration and incentive framework may effectively synchronize employees' individual objectives with the strategic objectives of the organization. This synchronization fosters the execution of the corporate strategy across all organizational echelons, bolstering employer appeal and bolstering employee retention rates.

Strategic HR development can be enhanced through the incorporation of the BSC for HR development into the design of compensation systems, ensuring a comprehensive assessment of organizational performance. Business Partners, acting as Total Rewards Stewards alongside line management and corporate leadership, are tasked with collaboratively devising a tailored compensation and incentive structure grounded in scientific insights drawn from both management and organizational research (Ilic, 2024, 282–287).

The amalgamation of compensation systems with HR development initiatives is pivotal for a company's sustained success. Financial incentives assume a pivotal and success-determining role in HR development. Monetary incentives like bonuses, premiums, or salary increments serve as potent motivators for employees. The promise of financial rewards can bolster performance readiness, motivating employees to engage in HR development initiatives, leverage provided opportunities, and attain the offered incentives.

8.6.5 Strategic Integration: Financial Incentives as Catalysts for HR Development Success

Business Partners, fulfilling the role of Total Rewards Stewards, must prioritize the establishment of incentives by tethering individual performance to financial rewards, thus incentivizing participation in HR development initiatives and fostering a drive for skill, competency, and knowledge enhancement (Lebrenz, 2020, 140–149). In the fiercely competitive labor market, securing and retaining qualified professionals poses a considerable challenge. HR development programs integrated with financial incentives can aid in retaining talented employees within the organization over the long term. Compelling HR development offerings can serve as a distinguishing factor among employers, attracting and retaining skilled personnel. This, in turn, curtails employee turnover rates, fostering stability and continuity within the organization.

The company's commitment to the professional advancement of its employees is demonstrated by providing financial resources for HR development and attractive incentives for participation. This commitment enhances employee retention, as evidenced by scientific research (Voß & Würtemberger, 2023, 261–269). The synergy between HR development and appealing participation incentives facilitates the achievement of individual objectives and career advancements, which typically correlates positively with heightened employee satisfaction. Furthermore, this strategy establishes a conducive work atmosphere and organizational climate, fostering employee engagement and satisfaction. Flexible financial incentives cater to individual employee needs, further reinforcing their commitment to professional development. In addition to financial incentives, non-monetary perks such as consideration of individual development interests, flexible work hours, and home office options can be offered to meet diverse employee preferences (Voß & Würtemberger, 2023, 261–269).

Business Partners, in their role as Total Rewards Stewards, must recognize that financial incentives serve as acknowledgment for employees' investment in professional growth. Participation in HR development programs demands additional time and energy from employees, resulting in heightened engagement and dedication. Employees perceive financial incentives as appreciation for their efforts, enhancing intrinsic motivation and encouraging further participation in HR development programs. Moreover, financial incentives contribute to fostering a conducive learning environment, where employees feel supported in their professional growth efforts. Strategic planning of incentives and rewards aligned with corporate goals and strategies enhances resource efficiency and fosters individual employee development. Offering market-competitive compensation aids in attracting and retaining talented employees, contributing to overall corporate success (Kruse, Mecke & Räss, 2024, 24–34).

In the realm of HR development, it is pertinent to align it intricately with corporate objectives by cultivating competencies pertinent to the prosperity of the company. The integration with the wage and salary framework offers inducements for employees to advance in requisite competency domains. This initiative not only fosters the company's capacity for innovation but also ensures perpetual possession of the requisite skills by employees to cater to evolving market exigencies. A strategically harmonized wage and salary structure, considering individual employee performance, serves as a catalyst for exemplary performance. By intertwining with HR development, employees can be meticulously groomed for their roles, thereby positively impacting the holistic performance of the organization. Performance-oriented remuneration, paired with tailored developmental prospects, engenders a mutually beneficial scenario for both businesses and employees.

In an ever-evolving business milieu, adaptability assumes paramount significance. Aligning wage and salary systems with HR development empowers companies to adeptly respond to changes. Employees, receiving continual support in their progression, exhibit heightened adeptness in confronting novel challenges. This bolsters the resilience of the organization and fortifies its enduring viability. Business Partners, as Total Rewards Stewards, must focus on the integration of HR development strategy elements with corporate objectives, emphasizing alignment with the broader corporate strategy. Achieving this alignment enhances their value contribution to the organization. It is recommended to conduct a comprehensive analysis of both current and desired states to pinpoint areas necessitating development. This analytical process demands that Business Partners possess the requisite competencies, skills, experiences, and resources to enact necessary changes and draw informed conclusions. Close collaboration with line management and corporate leadership is imperative for successful execution. A profound comprehension of strategic development goals is essential for Business Partners to derive the appropriate competencies, skills, and experiences required. Recognizing that these requirements may evolve over time, alongside the company's strategic objectives, underscores the need for a continuously expanding development trajectory over an extended planning horizon. Moreover, Business Partners, in their role as Total Rewards Stewards, must factor in the guiding function when aligning the salary and compensation structure with strategic HR development initiatives. This alignment establishes specific incentives aimed at fostering targeted competencies, skills, and experiences. Failure to closely align these incentives with future needs may result in a deficiency of requisite capabilities, thereby impeding task fulfillment and generating challenges for employees. Such challenges can provoke skepticism among employees regarding HR development programs, necessitating reorientation towards the correct objectives. This cycle of frustration can escalate costs associated with HR development while diverting resources away from preparing for future demands.

Additionally, employees may find themselves unable to fully utilize their acquired proficiencies within the organization, potentially prompting voluntary attrition in favor of opportunities with other employers. In a labor market characterized by skill shortages, the risk of voluntary turnover heightens, compounded by the loss of invested resources in HR development programs. Misguided HR development initiatives further diminish the organization's appeal as an employer, making it susceptible to employee poaching by rival firms. Consequently, such scenarios negatively impact HR recruitment efforts and exacerbate challenges associated with employee retention.

8.7 Credible Activist

The third and ultimate categorization of roles assumed by Business Partners concerns Core Drivers. Initially, Business Partners are tasked with prioritizing elements of HR development in their capacity as Credible Activists. As indicated by their designation, Business Partners are obligated to establish credible representations concerning the significance of HR development. It is incumbent upon them to persuade line managers regarding the criticality of HR development for both individual and organizational accomplishments.

8.7.1 Unlocking Corporate Prosperity in the Role of a Credible Activist: The Strategic Role of HR Development in Today's Business Landscape

In an epoch characterized by uncertainty and continual flux, strategic HR development assumes paramount importance in the endeavors of companies to adapt to novel circumstances and function effectively. The capacity to optimize employee development and unleash their potentials emerges as a pivotal determinant for sustainable corporate prosperity within this milieu. Business Partners, acting as intermediaries between corporate objectives and strategies for HR development, assume a pivotal role. In their capacity as Credible Activists, they wield significant influence by actively championing the advancement of HR development. The objective is to revolutionize HR development to realize value enhancement and actively strive to ensure a seamless integration between corporate strategy and HR development, instigating and fostering changes (Niehaus, Mocan & Hansen, 2024, 6–12).

Business Partners must view strategic HR development not as an isolated endeavor but as an intrinsic component of corporate strategy. The pertinence of strategic HR development necessitates persuading line management of its significance and integrating it more deeply into the corporate culture. To accomplish this, Business Partners must initially formulate a lucid vision and mission to steer them throughout the process, accentuating the value addition and ensuring alignment with overarching corporate objectives. In a milieu marked by technological progressions, globalization, and swiftly evolving markets, the imperative to enhance employees' skills and competencies becomes more acute. This backdrop underscores the strategic significance of HR development for firms to uphold their adaptability, innovativeness, and competitiveness. Acting as Credible Activists, Business Partners must bridge the chasm between the company's strategic aspirations and the operational facets of HR development, serving as intermediaries within this domain.

Leveraging their profound comprehension of corporate strategy, Business Partners can ensure that HR development endeavors not only address present requirements but also bolster long-term objectives. Their responsibilities encompass identifying competency deficiencies and crafting bespoke programs that mirror the strategic imperatives of the company. To advocate more vigorously for HR development and underscore its relevance based on its value addition, it is imperative for Business Partners to possess a pronounced strategic and operational acumen, thereby advocating the value addition, potential, and developmental capacity of HR through systematic methodologies derived from this understanding. Business Partners are tasked with compellingly advocating to line management for the implementation of HR development measures, leveraging a profound comprehension of requirements and comparing current situations with future needs. This role, particularly as Credible Activists, poses a challenge as line management bears direct responsibility for executing such measures. Persuading line management is pivotal, facilitating resource allocation and operational execution. Nevertheless, due to financial limitations and short-sightedness, convincing line management of the enduring significance of HR development and allocating essential resources can prove arduous. Yet, line management's conviction substantially impacts the efficacy of implementing HR development initiatives (Guggenberger, 2021, 309–318).

To credibly champion HR development and elucidate its indispensability and prospective triumphs, Business Partners acting as Credible Activists must adopt a methodical approach that comprehensively addresses all echelons of the organization. This involves disseminating the overarching corporate strategy throughout diverse levels of line management. Interaction at lower levels entails direct engagement with team leaders and staff, while alignment at higher tiers involves collaboration with department heads and senior executives. A profound grasp of individual needs and strategic objectives at each level is imperative to serve as an effective intermediary. The task of bridging divergent goals, negotiating compromises, and ensuring alignment with shared objectives, values, and visions also falls within the purview of the interface function. Business Partners must reconcile these disparities through appropriate methodologies and formulate programs conducive to goal attainment. Nonetheless, in practice, this often poses a formidable challenge, particularly amidst disparate perspectives, attitudes, expectations, and objectives among different levels of line management (Bauer, Dworschak & Zaiser, 2023, 125–130).

Different levels of line management exhibit variations in their acceptance and willingness to invest in HR development. Lower echelons may prioritize short-term achievements, while higher tiers prioritize long-term strategic alignment and success paradigms. Business Partners must comprehend these variances and strategically address individual concerns and requirements to effectively sway opinion. It has been empirically effective for Business Partners to envision themselves as Credible Activists beforehand, considering which arguments, evidence, and methodologies can effectively broaden the strategic purview of HR development and credibly advocate for its significance. At lower levels, arguments emphasizing immediate benefits such as heightened employee satisfaction, enhanced team performance, and increased productivity hold significance. Utilizing examples and success narratives from prior HR development initiatives can serve as corroborative evidence. At intermediate levels, Business Partners should highlight the adaptability and innovation potential of the organization. Positioning the development of expertise and leadership skills as pivotal contributions to long-term competitiveness can illustrate the tangible benefits of expanding strategic HR development at this stratum. At elevated tiers, Business Partners should accentuate strategic competitive edges, encompassing facets like talent retention, succession planning, and ensuring enduring corporate sustainability.

In order to bolster credibility and systematically synchronize the objectives of advancing strategic HR development, Business Partners, in the capacity of Credible Activists, confront the task of initially comprehending, categorizing, and subsequently harmonizing diverse aims. This endeavor not only fosters the evolution of a superior and more methodical approach but also facilitates the discovery of compromises amidst varied tiers while fostering awareness among them. Consequently, the involved parties can better discern their interdependence, with Business Partners assuming the role of interface agents capable of forging connections through their approach to maximize value contribution for the company (Schreyögg & Geiger, 2024, 55–64).

8.7.2 Maximizing HR Development Impact: The Imperative of Effective Communication and ROI Integration

A prerequisite for this entails that Business Partners, embodying the role of Credible Activists, possess efficacious communication strategies and methodologies. Central to this is transparent and continual information exchange. Business Partners ought to engage line management early in the developmental process to ensure that the strategic frameworks align with the actual requirements of the teams. Concurrently, line management should consistently relay feedback and insights from day-to-day operations to the Business Partners, enabling agile adjustments to HR development strategies.

Business Partners must tailor their communication strategy to the specific requisites and priorities at each echelon of line management. This necessitates a nuanced approach and the capacity to cogently communicate the enduring benefits of HR development. Furthermore, data and statistics can be leveraged to substantiate the ROI of HR development initiatives, alongside the value addition attainable through targeted expansion of strategic HR development. Implementation of this approach augments the resources accessible to Business Partners. Consequently, Business Partners can fortify their position within the company, amplify their influence, and substantially augment the value contribution.

Business Partners, acting as Credible Activists, must not only enact effective developmental measures but also demonstrate proficient communication of attained successes. The ROI serves as a pivotal metric, quantifying the financial efficacy HR development endeavors. Incorporating ROI into HR development practices is imperative for assessing the economic viability of training and developmental initiatives. It facilitates a quantitative evaluation of outcomes in relation to allocated resources. Business Partners are tasked not only with showcasing financial gains but also with considering qualitative dimensions, such as heightened employee satisfaction, improved teamwork dynamics, and enhanced innovation prowess. Measuring ROI enables a comprehensive evaluation of HR development effectiveness, encompassing both quantitative and qualitative facets.

Evaluating ROI proves challenging due to intricate interconnections, particularly when reliant on qualitative indicators and data collection methods. Effectively communicating ROI achievements transcends mere numerical presentations; it necessitates crafting a coherent and compelling narrative. Integration of individual employee success stories from training interventions is crucial. Furthermore, attention must be paid not only to quantitative metrics but also to qualitative factors like heightened employee motivation, enhanced problem-solving capabilities, and increased adaptability. Communication efforts should aim to foster a holistic understanding of positive impacts to secure stakeholder commitment (Hermann & Bittner, Fesseler, 2024, 106–109).

The multifaceted impacts of HR development on leaders' success are notable. Effective training programs serve to not only augment the skills and knowledge of employees but also facilitate leaders in employing more efficient and motivational leadership methodologies. Communication regarding the ROI should extend beyond general corporate objectives to encompass the individual achievements of leaders in employee development and team performance. Such communication sharpens the strategic awareness of leadership's significance in HR development and elucidates leaders' contributions to overall company performance. Business Partners, in their capacity as Credible Activists, should prioritize the perpetuation and intensification of HR development, especially in immediate augmentation of corporate success. Continuous enhancement of employee competencies, stimulation of innovation, and bolstering of competitiveness assume pivotal roles in this regard. When communicating the ROI, it's crucial not only to underscore short-term successes but also to address long-term strategic objectives. This fosters comprehension of the enduring impact of HR development on corporate success. Transparent communication of attained ROI fosters trust among decision-makers and validates further investments in HR development.

8.7.3 Strategic Collaboration: Maximizing HR Development Impact Through Synergy Approaches

Expanding on the aforementioned, Business Partners must, subsequent to formulating a systematic and strategic approach, ensure the seamless execution of developmental processes across all company levels, in close collaboration with line management within the intricate organizational framework. Emphasis should be laid on perpetuating the relationship continuity among Business Partners, line management, and employees to achieve effective individual development, thus positively impacting overall company success (Ludwig, 2024, 15–22).

A critical element contributing to the efficacy of HR development, the adept execution of Credible Activist duties, and the augmentation of value-added contributions hinges upon the symbiotic relationship between Business Partners and line management. This synergy fosters collaborative efforts, shared accountabilities, and underscores the significance of value augmentation while safeguarding the enduring prosperity of the enterprise. It ensures the seamless assimilation of development schemes into operational frameworks, encompassing the integration of HR developmental initiatives alongside continual efficacy assessments. In executing this, Business Partners manifest their deliberate dedication to HR development and its corresponding programs, objectives, and strategies, accentuating their pertinence and ardently advocating for triumph, streamlined execution, and resultant value amplification, which they strive to perpetuate further.

By adopting this methodology, Business Partners assume the role of in-house consultants for executives, actively aiding in the identification and cultivation of pivotal competencies within their teams. Line management is furnished with training to equip executives with the capability to discern individual potentials among their staff and implement efficacious developmental schemes. As Credible Activists, Business Partners must forge strategic alliances with executive line management to facilitate their empowerment in leadership development, fostering the establishment and execution of lucid frameworks and systems conducive to the strategic enhancement of their subordinates' competencies. The application of performance metrics and feedback mechanisms facilitates the continual tailoring of HR competency development to evolving business exigencies. Success metrics extend beyond financial parameters to encompass employee contentment, innovation, and adaptability (Troger, 2018, 126–133).

Through the synthesis and interpretation of gathered data, Business Partners in the capacity of Credible Activists synergistically contribute to the facilitation of interdepartmental coordination for HR development initiatives and the attainment of organizational alignment on a company-wide scale. Achieving this objective is viable as Business Partners scrutinize the efficacy of training schemes, workshops, and other HR development endeavors. Within this framework, the assessment of key performance indicators, employee contentment, and competency enhancement assumes centrality and necessitates the utilization of pertinent metrics and evaluation tools. Such methodical scrutiny enables the identification of strengths and weaknesses, laying the groundwork for ongoing adjustments. In addition to fostering adaptability, Business Partners must prioritize the analysis of HR development successes, delving into their causality and underpinnings to sustain the perpetual adaptation process.

The iterative nature of HR development adaptation mandates a flexible orientation towards organizational exigencies. Business Partners occupy a pivotal role in instituting feedback mechanisms that facilitate continuous responsiveness to shifts in the corporate landscape, market dynamics, and individual staff requisites. The capacity to promptly and efficiently respond to changes bolsters the company's enduring competitiveness. Business Partners are tasked with establishing clear linkages between developmental endeavors and corporate objectives, underscoring their pertinence to business triumph (Michl, 2024, 122–129). The coordination facilitated by this mechanism illustrates the interface function of Business Partners, showcasing their capacity to enhance value-added contribution through HR development measures, cross-team competency development, structured career planning, and deploying individuals with specific competencies across various company positions. This demonstration underscores their significance to line management executives and contributes to the expansion of HR development programs through tangible outcomes.

Business Partners must persuade line management through articulate communication and transparent presentation of success analysis outcomes. Presenting concrete impacts on business objectives, employee morale, and productivity reinforces line management's willingness to actively engage in the adaptation process. Collaboration between Business Partners and line management fosters more efficient resource allocation (Barbian & Knabenbauer, 2023, 414–416).

8.7.4 Strategically Aligned HR Development: Empowering Leadership, Enhancing Competitiveness

A thorough analysis of success, grounded in empirical evidence, facilitates the alignment of HR development initiatives with the specific requirements of the enterprise. This alignment serves to mitigate superfluous expenditures and optimize the ROI of HR development endeavors. Line management stands to gain from active engagement in HR development activities, as it fosters continual enhancement of leadership proficiencies. Through structured training and developmental interventions, leaders acquire the capacity to adeptly steer their teams, resolve conflicts, and augment employee productivity. Such empowerment directly contributes to heightened managerial efficacy and overall organizational performance.

Business Partners, operating in their capacity as Credible Activists, bear the responsibility of ensuring that organizational leaders duly recognize the indispensability, relevance, and augmentation of value-added contributions attainable through leadership development initiatives. The synergistic amplification effect witnessed in executive functions consequent to enhanced leadership merits acknowledgment, underscoring leaders' acknowledgement of the imperative nature of HR development and their advocacy thereof. Moreover, as the cultivation of leadership acumen necessitates a heightened comprehension of the collective accountability for HR development among executives, collaborative efforts between executives and Business Partners in the domain of HR development are enhanced (Wirtz, 2024, 759–762). The collaboration between Business Partners and line management facilitates the identification of established practices and the successful implementation of tested methodologies throughout the organization. This fosters a consistent approach to HR development across the company, promoting efficient scaling of successful initiatives across different departments and hierarchical levels.

The growing integration of Business Partners, line management, and HR development significantly enhances sustainable corporate success. Continuous employee development not only enhances adaptability to market changes but also boosts satisfaction and commitment. Close cooperation between Business Partners and executives fosters interdisciplinary exchange, mutual understanding, and strategic alignment, positively impacting value creation. Consequently, Business Partners can positively impact team dynamics, bolster innovation capabilities, and enhance overall productivity, directly influencing the company's competitiveness. In addition to maximizing employee potential, Business Partners, acting as Credible Activists, can establish HR development as a dynamic, respected, and effective aspect of corporate culture. Employees who experience continuous development are more engaged and contribute actively to fostering a positive corporate culture. Emphasizing agility in the learning culture is crucial, perceiving the need for change as an opportunity. Moreover, it's essential to recognize that strategic HR development and adaptation measures are vital for long-term success. Designing HR development to meet the organization's specific needs requires close collaboration and shared responsibility between Business Partners and line management. Both parties must understand their joint responsibility in achieving value addition, long-term competitiveness, and strategic goals.

The amalgamated impacts of strategically implemented and efficient HR development initiatives significantly contribute to augmenting the comprehensive performance of a company. Enhancing the skills and qualifications of employees, fostering a culture of continual learning, and aligning these endeavors with the strategic goals of the company synergistically bolster operational efficacy. Consequently, this synergy can yield heightened productivity levels, enhanced quality of both products and services, and an overarching elevation in competitiveness. As such, HR development, oriented towards fostering partnerships and driven by tangible outcomes, emerges as a pivotal instrument for contemporary organizations.

It is discernible that Business Partners occupy a pivotal position in the integration of HR development initiatives within the corporate strategy, while the commitment of line management ensures the successful execution of these endeavors. The collective interplay among these stakeholders is paramount in formulating and executing a cohesive and efficacious HR development strategy, one that not only prepares the organization for present challenges but also anticipates and addresses future ones (Nowoczin, 2023, 11–16).

8.8   Strategic Positioner

Within the category of Core Drivers, the Strategic Positioner is the second role. As inferred by its nomenclature, Business Partners are tasked with prioritizing strategic themes and facets of HR development crucial for organizational prosperity and advancement.

8.8.1 Navigating Corporate Development and HR Alignment for Long-Term Success

Other central areas encompass the intensive engagement with the company's strategic goals, corporate development, and timelines. Corporate development refers to the processes through which organizations implement and achieve their strategic plans and objectives. It is crucial to consider the economic environment, focusing on both internal and external factors, to ensure continuous and strategic adaptation, thereby securing long-term competitiveness. The strategic goals of a company are long-term guidelines that aid in achieving its mission and vision. These goals, in turn, influence corporate development, organizational structure, and corporate culture. Overall, Business Partners in the role of Strategic Positioners must be cognizant of the interdependence of these elements.

Another core task for Business Partners in the role of Strategic Positioners involves recognizing that within line management and corporate governance, HR development should be viewed not merely as a cost factor but as an investment that directly contributes to value creation and organizational outcomes, thus holding strategic importance. In strategic planning, as well as in associated corporate development and HR development, establishing clear and realistic corporate goals is essential for long-term success. These goals provide a clear direction for the company and serve as a practical guide for implementation. This process is complicated by uncertainties in external factors, notably the shortage of skilled workers (Wollmann & Püringer, 2024, 7–10).

The subsequent sections will explore these core challenges in greater depth, analyzing causes, backgrounds, and solution approaches, initially focusing on the corporate level and subsequently on the individual level.

Corporate leadership typically formulates the company's strategic goals and associated directions and guidelines to establish the company's trajectory and priorities. The formulation of a specific course and priorities necessitates a clearly defined analysis to determine resource requirements, relevant competencies and skills. This analysis identifies all essential resources of the company, including HR, thereby emphasizing human capital.

The strategic importance of HR development is evident in the need to anticipate future employee competency requirements. For instance, if a company aims to expand its global presence, intercultural communication skills and international market knowledge become critical for employees. Therefore, strategic corporate development provides a framework for identifying and developing these specific HR competencies.

Value-maximizing approaches emerge when Business Partners enhance the strategic alignment of HR development, demonstrated by accelerated implementation of corporate strategy and optimized efficiency in achieving objectives. A crucial prerequisite is that Business Partners not only comprehend the existing strategic goals but also align them with the dynamic requirements of the economic environment. This necessitates a proactive approach to ensure that HR development strategies adapt to changing conditions. However, Business Partners must be cognizant of their position as intermediaries between the operational business sector and HR management. Their responsibilities encompass conducting needs analyses and executing HR development initiatives. Business Partners are required to cultivate and sustain strong relationships with various departments. This facilitates the accurate identification of needs and the precise execution of relevant measures.

8.8.2 Strategic Positioners: Architects of Organizational Transformation

The Strategic Positioner role of Business Partners, characterized by close collaboration with different departments, line management, and corporate leadership, can significantly influence strategic HR development, potentially transforming organizational culture, structure, and interdisciplinary cooperation. Ideally, the Strategic Positioner plays a pivotal role in fostering an open, learning-oriented culture, alongside a flexible organizational structure that can readily adapt and support the implementation of new strategies (Rein, 2023, 64–69).

From a scientific perspective, the formulation of strategic goals and their determination can be elucidated through various frameworks and concepts developed within the domains of management, economics, and organizational theory. Two primary frameworks, the BSC and the RBV, have been extensively analyzed and discussed. All these approaches share a common foundation in deriving a company's strategic goals from meticulous analysis of both internal and external environments, employing established concepts and frameworks from diverse scientific disciplines to enhance performance and ensure long-term success.

Business Partners, in the capacity of Strategic Positioners, must possess an in-depth understanding of the various concepts and frameworks pertinent to the company to serve as genuine Strategic Partners. Furthermore, these Business Partners need a thorough comprehension of operational activities, their evolution, and the value-added contributions they generate. Thus, it is imperative that Business Partners exhibit profound business acumen. With this foundation, they can discern the implications of corporate strategy on HR strategy and develop effective approaches, processes, and methods to achieve a tight alignment between corporate strategy and HR strategy. However, the responsibility does not rest solely on the Business Partners. They must also take into account the implications for collaboration with corporate management and line management.

The complexity of this task is heightened by the fact that corporate management, during the formulation of corporate strategy, often does not fully consider the intricate interrelationships among various corporate areas. This oversight frequently stems from an incomplete understanding of these complexities by corporate management, which impedes their adequate incorporation into the strategy. This gap is often a result of corporate management's hierarchical position and their associated responsibilities, which distance them from the operational activities, unlike Business Partners who maintain close interaction with line management and operational employees (Jacob, 2023, 232–234).

In the implementation of corporate strategy, specific difficulties often arise, which in some cases cannot be resolved due to inherent contradictions or insufficient harmonization in detail. Business Partners, acting as Strategic Positioners, must aim to be extensively involved in the strategy formulation process, allowing them to contribute their competencies, experiences, skills, and knowledge. Given the increasing importance of HR and human capital, coupled with the adverse effects of skill shortages, Business Partners in the role of Strategic Positioners can offer valuable insights and recommendations during the formulation of corporate strategy. Business Partners must articulate and contribute their understanding of existing qualitative and quantitative competencies, skills, abilities, and experiences to ensure the formulation of corporate strategy is informed by these factors, thereby preventing strategies that overlook the company's HR and human capital (Lebrenz, 2020, 141–147).

8.8.3 Closing the Gap: Integrating Strategic HR Development for Corporate Success

In many organizations, skill shortages and their associated consequences restrict the company's strategic objectives. With more or better-skilled employees, companies could establish and ultimately achieve more ambitious strategic goals. This issue is increasingly recognized within corporate management, though it remains insufficiently addressed in many instances. Consequently, a mismatch often exists between the desired goals and the realistically achievable objectives at the outset of corporate strategy planning. Frequently, HR management and HR development are blamed for the subsequent failure to achieve goals and targets, despite the fact that closer collaboration would have revealed that the goals and targets are unattainable given the current HR and their developmental potential. Unfortunately, this close collaboration in formulating corporate strategy between corporate management and HR management remains underdeveloped in many companies. Insufficient coordination can lead to knowledge gaps and inefficiencies. Enhanced coordination can mitigate risks arising from a lack of qualified employees or inadequate competencies (Hillebrecht, 2021, 32–50).

The company management is missing a significant opportunity by not integrating the strategic aspect of HR management and development into the Business Partner role, specifically as Strategic Positioners. Leveraging their knowledge, experiences, and competencies, Business Partners can identify competitive advantages derived from existing and potential human capital, which can then be incorporated into corporate strategy formulation. Systematic competency interrelations within a company refer to the connections and dependencies among the individual skills, knowledge, and experiences of employees. A thorough understanding of these interrelations enables the identification and targeted enhancement of strengths and weaknesses in the competency portfolio.

Despite the evident advantages, challenges exist in practically implementing a deep understanding of competency interrelations. Based on this assessment and the resulting proposals, Business Partners can evaluate which strategic goals are realistically attainable, determine the necessary investments in HR development, and find a balance between corporate management's strategic goals and the potential objectives from the perspective of Business Partners, considering human capital resources. This facilitates the formulation of a realistic yet ambitious corporate strategy that is closely aligned with the HR strategy and feasible within the available financial resources (Grundei, 2024, 195–202).

The increasing significance of strategic HR development for corporate success is becoming apparent. Regardless of the initial situation, Business Partners in the role of Strategic Positioners must endeavor to achieve a progressively closer integration into the strategy formulation process. This integration is essential to contribute to corporate success, align corporate strategy with HR strategy, and enhance the company's value contribution and potential through HR development. To achieve these objectives, Business Partners in the role of Strategic Positioners must comprehend the interrelations within the company and actively drive strategic HR development and its efficiency. The cornerstone for this process consistently is the needs analysis.

Needs analysis and recognition of needs are fundamental aspects of strategic HR development. The importance of these processes lies in optimizing resource allocation, securing financial resources, and aligning HR development initiatives with the company's strategic objectives. This alignment helps to minimize resource wastage or misallocation in HR development and aims to optimize resource allocation. The needs analysis facilitates the targeted identification of skill gaps and development needs within the company. By concentrating on pertinent areas, resources can be utilized more efficiently to ensure higher productivity and effectiveness through HR development. It is imperative that the financial and HR allocated to HR development are connected to the desired goals and the strategic objectives of the company. Furthermore, a continuous analysis of existing HR development programs is necessary. This analysis should also consider aspects such as efficiency, effectiveness, employee and potential participant expectations, and the individuals responsible for implementing HR development. Evaluating experiences, attitudes, opinions, and HR development programs in terms of efficiency, relevance to current and future tasks, as well as the quality of preparation and implementation, can significantly enhance the effectiveness of strategic HR development.

The primary task is to ensure close alignment between the goals of HR development programs, the strategic goals of HR development, and the company's strategic objectives. Based on this foundation, it is possible to swiftly identify changes in the business environment that necessitate adjustments in required competencies. These changes can then be promptly addressed through modifications to HR development programs and strategic HR development. This ensures that Business Partners, in the role of Strategic Positioners, maintain a close link between strategic goals and HR development, thereby achieving a high value-added contribution (Lauer, 2019, 185–191).

In their capacity as Strategic Positioners, Business Partners specializing in needs analysis are responsible for aligning strategic HR development with the distinct requirements of various business units and integrating these needs effectively. The access to information, cross-functional knowledge, experience, and expertise that Business Partners possess as Strategic Positioners enables them to draw accurate conclusions. Consequently, they must emphasize the comprehensive overview of the company's HR development needs within the realm of strategic HR development and actively seek synergies to further align HR development initiatives with the strategic corporate objectives. This alignment can ensure that HR development activities are congruent with long-term corporate goals and contribute sustainably to organizational growth.

8.8.4 Strategic Positioning of Human Capital: Navigating Scarcity and Development for Corporate Success

Given the increasing scarcity of skilled labor and the resulting qualitative and quantitative deficiencies in HR, Business Partners in the Strategic Positioner role must ensure that the potential and developmental capacity of the company's human capital are evaluated in a manner that prevents significant misalignment with strategic goals from the outset. It is imperative that strategic goal planning considers the current status and capabilities of HR development. Overlooking HR development in strategic planning often leads to unmet corporate objectives. Conversely, an overly critical view of human capital and its development might allow strategic goals to be met, but it would result in underutilization of existing resources, opportunities, and potential.

In the role of Strategic Positioners, Business Partners must evaluate the current status and potential of human capital to identify and demonstrate strategic development opportunities for the company. This task involves integrating perceived development opportunities, value creation potentials, and strategic possibilities into the formulation of corporate strategic objectives. Through this integration, Business Partners significantly contribute to creating high value-added outputs and establishing long-term competitive advantages. This contribution is particularly effective when Business Partners possess a deep understanding of competencies, knowledge, experience, skills, and the potential for development within HR, which may be less developed in corporate management. Close collaboration with line management executives, interdisciplinary exchanges, and leveraging operational knowledge to identify necessary competencies, skills, experiences, and knowledge are crucial in this context. Furthermore, an in-depth understanding and experience in the time required for competency development are essential for providing strategically relevant HR. This necessitates the ability to connect directly with the current state of HR development processes, HR development programs, and their implementation.

Additional complexity arises from the need to accurately assess the development and improvement potential of HR development programs and processes. This assessment must also consider the realistic outcomes that can be achieved within specific timeframes given the available financial resources and HR. To present credible and detailed analyses of potential developments to corporate and line management, scenario analysis is recommended. This analysis should illustrate the current situation and potential developments under various conditions, outlining development paths that provide a framework for the desired scope of value-added contributions over time.

8.8.5 Strategic Positioning in HR: Aligning Business Partnerships for Sustainable Growth and Agility

Business Partners in the role of Strategic Positioners should also account for path dependency and its implications within different scenarios, ensuring that these factors are integrated into strategic planning (Nauendorf, 2023, 35–41). The analysis should encompass potential alterations in the business environment, with probabilities of such changes, as well as the subsequent competency requirements driven by various developmental factors, including technological advancements and the increasing scarcity of skilled labor, and their implications for HR development and the company's human capital.

A realistic projection of employee retention in critical areas, turnover rates, and the capacity to attract new employees with specific qualifications, competencies, experiences, and knowledge is also necessary. In this analytical and forecasting framework, employing competency models and skill mapping is recommended to visualize existing employee skills, align them with organizational requirements, and evaluate strategic potential, development, and value-added contributions. This approach aids in identifying bottlenecks and enables targeted strategic HR development planning, which should be closely integrated with the company's strategic goals and strategic HR development. The participation of employees, HR development program participants, coaches, mentors, and line management, who possess valuable insights into the utilization of newly acquired competencies, skills, and qualifications, is crucial in this process.

Such a participatory approach fosters transparency and harnesses firsthand insights, experiences, perceptions, and expectations, thereby enhancing acceptance and increasing awareness of the relevance and objectives of strategic HR development and the role of Business Partners as Strategic Positioners. This alignment drives the synchronization of HR development with the company's strategic objectives, considers HR development and human capital in the formulation of strategic company goals, and underscores the importance of investments in employee development. It becomes clear that there is a direct impact on the achievement of company goals associated with this alignment.

In this process, the collaborative efforts of HR strategists acting as Strategic Positioners and corporate strategists are vital in establishing a robust linkage between the company's requirements and the potential avenues for strategic HR development. Optimal strategic planning and design necessitate a comprehensive focus not solely on the individual and organizational growth of employees, but also on the enduring alignment of the organization. This necessitates a holistic perspective wherein the objectives of HR development are intricately intertwined with corporate objectives (Ilic, 2024, 279–282).

Such an approach, characterized by transparent processes and inclusive engagement of Business Partners, line management, and corporate leadership, bolsters the integration of strategic HR development both in day-to-day operations and in the medium to long term. It reinforces the recognition that strategic HR development holds significant importance in establishing sustained competitive advantage, driving corporate success, and augmenting value contributions. The deliberate collaboration and coordination role undertaken by Business Partners in the capacity of Strategic Positioners contribute to enhancing the company's agility and its capacity to swiftly respond to emerging demands, as HR, their development, and thereby strategic HR development are given heightened consideration. This elevation not only amplifies the company's adaptability but also augments its competitiveness within the market. Such enhancements are achieved through the cultivation of agility, which concurrently enriches the innovation prowess of the workforce. This necessitates employees equipped not merely with current expertise but also with the capacity for creative and flexible thinking (Zimmermann, Richter & Stuer, 2024, 13–24).

8.8.6 Strategic HR Development: Navigating VUCA Terrain for Organizational Adaptability and Success

The adaptability of a company pertains to its capacity to dynamically respond to alterations in the environment, encompassing technological transitions, market fluctuations, regulatory modifications, and other external stimuli. High adaptability facilitates swift and efficient adjustments to novel circumstances, critical in the contemporary volatile business landscape. The perpetually shifting business milieu is influenced by four factors delineated in the acronym VUCA, denoting Volatility, Uncertainty, Complexity, and Ambiguity. These factors epitomize the challenges organizations confront in an ever-evolving and unpredictable setting. Volatility denotes the velocity and magnitude of alterations transpiring; in a volatile milieu, conditions alter rapidly and often unpredictably. Uncertainty signifies the absence of predictability or the incapacity to precisely forecast future occurrences; within uncertain scenarios, making definitive forecasts or securing decisions is challenging. Complexity characterizes the myriad of elements and interactions within a specific context; in complex systems, causality is frequently non-linear and comprehension can be arduous. Ambiguity embodies the presence of multiple interpretations or potential meanings; within an ambiguous environment, information may be contradictory or permit diverse perspectives. The concept of VUCA finds particular resonance in management and organizational development spheres to dissect and tackle the escalating dynamism and uncertainty in the contemporary business realm. This analysis, predominantly instigated by corporate leadership, engenders numerous implications for strategic HR development. The central objective of this approach is for organizations to embody and sustain flexibility, adaptability, and innovation to thrive in such environments.

Strategic HR development endeavors to cultivate requisite skills among the workforce, thereby augmenting the innovation prowess of the company's operations. Accounting for anticipated shifts in the economic milieu presents both prospects and hazards. Enterprises proactively responsive to forthcoming trends stand to secure a competitive edge. Conversely, overlooking these dynamics entails the peril of lagging responses and impediments to adaptation. Owing to the scarcity of skilled labor, firms are compelled to exhibit heightened flexibility and ingenuity in delineating their objectives. Strategic HR development assumes a pivotal role in discerning competency deficiencies and effectuating initiatives to fortify the extant workforce, facilitating companies in aligning with the ever-evolving market requisites whilst adhering to their long-term objectives.

Optimal realization is contingent upon effective collaboration between Business Partners, assuming the mantle of Strategic Positioners, and the executive and line management, facilitating comprehensive data scrutiny that encompasses strategic proficiencies and ensures strategic resilience throughout the implementation phase. This necessitates meticulous attention to data quality, inclusivity of pertinent data, and proficiency in data analysis. The evolution of Big Data, the integration of AI into data analysis and interpretation, and the ensuing potential to discern interrelationships, causations, and repercussions, collectively augment the scope and purposefulness of data analysis, thereby affording deeper insights. Competencies, knowledge, and experiences in these domains are imperatives for Business Partners acting as Strategic Positioners, as well as for the executive and line management.

Strategic Positioners must elucidate to the management and leadership the pertinence and advantages of pronounced competencies in these realms, propelling the strategic enhancement of workforce competencies and leadership acumen through HR development, encompassing emotional intelligence and soft skills. Consequently, not only technical but also social and ethical considerations assume prominence in leadership cultivation.

Supplementary proficiencies requisite in the delineated VUCA environment encompass the ability to motivate guided teams towards goal attainment, fortifying decision-making capabilities amidst intricate scenarios, and nurturing an innovation-centric ethos to bolster agility and adaptability. Furthermore, these facets should be intricately interwoven with the company's strategy and distinct organizational domains. (Reinhardt, 2020, 247–250). Through meticulous collaboration across three hierarchical tiers, grounded in an appreciation of pertinence and developmental advantages, extant knowledge within the enterprise can be amalgamated and interconnected. This method fosters methodical and comprehensive cogitation directed towards the systematic and strategic enhancement of core competencies within the organization, propelled and refined by internal networking (Kollmann, 2022, 57–59). This objective becomes notably attainable when bespoke strategies and approaches to strategic HR development are deduced, enacted, and effectively operationalized from the delineation of core competencies and requisite organizational proficiencies, qualifications, and experiences by Business Partners functioning as Strategic Positioners (Hübler, 2020, 160).

Emphasis must be placed on accentuating core competencies pivotal for the sustained prosperity of the enterprise, contingent upon its strategic objectives, extant and potential resources, human capital, while taking into account the probable and foreseeable ramifications of external influencers, such as advancements in technology, AI, the evolution of labor scarcity, potentially mutable economic and political landscapes, and other idiosyncratic organizational influences. This fosters targeted talent cultivation and optimal utilization of extant resources. In talent cultivation and the concomitant HR domain, coherence across individual spheres must be meticulously appraised. Business Partners acting as Strategic Positioners must recognize that the attainment of optimal strategic HR development hinges upon the harmonization of HR development across individual spheres, engendering an ideal complementarity between domains, roles, and collaborations within the enterprise, thereby maximizing synergies and engendering positive ramifications on the organization's value-added contribution and potential.

Insufficient specification and assessment of requisite competencies within a particular domain of a company can result in detrimental ramifications for other domains. For instance, if essential competencies in product innovation fail to align with development, it invariably impacts production and subsequently, the sales department. Failure to attain planned competencies in these domains hampers their full utilization, thereby constraining the company's potential, value addition, and overall contribution. Furthermore, such instances often necessitate reduced HR allocation in subsequent domains, potentially leading to downsizing. Nevertheless, even in the absence of downsizing, neglecting to harness competencies and knowledge from HR development initiatives can breed discontent and demotivation. A probable consequence could entail talent migration due to skilled labor scarcities, resulting in the depletion of human capital and diminished ROI of HR development programs.

To optimize value generation and its potential, it is imperative for Business Partners assuming the role of Strategic Positioners to attain strategic alignment through continual evaluation of HR development initiatives and their methodologies, strategies, and achievements (Schreyögg & Koch, 2023, 431–432). The efficacy of strategic HR development necessitates measurement via performance indicators, encompassing the enhancement of employee competencies, employee satisfaction, and their contribution to company success. By means of regular, collaborative, and jointly accountable reviews by Business Partners, corporate management, and line management, the efficacy of deployed resources can be scrutinized. Subsequently, adjustments can be made as needed to enhance goal orientation and efficiency. Interdisciplinary collaboration, interconnected knowledge, and collective systematic and strategic analysis of the prevailing situation, aligned with the desired scenario across various timeframes, are imperative for this progression. All stakeholders must recognize that corporate strategy and HR development are iterative processes. Continuous monitoring and analysis are indispensable for making adaptations to ensure that HR development aligns with the evolving demands of corporate strategy. This is pivotal for sustaining progress and the outcomes of integrated strategic HR development. Effective controlling mechanisms are pivotal in facilitating appropriate adjustments to maintain the trajectory of HR development and thereby enhance the likelihood of attaining strategic objectives.

8.8.7 Strategic HR Development: Aligning Competencies Across Temporal Dimensions for Organizational Success

Business Partners acting as Strategic Positioners necessitate competencies in analytical prowess with a strategic orientation. The assessment of existing competencies mandates a meticulous scrutiny of employees' present skills and qualifications. This examination can be facilitated through methodologies such as employee surveys, performance evaluations, skills inventories, and other diagnostic approaches. For instance, qualitative and quantitative methodologies encompass interviews, focus groups, competency evaluations, data analytics, statistical modeling, and trend projection. The amalgamation of these methodologies facilitates a thorough and precise comprehension of HR requisites. The acquired data facilitates an accurate enumeration of extant competencies at both individual and organizational levels (Rein, 2023, 69–72).

Similar to the realm of current competencies, Business Partners necessitate strategic competencies concerning the envisioned scenario. The delineation of desired competencies hinges upon the strategic objectives of the enterprise. Close congruence with corporate strategy is imperative in this context. Benchmarking, needs assessments, technological trajectories, and market evaluations serve as tools to delineate future competency prerequisites. Consequently, desired competencies are markedly influenced by the company's long-term aspirations. Drawing from the scrutiny of both domains, Business Partners encounter the challenge of synthesizing them at a strategic developmental echelon. The amalgamation of findings from current and desired competency assessments lays the groundwork for strategic HR development. The objective is to pinpoint extant disparities between present and anticipated proficiencies. The formulation of training regimens, ongoing education endeavors, and targeted talent management strategies equips employees for forthcoming demands.

The ever-changing landscape of markets and technologies necessitates continual monitoring and adjustment of existing and desired competencies. Regular assessments and revisions of the analysis are imperative to ensure that strategic HR development remains synchronized with evolving demands. For the acquisition of requisite information and the harnessing of potentially accessible knowledge, close cooperation among Business Partners, line management, and corporate leadership proves advantageous in this domain. By accounting for various temporal dimensions, it can be assured that employees augment their performance through targeted training interventions and personalized development strategies. This not only fosters individual growth but also yields direct repercussions on the efficacy and productivity of the entire enterprise. A highly proficient workforce stands as a pivotal constituent within the value chain.

Business Partners assuming the mantle of Strategic Positioners must initially grasp the conventional tripartition of temporal dimensions along with the associated aims and imperatives pertinent to optimizing HR via HR development. Short-term objectives in strategic HR development pertain to the immediate exigencies and requisites of the organization. These may encompass transient training initiatives, the introduction of novel operational methodologies, or the mitigation of knowledge lacunae. Aligning these short-term objectives with the overarching strategy of the organization ensures the swift adaptability of employees to extant demands. The medium-term outlook pertains to developmental targets achievable within a span of several years. This might involve the implementation of talent management schemes, deliberate career mapping, and the cultivation of leadership proficiencies. Integrating these objectives with short- and long-term goals facilitates a cohesive progression of employees' adept at confronting both current exigencies and prospective challenges. Strategic HR development's enduring objectives center on the persistent synchronization of employee advancement with the organization's extended aims. This encompasses cultivating a learning-oriented entity, stimulating ingenuity, and securing talent for forthcoming progressions. The amalgamation of these durable objectives ensures the sustainability and perpetuity of HR development. Interlinking short-, medium-, and long-term objectives is pivotal to circumvent incongruities and guarantee the sustained progression of employees. Short-term measures should be intricately woven into the fabric of medium- and long-term strategies to assure cohesive employee progression and the efficacious realization of organizational aims.

When strategizing across all temporal scopes, ensuring the judicious allocation of resources while considering priorities and return on investments is paramount. This entails leveraging competencies and experiences predicated on requisites and developmental analyses from Business Partners, with optimization attainable solely through collaboration with corporate leadership and line management. Execution of these interrelated objectives mandates a lucid strategy, efficacious communication, and continuous monitoring in application. Introducing performance metrics and feedback mechanisms facilitates progress tracking and strategy adjustments as needed. Engaging leadership is equally vital in fostering an organizational ethos conducive to strategic HR development. A deliberate amalgamation of these temporal dimensions not only assures the immediate adaptability of employees but also guarantees sustained, long-term development aligned with overarching organizational objectives. This comprehensive approach is indispensable for adeptly navigating the perpetual alterations in the contemporary workplace. Nonetheless, it is imperative to infuse flexibility into development schemes to address the evolving exigencies of the business milieu.

Incorporating the temporal dimension, the HR development strategy must account for the diverse developmental stages experienced by a company. During the growth phase, heightened training initiatives may become imperative to address emerging challenges, contrasting with the consolidation phase where prioritizing the enhancement of leadership qualities is paramount. The temporal dimension within HR development, intricately intertwined with corporate strategy, plays a pivotal role in ensuring enduring corporate success. Numerous scientific inquiries and research endeavors have emphasized the criticality of temporal considerations in strategic HR development. These investigations underscore that firms adhering to prolonged developmental schemes generally exhibit higher levels of productivity, adaptability, and employee satisfaction. The discernment and cultivation of specific competencies aligned with long-term corporate goals facilitate sustainable and targeted HR development. Augmenting long-term HR development, succession planning emerges as a key strategy, ensuring the availability of executives possessing requisite skills when pivotal positions become vacant (Wirtz, 2024, 762–786).

8.8.8 Unlocking Organizational Resilience: Strategic HR Development in a Dynamic Landscape

Consideration of temporal aspects within the framework of strategic HR development is intricately intertwined with competency management and succession planning, pivotal in fostering organizational resilience. Longitudinal developmental strategies afford enterprises the ability to discern, cultivate, and retain talents across extended time horizons. Proactive HR initiatives forestall talent voids within the organizational fabric, thereby facilitating the seamless integration between strategic imperatives and operational realities. The integration of empirical cases and exemplary methodologies furnishes pragmatic insights into the efficacious adaptation of HR paradigms to dynamic economic landscapes. This empirical grounding elucidates the efficacy of specific interventions while furnishing a blueprint for crafting bespoke strategies tailored to organizational exigencies.

The deployment of a value-centric and outcome-driven strategic HR schema necessitates meticulous orchestration and execution at the grassroots level. Diverse tools, ranging from bespoke development blueprints to targeted training regimens and regular performance appraisals, feature prominently in this endeavor. Their efficacy hinges on their alignment with overarching strategic objectives and their direct correlation with value augmentation. Deliberate investment in employee upskilling augments task proficiency, thereby concretizing the link between individual performance and organizational success. Collaborative synergies between operational entities and Business Partners engender personalized developmental trajectories, meticulously calibrated to accommodate the idiosyncratic aptitudes and proclivities of individual employees.

The ontogenetic theories propounded by Erikson or Piaget underscore the dynamic interplay between psychological development and vocational progression. Assimilating these developmental milestones into HR stratagems facilitates bespoke support mechanisms tailored to individual growth trajectories. Employee surveys serve as a linchpin for gauging employees' self-assessment vis-à-vis their competencies, thereby facilitating a nuanced juxtaposition against objective benchmarks. This dissonance delineates avenues for targeted interventions, thereby enriching the individualized HR development schema. The individual advancement of employees contributes significantly to the establishment or advancement of proficient teams that complement and reinforce one another in their entirety and progression. This leads to a heightened sense of attachment among employees to the company, thereby positively impacting employee retention rates and consequently reducing turnover and recruitment expenses. At the organizational level, such initiatives can foster a sustainable augmentation in competitiveness. Moreover, employees exhibit a greater sense of affinity towards the company when their personal career aspirations align with the overarching strategic objectives. In such instances, there typically ensues heightened employee engagement and motivation (Peterke, 2021, 89–93).

Business Partners, in their capacity as Strategic Positioners and line managers, must not excessively fixate on the individual level, notwithstanding its significance and influence, to ensure continued consideration of the broader strategic context of the corporation. The interface between organizational and individual levels is paramount. By conducting meticulous analysis and systematically examining connections, dependencies, and repercussions, targeted career trajectories can be devised that not only resonate with individual competencies but also fulfill the company's needs and strategic objectives. The integration of both individual levels and their interconnection ensures the establishment of a continuous process, thereby bolstering the agility and competitiveness of the company while ensuring a substantial value-added contribution. This process prioritizes not only short-term HR requisites but also the long-term security and optimization of resources (Holtmeier & Mertin, 2023, 245–251).

An essential challenge within this domain involves establishing corporate objectives intricately intertwined with the resolution of the skills deficit. Strategic HR development emerges as an indispensable tool for ameliorating the repercussions of this skills deficit and ensuring sustained growth and competitiveness over the long term. Firms must possess the capability to adeptly respond to fluctuations in the labor market while continually refining their HR development strategies to effectively pursue their objectives amidst the multifaceted challenges posed by the VUCA environment. Business Partners, in their capacity as Strategic Positioners, alongside corporate leadership and line management, must recognize that strategic HR development, orchestrated and executed by adept Business Partners, stands as a pivotal determinant of success for companies. Amidst an environment characterized by perpetual change, adaptability, innovation, and personalized employee growth assume paramount importance for enduring prosperity. Enterprises that grasp and implement these principles will effectively confront the challenges of the future (Karl, 2023, 338–343).

8.9 Paradox Navigator

The final role of the Core Driver category is the Paradox Navigator. Business Partners operating within this capacity are entrusted with the coordination of activities among the remaining eight roles. This responsibility demands a significant cognitive capacity to comprehend the interdependencies and repercussions of said activities and methodologies. Strategies, activities, methodologies, and programs spanning short-, intermediate-, and long-range horizons must be synchronized to ensure an augmentation in HR development congruent with organizational strategy.

8.9.1 Paradox Navigators: Unraveling Complexity in Strategic HR Development

In their capacity as Paradox Navigators, Business Partners endeavor to amalgamate and synthesize the preceding eight roles of Business Partnering. As the nomenclature suggests, numerous challenges ensue, primarily stemming from the diversity, complexity, and conflicting objectives of HR development. These complexities are exacerbated by the intricacies of reconciling the interests of the three involved groups – Business Partners, line management, and corporate leadership – which vary depending on the specific circumstances of the company. In addition to content-related aspects, factors such as the financial resources, current organizational status, historical development, future projections, attitudes, temporal dimensions, incentive structures, and the scarcity of skilled labor all wield significant influence (Kaehler, 2023, 22–25).

From a business standpoint, it is imperative for corporate leadership, line management, and Business Partners in the role of Paradox Navigators to ensure a substantial value contribution through HR development, adequately anticipated in advance. A particular challenge in implementing strategic HR development, closely intertwined with corporate strategy, lies in the initial necessity for investments that yield returns only in the (considerably) distant future. This commitment of financial resources and working hours for HR development constrains resources otherwise available for ongoing operational endeavors within the company. Notably, regarding the scarcity of skilled labor, a paradox emerges wherein present operational activities suffer to enhance future prospects. Moreover, the requisite collaboration among the three aforementioned groups, alongside the myriad activities and responsibilities of Business Partners, monopolizes resources not available for alternative purposes within the company. Depending on the specific circumstances of the company, the outlined issues and the interests of the involved groups, varying degrees and intensities of paradoxes may arise, necessitating Business Partners to navigate and surmount them to propel strategic HR development and optimize value contribution and resource allocation within the company (Romeike & Hager, 2020, 393–399).

It is evident that Business Partners, acting as Paradox Navigators, are confronted with challenges that initially exhibit a high degree of paradoxical nature. Within this capacity, Business Partners are tasked primarily with resolving some of these paradoxes by fostering understanding among corporate leadership and line management. This can be achieved through persuasive discourse, ROI prognostication, and analysis of realized outcomes. In their role as Paradox Navigators, Business Partners are obliged to discern current and future HR competency requirements, taking into account the prevailing circumstances, corporate strategy, and directly associated corporate evolution. This necessitates regular intercommunication among Business Partner roles, the gathering and scrutiny of performance metrics, and a comprehension of long-term corporate objectives to evaluate the status of extant HR competencies, ascertain alignment with present and future demands, and consequently instate effective and efficient HR development initiatives.

The fundamental proficiency of Business Partners resides in their capacity for analysis, data interpretation, trend identification, and extraction of pertinent insights for HR development. This constitutes the bedrock for informed strategic decisions that exert direct influence on adjustments in HR development as well as on strategies and methodologies (von Borcke & Plohr, 2024, 15–20). As Paradox Navigators, Business Partners must extrapolate specific conclusions from needs assessments or adeptly establish them to pinpoint the requisite competencies within the organization. Drawing from the analyzed data, Business Partners can formulate customized training schemes aimed precisely at addressing identified competency lacunae. This ensures efficient and targeted HR development. However, a prerequisite entails clear delineation or specification of roles for Analytics Designers and Interpreters, as well as for the Technology and Media Integrator within the ambit of Paradox Navigators.

Analytical tools and technologies should be harnessed in a manner conducive to precise data interpretation and analysis. The better this is achieved, the more effectively HR development needs can be discerned, and targeted strategies and methodologies devised accordingly. A robust data infrastructure, coupled with the utilization of modern technologies and analytical tools, serves to surmount resistance and uncertainties on the part of line management and corporate leadership during the execution of enhancement measures. This is particularly pronounced when a substantial enhancement in value contribution and a tighter integration between corporate strategy and HR strategy are demonstrable. Business Partners must exhibit leadership qualities in this respect, while also demonstrating the beneficial and highly favorable nature of augmented analytical prowess for corporate advancement, resulting in a significant elevation in value contribution (Rump, Kreis, & Schmoll, 2017, 241–254).

Efficient utilization and connection of all elements within a company's operations depend on its specific circumstances. Individual disparities, influenced by factors such as company culture, structure, and financial resources, necessitate the identification of tailored solutions by Business Partners. Consequently, there exists no singular optimal approach. The selection of a methodology is contingent upon the magnitude of seemingly conflicting demands posed by the three stakeholder groups. The intensity of paradoxes within organizational frameworks correlates with the divergence in mental models among these groups, alongside cognitive parameters and challenges. Furthermore, existing resources and incentive structures exert a significant influence. For instance, incentive systems skewed towards short-term objectives may offer limited support for long-term and strategic HR development initiatives. Such scenarios pose challenges for stakeholders in devising coherent pathways for organizational advancement. They are compelled to navigate a complex landscape characterized by contradictions and unpredictable shifts in scope and scale, thereby impeding strategic planning efforts. Notably, discrepancies arise concerning the trajectory of company progression, particularly concerning its implications for HR development (Ilic, 2024, 283–285).

8.9.2 HR Development in the Age of Paradox: Navigating Technological Advancements and Organizational Dynamics

In the realm of HR development, paradoxes may manifest as a consequence of exogenous factors, notably illustrated by advancements in technology. The swift emergence and progression of AI give rise to disparate perspectives regarding the present and future proficiencies requisite of employees within the organization, amid the three implicated cohorts. This dynamic can impact both the breadth and velocity of HR activities within the company, contingent upon temporal prognostication, which holds considerable sway. Conversely, there may also exist incongruous evaluations concerning the temporal forecasts of HR development, as technological progress permeates HR endeavors, facilitating novel technologically-driven pedagogical methods, thereby expediting HR development initiatives. As elucidated by this instance, Business Partners, in their capacity as Paradox Navigators, are tasked not only with engaging with the aims, attitudes, assessments, forecasts, and goals of corporate and line management but primarily with addressing the other eight roles of Business Partnering and comprehending their implications (Peterke, 2021, 1–6).

This is paradoxically achieved most effectively when in close collaboration with line management and corporate leadership at the operational level, affording them greater precision in informing about the ramifications of their actions, a deeper understanding thereof, and, drawing upon extensive interdisciplinary knowledge of strategic and systematic methodologies to enhance value proposition, enabling them to maximize it and contemplate the purposive systematic advancement of HR development.

It becomes evident that delving into the origins, rationales, repercussions, and correlations in the capacity of Paradox Navigators fosters a heightened understanding of complexity, or endeavors to achieve such understanding. This comprehension could be harnessed in refining navigation algorithms, crafting cognitive training modalities, or bolstering technological systems. A robust engagement with the challenges in the role of Paradox Navigators can prompt a retrospective examination of the mental frameworks of the other eight roles, thereby catalyzing an ameliorative process within them as well. This unfolds because Business Partners, in the role of Paradox Navigators, grapple with the comprehensive panorama of their function, their undertakings, and the outcomes attained, thereby strategically positioning themselves to discern the interrelations among the nine roles and the resultant outcomes, including value contribution. Building upon this foundation, they can discern avenues for improvement and implement corresponding initiatives and strategies (Becker & Bader, 2019, 431–435).

8.9.3 Unlocking Strategic Synergy: The Crucial Role of Paradox Navigators in HR Development

Business Partners, acting as Paradox Navigators, must fortify their analytical prowess to comprehend causes, interdependencies, and ramifications effectively. Strengthening analytical capabilities involves self-critical examination, conducting literature reviews, analyzing case studies of both successful and unsuccessful HR development endeavors within and beyond the organizational scope, engaging in expert interviews, and scrutinizing best practices along with their adaptability and applicability to the company's unique context. Adaptability stands as a paramount necessity in the contemporary globalized landscape marked by incessant innovation and digital metamorphosis. This methodology enables Business Partners to attain profound insights into the intricacies of workflows, tasks, and objectives within the organization, thus facilitating the formulation of bespoke HR development strategies that accommodate the distinctive requisites of various departments and roles. Particularly in the milieu of escalating corporate intricacies mandating interdisciplinary cooperation and comprehension, a siloed understanding of departments no longer suffices to devise efficacious HR development initiatives.

Proficiency in discerning interconnections assumes significance, contingent upon the aptitude of Business Partners to discern patterns, interactions, and repercussions within intricate systems (Huf, 2022, 104–105). This proficiency spans across multiple dimensions. The primary dimension pertains to systems thinking, delineating the capacity to perceive the entirety of the business milieu as an unified system rather than disparate occurrences or departments. The second dimension pertains to the cognitive prowess of individuals, specifically focusing on their capacity for data analysis and information processing to discern pertinent correlations and patterns. The third dimension, termed contextualization, encapsulates the adeptness to contextualize information within the framework of corporate objectives, market dynamics, and strategic congruence. The amalgamation of these three dimensions empowers Business Partners to facilitate more targeted HR development strategies aligned with corporate visions and objectives. This efficacy primarily manifests through their aptitude for making judicious decisions.

Business Partners endowed with refined correlation recognition skills exhibit a propensity for making well-informed and strategic decisions. By comprehending the interplay among variables, they gain insight into how decisions reverberate across various facets of the organization. This acumen proves particularly efficacious in early identification and proactive mitigation of both opportunities and risks. Thereby, they catalyze the prompt execution of measures and HR development initiatives, fortifying the company's competitive standing and potentially positioning it as a frontrunner in its industry. The discernment of correlations also fosters enhanced collaboration between Business Partners and diverse internal departments as well as external stakeholders. This fosters procedural integration and optimizes the entirety of the value chain, bolstering collaborative efforts and propelling integration initiatives (Tolimir, 2022, 121–126).

Through this lens, the advancement of Business Partners' competencies assumes a paramount significance, facilitating enrichment in both theoretical underpinnings and the application of empirical evidence and case studies. Business Partners endowed with pronounced competencies in this realm can more effectively showcase the tangible contributions of their actions and proposed HR developmental initiatives towards the intended organizational objectives. Consequently, nurturing competencies, knowledge, and skills becomes imperative within training and developmental frameworks for Business Partners to underpin the enduring success and competitive edge of enterprises (Schüll, 2020, 1–2). Business partners serve as pivotal entities establishing a linkage between business strategy and HR development initiatives. Their role is paramount in facilitating the acquisition of requisite skills and competencies among employees to fulfill the strategic objectives of the company. This necessitates their consideration of the company's adaptability as a fundamental cornerstone.

8.9.4 Charting the Course: Navigating HR Development in the Complex Business Landscape

In the contemporary landscape of business, characterized by rapid change and heightened complexity, the challenge confronting HR development is significant.

Business partners are tasked with ensuring that training and development programs exhibit the requisite flexibility to seamlessly adjust to evolving demands. To foster adaptability effectively, Business Partners ought to actively engage in formulating long-term HR development strategies. This encompasses the identification of enduring key competencies resilient to uncertainties and the integration of agile methodologies into training initiatives (Michl, 2024, 274–279).

The cultivation of competencies must be viewed as an ongoing endeavor aligned with the dynamic requisites of the business realm. Business Partners should institute mechanisms supporting employees in assuming responsibility for continually enhancing their skill sets. Amidst an era dominated by incessant technological advancements, Business Partners must guarantee the workforce's possession of essential digital proficiencies. It is imperative for training schemes to encompass the latest technological trends, equipping employees with the requisite digital acumen. The efficacy of adaptability can be gauged through the implementation of performance metrics. Business Partners should conduct regular evaluations to ascertain the alignment of developed competencies with evolving demands. In the context of advancing technical content, fostering autonomy, cultivating entrepreneurial thought, and encouraging proactive engagement among employees, the role of Business Partners remains pivotal. They must comprehend the intricate interplays within diverse realms of the enterprise. This comprehension empowers them to delineate HR developmental requisites and devise pertinent HR development strategies, initiatives, and schemes that meticulously leverage synergies for sustainable corporate advancement and substantial value augmentation, while surmounting impediments in corporate and HR developmental endeavors. Through collaborative synergy, a comprehensive methodology, and shared accountability within the strategic planning framework, Business Partners ensure the resolution of paradoxes, alignment of HR development endeavors with overarching corporate objectives, and the facilitation of a sustainable nexus with strategic alignment (Zayats, 2020, 38–42).

It becomes apparent that Business Partners, particularly in their role as Paradox Navigators, necessitate not only expertise in their domain but also a profound grasp of the business architecture, market dynamics, and organizational flux. This acumen is pivotal for their efficacy in HR development schemes, value augmentation, and the seamless harmonization of corporate strategy with HR developmental strategy. In addition to the internal intricacies faced by Business Partners as Paradox Navigators, they confront external, dynamic, and complex influences, from which they must derive strategic developmental imperatives and correspondingly tailor HR development approaches. Thus, the Paradox Navigator occupies a pivotal locus not solely within the Business Partner spectrum but also for the corporation and its developmental trajectory, which increasingly hinges upon human capital and its strategic evolution in tandem with corporate objectives. In this role, alongside corporate leadership, particular emphasis is placed on addressing paradoxes and conflicting challenges within the business environment.

Business Partners functioning as Paradox Navigators assume responsibility for guaranteeing a tight alignment of HR with requisite competencies. The attainment of high alignment predominantly relies on their personal competencies, skills, and experiences, augmented by substantial input from interdisciplinary knowledge and collaboration. To achieve a targeted alignment of HR development with the strategic objectives of the company, Business Partners necessitate profound insights into not only the developmental trends and influencing factors within the business environment but also the operational undertakings of the company. Furthermore, they require expertise in domains such as management, organizational psychology, organizational development, leadership, change management, team competencies, social skills, trend sensitivity, communicative abilities, and value orientation. Even amidst the escalating complexity and dynamism in the business milieu, Business Partners must grasp the company's value chains to continually enhance and adapt them to changes effectively. The adeptness of Business Partners in discerning interconnections significantly augments the potential value creation, as the efficacy and suitability of HR development initiatives hinge upon this capability. Consequently, Business Partners must perpetually hone their skills to directly contribute to the value generation process. Through continual adaptation and refinement of their skills, Business Partners can enhance the efficiency of their services, thereby positively influencing the entire value chain. Thus, it is imperative for Business Partners to advocate for continuous investment by companies in the development of their Business Partners to secure long-term success and competitiveness (Wienkamp, 2021, 107–110).

8.9.5 Unlocking Success: The Role of Paradox Navigators in Maximizing Value-Added Contribution

In the modern business landscape, Business Partners serve as strategic allies and proponents, crucial in navigating the myriad paradoxes that may emerge suddenly. Acknowledging that there's no ideal resolution, they must strive to balance conflicting objectives, recognizing the inability to fully align with all involved parties. Understanding themselves as Paradox Navigators, Business Partners facilitate mediation between divergent interests and priorities. Their primary duty lies in harmonizing short-term objectives with long-term strategies, fostering innovation alongside efficiency, and balancing risk-taking with stability in HR development, all while maximizing value contribution. The aim is to capitalize on synergies and transform apparent contradictions into advantageous prospects (Wagner, 2021, 310–318).

Functioning effectively in this role necessitates ongoing analysis of both the business environment and internal dynamics, pinpointing (potential) paradoxes for further examination. Armed with this understanding, integrative strategies can be devised to reconcile conflicting objectives, foster value-centric approaches, and mitigate contradictions holistically. Moreover, as Paradox Navigators, Business

Partners must collaborate closely with corporate and line management, ensuring all stakeholders comprehend the situation, its causes, and ramifications. Such collaboration fosters knowledge exchange, deepening collective comprehension and facilitating the joint development of solutions. Effective communication is paramount for Business Partners in navigating HR development challenges, relying on insights, metrics, initiatives, and objectives to underscore the pursuit of value maximization and long-term success. Thus, communication competence emerges as a crucial prerequisite, prompting continual self-assessment and the pursuit of competency enhancements in communication skills, strategies, and objectives (Foelsing & Schmitz, 2021, 236–238).

Central to this concept is the pivotal role of Business Partners acting as Paradox Navigators, who assume a leadership role in informing stakeholders about the necessity, challenges, and approaches for enhancing value-added contributions. This is imperative due to the tendency for HR development programs, especially when viewed through a systematic and holistic lens, to be perceived and evaluated more keenly by Business Partners rather than by line management or corporate leadership. Particularly in situations where collaboration between Business Partners and corporate leadership or line management is limited, the imperative is to foster greater cooperation. This can be best achieved through presenting integrated strategies that emphasize overall success and resultant value-added contributions. Changes that yield clear benefits and enhanced value-added contributions are most persuasive to corporate leadership and line management. Business Partners can heighten support for HR development initiatives by ensuring they demonstrate swift successes in practical contexts, thereby enhancing value-added contributions. Typically, corporate leadership and line management are swayed by improvements in profit margins or productivity. Intensive collaboration efforts are essential for Business Partners to establish and expand interconnected knowledge networks. Alongside content-based strategies, it is vital for Paradox Navigators to ensure that promising strategies, progress, and successes are effectively communicated to corporate leadership and line management.

8.9.6 Empowering Paradox Navigators: Enhancing Collaboration and HR Development for Competitive Advantage

Business Partners, in their role as Paradox Navigators, must evaluate their competencies, experiences, and what is required to further persuade corporate leadership and line management towards closer collaboration. This awareness is crucial for enhancing value-added contributions and integrating HR development into corporate strategy and financial considerations. Fundamentally, the imperative for development arises from the necessity of comprehensively understanding company activities and interrelationships. This understanding is indispensable for devising effective measures to enhance HR competencies, address quantitative and qualitative skills shortages, and optimize HR potential within the organization (Ludwig, 2024, 97–104).

A robust collaboration, coupled with the amalgamation of knowledge, expertise, and experience among Business Partners, significantly bolsters the company's adaptability and agility. This synergy is particularly crucial in the contemporary business landscape marked by VUCA, where rapid and profound alterations in business conditions necessitate corresponding shifts in HR competencies. Enhancing one's own skills, competencies, and knowledge involves a deep understanding of operational activities, primarily influenced by external changes. This entails a systematic and comprehensive assessment of the present situation and its anticipated evolution. Business Partners, acting as Paradox Navigators, must ensure continuous advancement of competencies, skills, and knowledge among line management and corporate leadership. Hence, Business Partners in the role of Paradox Navigators must assert leadership and HR development initiatives alongside line management and corporate leadership. This approach not only fosters insight but also augments competencies, experiences, knowledge, and reflective capabilities, ultimately heightening awareness and recognition of paradoxes within the organization. The cultivation of problem-solving prowess underpins the establishment of interconnected knowledge networks and collaboration, facilitating the identification of innovative solutions for seemingly contradictory challenges and paradoxes (Sanabria, 2024, 353–360).

Drawing upon their own expertise and experiences from various roles, Business Partners in the role of Paradox Navigators forge close collaborations with corporate leadership and line management, ensuring that HR development aligns closely with the company's strategic objectives. This cultivates a keen awareness of the importance of HR development, optimal resource allocation, and collaborative efforts to enhance value creation situations, particularly in light of the evolving skilled labor shortage, thus bestowing sustainable competitive advantages upon companies.

Creating competitive advantages cannot exclusively rely on the enhancement of collaboration with corporate leadership and line management; it must also consider the engagement of employees. The advancement of HR competencies encompasses not only the potential of employees and its utilization but also the alignment with HR interests, thereby potentially involving Business Partners in HR development initiatives. Successful HR development, strategically oriented, necessitates alignment with the interests, motivation, insight, and understanding of the workforce. Furthermore, identified paradoxes, developmental needs, and objectives should be transparently communicated to the workforce, fostering awareness and comprehension regarding the rationale behind the implementation or adaptation of HR development programs. Business Partners and line management should collaboratively develop communication and persuasion strategies to effectively engage the workforce in this regard.

Additionally, it's crucial to recognize challenges and difficulties stemming from paradoxes within the workforce and support their transition between old and new paradigms. This involves surmounting resistance and facilitating continuous development while discouraging regression to previous behavioral patterns and coping mechanisms. Strategic positioning also necessitates addressing how the design of HR development programs, acknowledging paradoxes and implications at the employee level, influences retention and motivation. Particularly in collaboration with line management, it's imperative to assess which supplementary measures, approaches, and strategies can be employed to ensure that employees perceive alignment between their personal and professional development and the objectives of HR development programs and corporate goals (Stulle & Thiel, 2023, 240–245).

Business Partners are tasked with establishing a conducive learning culture, meticulously tailored to the unique circumstances of employees, predicated upon the organizational stratum. They must factor in the principles of continuous learning and adaptive learning, all the while crafting and upholding an inception point perceived by teams as stimulating and propitious for their advancement. A favorable learning culture serves not only to nurture individual progression but also to facilitate the exchange of knowledge and competencies within the organization, thereby augmenting the collective competence of the workforce. This underscores the nexus between the individual, team, and overarching organizational levels. The amalgamated strategy spanning these tiers fosters a dynamic and flexible operational milieu alongside individual career advancement. In sum, this bolsters the competitiveness and enduring prosperity of the company (Gabathuler & Bajus, 2021, 177–183).

9   The Challenge of Competency and Strategic Relatedness of HR Development in HR Business Partnering

The various roles described present distinct challenges necessitating individual coordination. Business Partners confront notable challenges in efficiently, purposefully, and harmoniously managing the components of each role. However, a significantly greater challenge arises for Business Partners in coordinating these components across different roles. Particularly, the multitude of potential connections between the challenges of individual roles and their mutual influence intensifies the challenges for Business Partners. Through coordination, analysis of mutual influence, systematic connections, and implications for further development of individual challenges, the work of Business Partners becomes more arduous. A systematic understanding and analysis, grounded in well-developed operational knowledge, current state, and implementation of Business Partnering, are imperative. This understanding should recognize trends, developments, and their implications for the work and development potential of Business Partnering, alongside a clear reference to corporate strategy and value contribution (Fallgatter, 2020, 210–212).

Another significant factor contributing to the major challenge is the imperative for Business Partners to comprehend and consider the company-specific situation. Best practice approaches are suboptimal in many cases as they fail to adequately account for the company-specific context. Business Partners must recognize the coordination of tasks and associated challenges as integral to the role of the Paradox Navigator. This role assumes an integrating function, mandating Business Partners to ensure effective coordination and cooperation aligned with the company's strategy or potential.

The forthcoming exposition will elucidate the challenges and responsibilities of each role, emphasizing their interconnectedness. A chronological framework will be employed to establish linkages between the challenges encountered by successive roles, thereby preventing redundancy. This sequential arrangement ensures that Foundational Enabler roles are intertwined with Strategic Enablers and Core Drivers, while Strategic Enabler roles are connected to Core Drivers. This methodology underscores the significance of strategic considerations and Core Drivers in fostering cohesion among individual roles. Furthermore, references will be made within each category to subsequent roles, maintaining consistency in the chronological sequence. The role of Paradox Navigators is not explicitly addressed, as the coordination of preceding connections, impacts, and implications falls within the purview of Business Partners, as elucidated. To maintain coherence with the chronological structure, connections to subsequent roles will be delineated in their chronological progression. In cases where a role's challenges pertain to multiple subsequent roles, a succinct summary will be provided to obviate repetition. The comprehensive exposition of connections within a task area will be predicated on the role occupying the lowest rank therein. References to connections with other roles will also be made, preserving the chronological order.

9.1 The Connection between the Roles of the Foundational Enablers and the Additional Categories

9.1.1 The Connection between the Technology and Media Integrator and the Other Roles

A conspicuous correlation manifests between the functions of Technology and Media Integrators and Analytics Designers and Interpreters. In the context of introducing and expanding VR, AR, and Blended Learning, Business Partners, occupying the role of Technology and Media Integrators, are reliant upon the analyses and insights furnished by Analytics Designers and Interpreters. Their focus pertains specifically to needs analysis, technical competencies, learning preferences, resource management, as well as acceptance and readiness to learn. Within the realm of needs analysis, grasping the requisite skills and knowledge for effective task fulfillment by participants emerges as pivotal. Through scrutinizing potential participants, precise learning objectives and training content can be tailored to suit their requirements.

Not all prospective participants possess familiarity with the essential technical proficiencies for utilizing VR, AR, and Blended Learning. Analysis aids in gauging technical comprehension and receptivity to embracing novel technologies, facilitating the implementation of appropriate training interventions. Diverse individuals exhibit varying learning preferences and modalities. Whereas some thrive in hands-on experiences afforded by VR and AR, others lean towards more conventional learning approaches. Analyzing potential participants assists in identifying preferred learning styles, thereby enabling adjustments in the learning curriculum accordingly.

The advent of new technologies like VR and AR often entails substantial resource allocation in terms of time, finances, and expertise. Through analyzing potential participants, enterprises can ensure judicious allocation of resources by customizing training content and methodologies to align with the needs and capacities of the participants.

Participant engagement stands as a pivotal determinant for the efficacy of training programs. Comprehensive analysis aids in pinpointing potential impediments to the acceptance of new technologies or training methodologies, facilitating the formulation of strategies to surmount them. Thus, companies can ascertain that their training endeavors evoke a positive reception from participants, fostering their active involvement (Peterke, 2021, 44–45).

The comprehensive evaluation of prospective participants in the integration of VR, AR, and Blended Learning into the HR development of Business Partners holds paramount importance in guaranteeing the efficacy of training initiatives, catering to participant requisites, and fostering sustainable value addition for the enterprise. This significance is accentuated by the escalating prominence of technological methodologies and mediums within HR development, presenting increasingly efficacious avenues for employee training, advancement, and skill cultivation through technological progression. Nonetheless, prudent consideration of cost-benefit dynamics and the discernment of enhancement potentials is imperative during implementation. Technological interventions in HR development often entail substantial costs, encompassing bespoke software development, learning platform deployment, and learning content procurement. Hence, a meticulous evaluation of costs vis-à-vis anticipated benefits is pivotal to ensure the investment's efficiency and yield a positive ROI, with due regard to technology effectiveness and alignment with employee requisites. The efficacy of technological interventions and mediums in HR development hinges significantly on their quality. It is imperative to ascertain whether selected technologies bolster learning outcomes, realize learning objectives, and facilitate the acquisition of targeted competencies and proficiencies. Identification of enhancement potentials is indispensable for continual optimization of technology. Frequently, technological solutions are either developed or furnished by external providers. Conducting cost-benefit analyses and identifying enhancement opportunities aids in the discernment of suitable partners and the establishment of enduring partnerships. Partnerships should not only be economically viable but also ensure technology quality and relevance (Winkler & Fink, 2022, 74–76). Technological solutions must exhibit scalability to synchronize with the expansion of the company and its workforce, ensuring efficacy and efficiency. Through meticulous assessment of costs and benefits, alongside the discernment of potential enhancements, corporations can ascertain the sustainability of their investments over prolonged periods, thus accommodating evolving requisites.

A fundamental prerequisite for Business Partners entails contemplation of AI and its applicative potentials, predominantly through data analysis, customized to individual advancements. Within the purview of the Analytics Designer and Interpreter's function, soliciting feedback from participants and alumni of HR development programs assumes paramount importance, especially concerning the temporal and spatial adaptability of such programs, the relevance of their content, and adherence to specific corporate exigencies. Beyond the purview of analytics design and interpretation lies a direct nexus with the role of the Compliance Manager in ensuring that the utilization and integration of technologies and media conform closely to corporate protocols and compliance standards (Johannsen & Kant, 2022, 276–278).

Furthermore, within the domain of association with the Analytics Designer and Interpreter role, scrutinizing the utilization of AI in HR development vis-à-vis the

9.1 The Connection between the Roles of the Foundational Enablers

company's strategic alignment necessitates consideration, which also entails linkage with the Strategic Positioner's role. The assessment of costs and benefits, alongside the identification of areas for enhancement, are pivotal factors in leveraging technological methodologies and media within HR development. This ensures efficiency in investments, alignment with employee requirements, sustenance of long-term success and expansion, and the facilitation of high-value creation. Furthermore, there exists a profound correlation between this process and the role of the Analytics Designer and Interpreter, highlighting a direct linkage to the Culture and Change Champions. The integration of novel technological methodologies necessitates alignment with the HR development culture and underscores the imperative of lifelong learning. Additionally, a significant nexus exists between the utilization of technologies and media for individualized learning support and the deliberate preservation of workforce employability, coupled with associated self-responsibility. Notably, the role of the Compliance Manager is directly referenced, emphasizing the imperative for HR development to adhere to stringent compliance standards. The instillation of self-responsibility and employability preservation within the organizational culture is reinforced through the efforts of the Culture and Change Champions (Helmold, 2024, 23).

Moreover, a correlation emerges with the role of the Human Capital Curator, particularly concerning the selection of technological deployment and the cultivation of human capital, especially in nurturing Future Skills vital to central and success-critical domains of corporate strategy. This juncture also implicates the role of the Strategic Positioner.

The deployment and utilization of Technology and Media are intricately intertwined with the roles of the Analytics Designers and Interpreters, the Culture and Change Champions, the Human Capital Curators, the Credible Activists, and the Strategic Positioners in the realm of knowledge networking facilitated by technology. In their capacity as Analytics Designers and Interpreters, Business Partners are tasked with designing and implementing analytical technologies for data collection, analysis, and interpretation. Leveraging technology enables them to glean crucial insights that facilitate knowledge generation and utilization, thereby advancing knowledge networking within the organization.

In the capacity of Culture and Change Champions, Business Partners concentrate on instituting a milieu conducive to transformation and information interchange within an entity. Leveraging technology and media, they facilitate the dissemination of information and collaborative efforts, thereby fostering the establishment of an open and knowledge-driven corporate culture.

Functioning as Human Capital Curators, Business Partners undertake the task of advancing and honing the competencies and expertise of employees. Utilizing technology, they furnish learning platforms and resources that empower employees to continually acquire fresh insights and enhance their skill sets (Lohmüller & Greiff, 2022, 234–235).

In their role as Credible Activists, Business Partners direct their attention towards individuals advocating for the propagation of pertinent knowledge and information internally and externally. Harnessing technology and media, they amplify their credibility and outreach, thereby stimulating change and disseminating knowledge.

Assuming the mantle of Strategic Positioners, Business Partners shoulder the responsibility of fortifying the organization's standing within the knowledge domain and forging strategic alliances. By deploying technology, they facilitate networking with external entities and knowledge reservoirs to glean insights and propel innovation.

Collectively, these roles epitomize the utilization of technology and media for networking, advocacy, and dissemination of knowledge, thus fortifying the development of an organizational culture steeped in knowledge. Incorporating technological advancements and subsequent opportunities into organizational culture is imperative. This process should consider various forms of learning and their motivational influences, thereby ensuring their sustainable integration into the learning and HR development culture. Within the HR development process and learning culture, it's essential to foster autonomy and individual responsibility, particularly in self-Blended Learning initiatives.

The synergy between Technology and Media Integrators and Human Capital Curators within HR development is pivotal for optimizing return on investment and facilitating efficient learning processes. Business Partners, functioning as Technology and Media Integrators, bear the responsibility of seamlessly integrating technology and media into learning frameworks. They identify appropriate technologies and media formats to enhance learning experiences, encompassing e-learning platforms, interactive modules, simulations, and VR. The selection and incorporation of these tools should be tailored to learners' needs, ensuring an engaging and effective learning journey.

Human Capital Curators are tasked with sourcing, creating, and curating high-quality learning content tailored to employees' developmental needs. They collaborate closely with Technology and Media Integrators to integrate content into chosen platforms, ensuring easy accessibility for learners. This collaborative effort aims to maximize the ROI of HR development initiatives. Technology enables tracking and analyzing learning activities, facilitating the quantification of training success and ensuring tangible benefits for the company. By amalgamating technology with curated content, personalized learning experiences can be crafted. Technology and Media Integrators empower employees to personalize their learning paths and adapt content to their unique needs and learning styles. Human Capital Curators are instrumental in identifying pertinent content and adjusting learning programs to meet employees' specific requirements (Ilic, 2024, 284–287).

Consideration may be given to the incentive mechanism through pricing in gamification within HR development, establishing a linkage that extends the role of Human Capital Curators to that of Total Rewards Stewards. The symbiotic relationship between the Technology and Media Integrator and the Credible Activist in HR development holds significant relevance, particularly in the contemporary digital epoch, where technology and media exert pivotal influence.

Leveraging their proficiency and expertise, Technology and Media Integrators ensure the alignment of chosen technologies and media with organizational requisites, facilitating their effective utilization. Concurrently, the Credible Activist bolsters these endeavors by advocating for the adoption of novel technologies and media. Through their accrued credibility and sway, they foster acceptance and utilization of these new tools among fellow employees (Kobi, 2021, 381–385).

In the swiftly evolving milieu of work, it becomes imperative for organizations to synchronize with the latest technological advancements and media to sustain competitiveness. Technology and Media Integrators play a pivotal role in ensuring that HR development remains abreast of such transformations. The Credible Activist, meanwhile, contributes to cultivating acceptance and significance in the utilization of technology and media by elucidating their inherent benefits and opportunities. Additionally, they address and surmount apprehensions or resistance towards novel technologies and media.

9.1.2 The Connection between the Analytics Designers and Interpreters and the Other Roles

In HR development, the functions of the Analytics Designer and Interpreter and the Compliance Manager are intricately intertwined, mutually supporting each other across various dimensions. Analytics Designers and Interpreters employ data analysis techniques to identify gaps in knowledge within the workforce. These insights inform adjustments to HR development programs to enhance the congruence between employees' competencies and organizational demands. Compliance Managers ensure that these programs adhere to legal mandates and mitigate regulatory risks. By continuously scrutinizing objectives and attained outcomes, both parties assess the efficacy of HR development endeavors. Such analysis facilitates ongoing program adaptation and evaluation to ensure effectiveness, efficiency, and alignment with organizational requisites. Compliance Managers oversee the alignment of all HR development endeavors with legal and regulatory stipulations. Analytics Designers and Interpreters complement this effort by scrutinizing data to ascertain program adherence to internal protocols and external regulations. Collaboratively, they steer HR development towards congruence with the organization's strategic objectives. They share accountability for program efficacy and the cultivation of employee skills essential for achieving corporate goals. Analytics Designers and Interpreters leverage data analysis to appraise coach effectiveness and ensure requisite skills and qualifications. Compliance Managers guarantee that coach selection and training comply with relevant compliance benchmarks. By monitoring and regulating educational activities, both parties optimize resource allocation and ensure HR development initiatives yield desired outcomes while adhering to legal frameworks and averting organizational risks. Furthermore, attention must be given to guidelines and standards pertaining to individual learning cultures and employees' learning preferences, particularly regarding the utilization and analysis of AI in HR development. This aspect also intersects with the role of the Human Capital Curator in fostering human capital development and with that of the Strategic Positioner in ensuring strategic alignment.

The engagement of Analytics Designers and Interpreters within HR development intricately intertwines with that of the Culture and Change Champions, as they collectively contribute to catalyzing and fostering a paradigmatic shift within the organizational framework. Both entities, the Analytics Designers and Interpreters, alongside the Culture and Change Champions, are instrumental in steering HR development away from short-term reactive measures towards the formulation and execution of medium- and long-term strategic initiatives. By harnessing the power of data and deploying analytical methodologies, they engender a profound comprehension of both employee exigencies and corporate imperatives, thereby augmenting the sustainability quotient of HR development endeavors.

Leadership and stewardship in the domain of HR development are assumed by both the Analytics Designers and Interpreters and the Culture and Change Champions, manifested through their orchestration of team dynamics, judicious allocation of resources, and vigilant monitoring of developmental trajectories. Their concerted efforts converge to ensure the congruence of HR development undertakings with overarching corporate objectives and culture. Analytics Designers and Interpreters in particular leverage data-driven insights to fortify synergies across disparate teams and organizational silos. By scrutinizing performance metrics, soliciting employee feedback, and mining pertinent datasets, they discern common objectives and shepherd employees towards a collective ethos of alignment.

The indispensability of data in sculpting a culture predisposed towards continuous learning and fostering the professional evolution of employees cannot be overstated. Analytics Designers and Interpreters wield data as a potent tool to craft bespoke developmental blueprints, predicated on the analysis of learning trajectories, identification of training requisites, and delineation of competency lacunae, thereby instilling a culture of developmental ascendancy within the organizational milieu.

Culture and Change Champions shoulder the responsibility of articulating the imperatives, significance, and rationale underlying HR development initiatives. In close collaboration with Analytics Designers and Interpreters, they strive to imbue communication strategies with data-derived insights, galvanizing employees to actively engage in developmental pursuits. Moreover, both Culture and Change Champions and Analytics Designers and Interpreters play a pivotal role in disseminating and dissecting corporate culture. Through a regimen of coaching and mentoring, they cultivate a milieu wherein employees internalize and embody corporate values in their quotidian endeavors (Schermuly & Graßmann, 2023, 204–210).

In light of the skills deficit, strategic alignment of HR development tools becomes paramount. Utilizing Analytics Designers and Interpreters can facilitate the identification of HR development initiatives aimed at addressing organizational skill gaps through data analysis. This pertains to the functions of the Human Capital Curator, the Credible Activist, and the Strategic Positioner, as the development, advocacy, and alignment of human capital are imperative. These roles are instrumental in refining best practices through data-driven identification, analysis, and dissemination of effective HR development methodologies. By iteratively enhancing these practices, they ensure the efficacy and adaptability of HR tools to evolving organizational needs. The adoption of best practices is critical not solely for the Culture and Change Champion but also for the Credible Activist and Strategic Positioner, as they must sway corporate leadership and harmonize their efforts with strategic objectives for value optimization. Analytics Designers and Interpreters are pivotal in bolstering the competencies and analytical acumen of Business Partners. Through provision of training, resources, and involvement in data-driven HR development, they equip Business Partners with the requisite skills for informed decision-making and effective support of HR initiatives. This endeavor is indispensable for fostering human capital development and strategic congruence, directly correlating with the roles of the Human Capital Curator, Credible Activist, and Strategic Positioner.

The symbiotic relationship between Analytics Designers and Interpreters and Human Capital Curators in HR development is pivotal, contributing significantly to human capital advancement within enterprises. In ensuring the adequacy of competencies within organizations, Analytics Designers and Interpreters, alongside Human Capital Curators, must orchestrate a meticulously planned developmental trajectory. This trajectory encompasses delineating clear timelines for discerning competency lacunae, formulating training regimens, and executing developmental endeavors. HR development necessitates an investment predicated on empirical data. The costs of short-term training and programs are counterbalanced by medium- and long-term achievements. Employing a ROI methodology is paramount for gauging the efficacy of HR developmental initiatives and ensuring judicious resource allocation (Hendrischke, 2024, 330–336).

Managers wield significant influence in nurturing human capital. They must grasp the significance of HR development, advocate for the advancement of their personnel, and cultivate an environment conducive to learning and progression. Harnessing data empowers enterprises to streamline their HR developmental endeavors. Analytics Designers and Interpreters facilitate the acquisition, analysis, and interpretation of pertinent data to inform decisions concerning developmental undertakings.

Coaches are instrumental in fostering human capital development by furnishing individual employees with support to enhance their competencies, actualize their potential, and surmount obstacles. By embracing data-driven HR development and perpetual competency enhancement, enterprises can fortify their adaptability to swiftly respond to evolving market dynamics and attain competitive supremacy. This pertinence extends to the roles of the Credible Activist and the Strategic Positioner, who advocate for the primacy of HR development and align it with the company's strategic imperatives.

The formulation of the evaluation should serve to enhance the efficacy of human capital advancement. This entails harmonizing analytical approaches and metrics across the enterprise, alongside a strategic synchronization with organizational objectives and requisites – rendering it pertinent to the function of the Strategic Positioner. Metrics ought to be tactically employed for gauging and perpetually enhancing the efficacy of initiatives in HR development. This entails establishing precise delineations of performance metrics and their routine appraisal within the ambit of a comprehensive plan for human capital development. Such endeavors must also find support within the purview of the role of the Strategic Positioner (Blaha, 2021, 78–82).

The role of the Analytics Designer and Interpreter, as well as the role of the Total Rewards Steward, are pivotal for HR advancement, particularly in data analysis and incentive system optimization within Business Partnering. Analytics Designers and Interpreters employ data analyses to discern patterns and trends within employee data, facilitating the identification of correlations between incentives, employee retention, and the ROI of HR developmental initiatives. Leveraging these insights, the Total Rewards Steward designs incentive systems aimed at bolstering employee retention and enhancing the ROI of HR development endeavors. Through appropriate incentive structuring, companies can concurrently retain talent and improve financial performance.

Analytics Designers and Interpreters conduct data analyses to assess the efficacy of HR development programs and the motivation levels of frontline management executives in participating in these initiatives. Total Rewards Stewards utilize these findings to refine incentive frameworks, ensuring proper recognition for frontline management engagement in team development efforts. This adjustment enhances the efficacy of HR developmental initiatives (Dohmen, 2023, 15–18). Analytics Designers and Interpreters contribute to evaluating the ROI of HR development programs by quantifying the benefits through data analysis. Total Rewards Stewards utilize these evaluations to design incentive structures that effectively communicate the benefits of HR developmental programs to both employees and executives. This approach enhances employee motivation to engage in such initiatives, ultimately optimizing the success of HR developmental endeavors.

The role of the Analytics Designer and Interpreter is pivotal in the advancement of HR, particularly when synergized with the function of the Credible Activist within the organizational framework. Leveraging data analytics, the Analytics Designer and Interpreter discerns trends, patterns, and aberrations in employee performance and growth trajectories. These data-derived insights form the foundation for the design and refinement of HR development programs, crucial for optimizing organizational performance. The Credible Activist utilizes this analytical output to articulate the significance of impending changes and galvanize employees towards adaptive evolution. Discrepancies between anticipated and actual employee performance are meticulously identified by the Analytics Designer and Interpreter, serving as catalysts for recalibrating HR developmental strategies.

The Credible Activist lends support to this process by effectively communicating the import of these alterations and emphasizing the imperative for adaptation and enhancement.

Both the Analytics Designer and Interpreter and the Credible Activist acknowledge the indispensability of ensuring the enduring relevance and efficacy of HR development endeavors for both the workforce and the overarching organization. Through the adept utilization of data analytics and lucid communication strategies, they collaborate to guarantee that HR developmental initiatives not only fulfill short-term objectives but also endure as pertinent and impactful instruments for organizational advancement (Macharzina & Wolf, 2023, 630–633).

In the realm of HR development, the role of Analytics Designer and Interpreter is pivotal, intricately intertwined with the one of the Strategic Positioner. They serve to ensure strategic alignment and concentration within HR development. Utilizing data analysis, they discern organizational needs, thereby establishing HR strategic objectives. Their collaborative efforts unveil enduring technological, economic, and societal trends, facilitating the formulation of long-term perspectives for HR development, thereby fortifying the organization's future prosperity. Analytics Designers and Interpreters employ data analysis to garner strategic insights, facilitating adjustments within HR development programs. Retrospective analyses enable the assessment of past performance and identification of success determinants, while a predictive stance aids in anticipating future requisites and hurdles, facilitating program adaptations.

The strategic evolution of HR development stands as a paramount responsibility for executives. Collaborating with Strategic Positioners, Analytics Designers and Interpreters furnish executives with data-centric insights, empowering informed decision-making and fostering the enduring growth of employees and the organization. Thus, they substantially contribute to the attainment of organizational objectives (Senn, 2022, 560–563).

9.1.3 The Connection Between the Compliance Manager and the Other Roles

In HR development, the roles of the Compliance Manager and the Culture and Change Champion are intricately interwoven. These roles collaborate to synchronize HR development with the cultural ethos and norms of the organization. They play pivotal roles in fostering a culture of learning, adhering to established guidelines and standards for compliance with policies and legal mandates. Both positions facilitate the integration of social dimensions into HR development endeavors. Coaches, mentors, and leaders are urged to factor these dimensions into their developmental initiatives and daily operations, ensuring alignment with cultural imperatives. Regular reviews of compliance with standards and requisites are conducted by the Compliance Manager, while the Culture and Change Champion ensures the congruence of these standards with the organizational culture and strategic trajectory. The Compliance Manager delineates clear-cut guidelines and standards that all employees must abide by, serving as the yardstick for HR development initiatives. Both roles collaborate closely with line management to ensure the pragmatism and suitability of HR development initiatives for their respective domains of operation.

The Compliance Manager and the Culture and Change Champion jointly monitor the execution of developmental measures by coaches, mentors, and executives, ensuring regulatory compliance and attainment of desired outcomes. This endeavor also establishes a direct linkage with the role of the Human Capital Curator, given the paramount importance of the effectiveness of human capital development. Both roles, acting as Business Partners, are tasked with overseeing the outcomes of HR development initiatives and, when necessary, implementing modifications to ensure goal attainment. This domain also exhibits an intersection with the Human Capital Curator, stemming from its involvement in both oversight and the advancement of human capital.

The close collaboration between the Compliance Manager and the Culture and Change Champion serves to optimize the efficacy of HR development endeavors in day-to-day operations, ensuring alignment with both regulatory standards and cultural as well as strategic objectives. This underscores the relevance of the Human Capital Curator and Strategic Positioner.

Compliance delineates the regulatory prerequisites essential for inclusion in development schemes to uphold legal standards. Culture and Change Champions identify the cultural proficiencies and behaviors imperative for sustained corporate success, integrating them into development initiatives, thus underscoring the indispensability of the Human Capital Curator's role and scope.

Compliance assesses the ROI of development programs through adherence to legal stipulations and risk mitigation. Culture and Change Champions gauge ROI by evaluating the cultural shifts and organizational metamorphosis engendered by these programs, implicating the roles of Human Capital Curators, Credible Activists, and Strategic Positioners.

Compliance ensures program alignment with regulatory mandates and documents their efficacy concerning compliance. Culture and Change Champions articulate the advantages and value generation of programs in terms of cultural evolution and organizational adaptability, thereby integrating the roles of Human Capital Curators, Credible Activists, and Strategic Positioners.

Compliance conducts retrospective evaluations of development programs to ensure conformity with prevailing regulations and strategically plans future adaptations. Culture and Change Champions retrospectively assess cultural transformations and chart future development endeavors based on these insights. Compliance underscores the application of acquired proficiencies and knowledge from programs within the daily work milieu to ensure regulatory adherence. Culture and Change Champions advocate for the assimilation of new behaviors and competencies into the corporate ethos, facilitating their practical implementation (Schirrmacher, 2023, 36–41).

Compliance initiatives promote engagement in developmental programs aimed at equipping employees with requisite competencies and knowledge for adhering to compliance standards. Culture and Change Champions incentivize employees to confront the challenges posed by cultural shifts and aid in their adaptation. Analogous to the aforementioned associations, there exists a symbiotic relationship with the Business Partner and the Strategic Positioner. Compliance offers guidance on reconfiguring organizational frameworks to streamline adherence to legal mandates and mitigate potential risks. Culture and Change Champions advocate for structural modifications conducive to fostering cultural transformations and enhancing organizational agility, with a specific emphasis on strategic dimensions, thus establishing a correlation with the Strategic Positioner (Geissler, 2023, 176–179).

The connection between the Compliance Manager and the Human Capital Curator in HR development is intricately interlinked and mutually reinforcing across diverse dimensions. Compliance Managers uphold standards and objectives, while the Human Capital Curator orchestrates competency development congruent with these benchmarks. This nexus substantially fosters the cultivation of human capital by adhering to standards and fostering competency growth. Collaboratively, both roles ensure that competency development evolves congruently with organizational objectives and standards. Compliance oversees the adherence to established parameters for competency development, whereas the Human Capital Curator ensures that the development process fulfills requisites and effectively nurtures essential skills.

The collaborative efforts between the Compliance Manager and the Human Capital Curator are geared towards efficiently allocating resources in HR development. By adhering to compliance protocols and strategically directing resources towards competency enhancement, the efficacy of HR development is optimized. Crucially, both roles are pivotal in appraising and evaluating the cultivated human capital. Compliance Managers uphold assessment standards and procedures, while the Human Capital Curator ensures that assessments accurately reflect the actual growth and advancement of employees.

In the pursuit of bolstering employee retention, Compliance Managers and the Human Capital Curator synergistically engage in the cultivation of human capital. They facilitate developmental avenues and ensure conformity to corporate regulations, thereby fostering an environment conducive to employee appreciation and active participation. Integral to this endeavor is the establishment of connections with the Total Rewards Steward and the Strategic Positioner, emphasizing the necessity of a comprehensive approach to organizational development.

Employing the Balanced Scorecard framework, Compliance Managers and the Human Capital Curator collaboratively monitor and augment the value proposition and efficacy of HR development initiatives. Their cognizance of strategic imperatives enables the identification of improvement areas and judicious resource allocation, thereby substantiating quantifiable contributions to the company's value proposition.

Recognizing the pivotal role they assume, Business Partners must embody the attributes of Credible Activists while aligning themselves as Strategic Positioners to facilitate the seamless execution of organizational strategies. Through collaborative efforts, Compliance Managers and the Human Capital Curators discern and address deviations in HR development outcomes. Their concerted actions aim to surmount barriers and challenges impeding progress, with the overarching objective of positively influencing organizational outcomes, thereby underscoring the significance of their roles as Credible Activists and Strategic Positioners.

In navigating dynamic business landscapes, Compliance Managers and the Human Capital Curator exhibit adaptability by comprehensively assessing the impact of environmental changes on compliance and HR development endeavors. They adeptly tailor their strategies to maintain credibility and augment effectiveness in line with evolving organizational needs.

The intertwined responsibilities of needs analysis and HR development alignment are shared between Compliance Managers and the Human Capital Curator. While compliance ensures adherence to legal requisites in analysis, the Human Capital Curator ensures developmental initiatives are aligned with both present and future organizational needs, with strategic alignment remaining paramount throughout the process.

The roles of the Compliance Manager and the Total Rewards Steward are pivotal in the realm of HR development and exhibit a close interconnection. Compliance entails the adherence to statutory mandates, organizational protocols, and moral principles, thereby establishing a framework for ensuring the quality assurance within HR developmental initiatives. This framework ensures that all developmental undertakings are executed in alignment with pertinent norms and optimal methodologies.

A Total Rewards Steward significantly contributes to this framework by ensuring that remuneration frameworks and incentive mechanisms not only conform to legal requisites but also align with corporate objectives, effectively fostering employee performance. Compliance assumes a pivotal role in guaranteeing the equity and transparency of incentive schemes and remuneration frameworks. Adherence to compliance protocols serves to mitigate potential risks associated with unjust compensation practices. The Total Rewards Steward underscores and propagates the incentivization function within HR development, ensuring that reward structures incentivize desirable behaviors and performances. This encompasses adherence to compliance directives, as violations often result in penalties that may attenuate the incentivization efficacy. Business Partners, in their capacity as Credible Activists, are tasked with advocating for the dissemination of equitable rewards and emphasizing the linkage between HR development and reward (Helmold, Dathe & Dathe, 2022, 231–235).

The symbiotic relationship between the Compliance Manager and the Strategic Positioner in HR development underscores their interconnectedness, particularly in addressing employees' expectations, perceptions, attitudes, and goals. The Compliance Manager's primary duty lies in guaranteeing adherence to both internal and external protocols and regulations. This encompasses upholding labor laws and regulations that reflect employees' expectations concerning equitable labor practices and workplace safety. By satisfying these expectations, the Compliance Manager aids in cultivating an environment conducive to meeting employees' needs and expectations.

Conversely, the Strategic Positioner endeavors to realize the organization's enduring objectives by optimizing the talents and proficiencies of its workforce. This entails discerning the individual aspirations and aims of employees and formulating developmental strategies that align with these objectives. Through tailored assistance aimed at advancing employees' aspirations and goals, the Strategic Positioner fosters the cultivation of a motivated and committed workforce.

Integration between the Compliance Manager and the Strategic Positioner is imperative to ensure the comprehensive consideration of employees' expectations, perceptions, attitudes, and goals. This entails viewing compliance initiatives not in isolation but as an integral component of a comprehensive HR development strategy that prioritizes the individual needs and objectives of employees.

9.2 The Connection between the Roles of the Strategic Enabler and the Other Categories

9.2.1 The Connection between the Culture and Change Champion and the Other Roles

The function of Culture and Change Champions is intricately intertwined with that of Human Capital Curators in the realm of HR advancement. In the capacity of a Culture and Change Champion, individuals facilitate the establishment of an atmosphere conducive to the generation of human capital through the advocacy of a culture that nurtures continual enhancement and individual advancement. This endeavor significantly bolsters HR development, as personnel within a supportive cultural milieu exhibit heightened motivation towards self-improvement and acquisition of novel competencies.

In their role as Culture and Change Champions, individuals prioritize the welfare of employees by cultivating a culture that fosters active involvement and commitment. This endeavor not only contributes to HR advancement but also amplifies the organization's capacity for innovation, given that employees are incentivized to proffer fresh concepts and devise innovative resolutions. Through the cultivation of a culture that nurtures talent and reinforces measures for employee retention, Culture and Change Champions play a pivotal role in the formation of a robust talent reservoir. Consequently, this augments the organization's innovation prowess and adaptability, as proficient personnel spearhead the progression of novel concepts and swiftly adapt to transformations. As Culture and

Change Champions, individuals continuously refine their aptitude in change management by accruing experience and utilizing feedback for further enhancement. This endeavor contributes to their personal human capital development and equips them with the prowess to efficaciously instigate and oversee changes within the organization (Kaune, Glaubke & Hempel, 2021, 30-39).

By fostering a culture characterized by transparency and continuous learning, the Culture and Change Champion contributes to enhancing the comprehension of performance dynamics within the organizational framework. This facilitates a more nuanced understanding of the individual strengths and weaknesses of employees, paving the way for tailored developmental interventions. In this context, there exists a pertinent necessity for the involvement and extrapolation of insights to all other roles of Business Partnering, categorized as Strategic Enablers and Core Drivers.

The Culture and Change Champion systematically gathers and evaluates operational data to lay the groundwork for organizational transformations and enhancements. An in-depth comprehension of the present organizational landscape empowers targeted initiatives aimed at driving change and progress. These initiatives can be synergistically reinforced in conjunction with the role of the Credible Activist.

Assuming the mantle of a Culture and Change Champion entails an active commitment to enhancing one's proficiency in succession planning and career development. This proactive approach contributes to the mastery of these domains, ensuring the availability of adept successors and facilitating the fruitful progression of employees' careers. Business Partners assuming the role of the Credible Activist are tasked with advocating for such career trajectories and effective succession planning.

The Culture and Change Champion assumes a pivotal role in fortifying knowledge management practices and delineating coherent career trajectories within the organizational context. This endeavor bolsters succession planning efforts and safeguards the organization's reservoir of knowledge and talent, thereby aligning with both the objectives of the Credible Activist and the Strategic Positioner. Moreover, a nexus is evident between the Culture and Change Champion, the Credible Activist, and the Strategic Positioner in subsequent roles emphasizing the Human Capital Curator (Wißfeld, 2023, 318-322).

The synergy between Culture and Change Champions and Human Capital Curators is indispensable for cultivating leaders proficient in steering agile, digital, and complementary strategies within a swiftly evolving milieu. This entails a symbiotic relationship to ensure leaders acquire requisite proficiencies and aptitudes to steer teams through transitions and nurture inventive resolutions. Culture and Change Champions, alongside Human Capital Curators, collaborate to forge interdisciplinary cohorts and foster interdepartmental cooperation. This process entails honing competencies enabling employees to operate effectively within diverse teams and environments, fostering mutual learning. Close collaboration between these roles is pivotal in fostering a culture of adaptability and nimbleness.

9.2 The Connection between the Roles of the Strategic Enabler and the Other Categories

Culture and Change Champions aid in shaping an environment where change is embraced as an opportunity, while Human Capital Curators ensure employees receive necessary skills and support to thrive amidst change.

Through collaboration, non-monetary competencies are cultivated, augmenting employees' value proposition. These may encompass interpersonal skills like communication, teamwork, and problem-solving, deemed vital for navigating an increasingly interconnected and intricate professional landscape. Culture and Change Champions, in tandem with Human Capital Curators, collaborate to instigate a culture of perpetual learning, advocating continuous knowledge exchange. This involves crafting learning avenues and strategically linking employees to facilitate knowledge accrual and dissemination (Kaehler, 2023, 20–26).

The intimate interrelation between Culture and Change Champions and Human Capital Curators facilitates a precise concentration on Performance Management. This encompasses the delineation of explicit objectives and anticipations alongside perpetual surveillance and assessment of performance, ensuring employees optimize their capabilities and bolster the company's success. Collaboratively, this fosters a performance-centric approach in HR development, entailing the identification of developmental requisites and implementation of tailored developmental interventions, thereby fostering continual enhancement in employee performance and goal attainment.

Collectively, these connections underscore the synergistic functioning of Culture and Change Champions and Human Capital Curators, culminating in the promotion of comprehensive HR development. This not only nurtures individual employee growth but also propels the realization of the company's strategic objectives.

The involvement of Culture and Change Champions in HR advancement is intricately linked with the responsibility of Total Rewards Stewards, particularly in the context of enhancing employee retention through equitable compensation structures and incentive mechanisms, alongside the infusion of a novel learning ethos into the reward framework. Culture and Change Champions endeavor to establish a corporate milieu conducive to retaining employees, encompassing the assurance of equitable compensation packages and bonuses to bolster workforce drive and tenure. Total Rewards Stewards wield pivotal influence by ensuring that remuneration and incentive frameworks aptly acknowledge the contributions and performance metrics of employees. Through concerted collaboration, they facilitate the judicious utilization of financial incentives to sustainably incentivize and retain personnel. The advocacy for a fresh learning paradigm necessitates its alignment within the incentive infrastructure. Culture and Change Champions labor towards fostering an ambience where perpetual learning is championed, granting employees avenues for continuous self-improvement. Total Rewards Stewards fortify these endeavors by guaranteeing that monetary incentives and avenues for career progression are accessible to employees who actively pursue further education, thereby fostering ongoing enhancement of the organization. By integrating learning incentives into the reward apparatus, employees can be galvanized towards continual self-development, thereby enriching their contributions to the company's prosperity (Hungenberg & Wulf, 2021, 253–261).

The function of the Culture and Change Champion correlates closely with the role of Credible Activists within HR development. In their capacity as Culture and Change Champions, it becomes imperative to employ data-driven methodologies for the assessment and enhancement of HR development initiatives' efficacy. Credible Activists leverage their credibility to gather, analyze, and furnish informed suggestions on optimizing HR development processes through data scrutiny. Culture and Change Champions actively champion for HR development by nurturing an environment conducive to perpetual learning and advancement. In tandem, they invest in their personal growth to serve as Credible Activists, thereby motivating others to follow suit. These dual roles are geared towards comprehending the intricacies of the corporate milieu and its ramifications on HR development. Culture and Change Champions acknowledge the necessity for adaptability and spearhead initiatives to ensure alignment of HR development with present and future demands. They endeavor to generate favorable outcomes and value for HR development program participants. By functioning as Credible Activists, they bolster motivation and engagement in the learning journey by articulating the significance and advantages of active involvement. Both Culture and Change Champions and Credible Activists grasp the importance of contemporary learning methodologies and flexibly adjust to the requisites of Industry 4.0 and agility. They advocate for innovative learning strategies and facilitate the cultivation of a learning ethos that seamlessly integrates novel technologies and work methodologies.

The interconnections observed between roles within the domain of Human Capital Curators pertain equally to the roles of Credible Activist and Strategic Positioner, as they predominantly center on effecting structural changes and ensuring strategic congruence. Culture and Change Champions assume a pivotal function in nurturing competencies that transcend present temporal constraints. They cultivate an ethos of continual learning and adaptability, empowering personnel to evolve sustainably amidst perpetual exigencies. These roles synergize to propel alterations in organizational architecture, configuration, and methodologies. Culture and Change Champions discern and instigate changes conducive to the strategic alignment of the organization, while Credible Activists facilitate the effective implementation of these changes through their credibility and persuasive prowess. Both roles engage in short-term adjustments while maintaining a steadfast focus on long-term strategic objectives. Culture and Change Champions furnish a vista for enduring development, whereas Credible Activists ensure that immediate adaptations harmonize with this vista. This nexus encompasses the refinement of organizational frameworks to optimize talent development and strategic alignment. Culture and Change Champions identify the imperative for such refinements, while Credible Activists aid in their successful execution by garnering employee support and endorsement.

Culture and Change Champions and Credible Activists collaborate closely with line management in their capacity as Business Partners to ensure the alignment of

9.2 The Connection between the Roles of the Strategic Enabler and the Other Categories

talent development initiatives with the organization's strategic imperatives. They share accountability for conceiving and implementing developmental measures tailored to the organization's exigencies. Both roles wield adept communication skills essential for efficaciously embedding and fortifying a novel culture of learning and talent development. They substantiate the relevance of developmental measures and sway employees regarding their utility and significance for the organization. Culture and Change Champions and Credible Activists necessitate tight collaboration with line management and corporate leadership to effectuate changes in talent development successfully. They rely on the backing and allocation of resources from senior management to realize their objectives and fortify the organization in the long haul.

The involvement of Culture and Change Champions in HR development closely correlates with that of Strategic Positioners, particularly in integrating HR development within the strategic framework and organizational culture, and in aligning change processes with strategic aims. As intermediaries between HR development and the company's strategic objectives, Culture and Change Champions grasp both the existing corporate culture and the envisaged culture delineated by strategic goals. They identify and advocate for pivotal competencies and behaviors that harmonize with strategic objectives, thereby aiding the seamless integration of HR development into the strategic discourse of the organization. Their efforts ensure that HR development is perceived not in isolation but as an indispensable element of corporate strategy, guaranteeing that training and developmental endeavors mirror and bolster strategic imperatives.

In their capacity as Culture and Change Champions, they wield significant influence in harmonizing change initiatives with the company's strategic direction. They comprehend the imperative and context of changes and can tether them to overarching corporate aspirations. Their communication and facilitation of changes underscore the company's strategic aims, aiding employees in grasping the nexus between changes and the company's enduring vision. Leveraging their awareness of cultural dynamics, they mold changes to be embraced and endorsed by employees, fostering a culture of adaptability and change that converges with strategic objectives (Helmold, 2023, 184–185).

9.2.2 The Connection between the Human Capital Curator and the Other Roles

The Human Capital Curator and Total Rewards Steward jointly wield pivotal influence in the progression of HR, complemented by the Strategic Positioner's pertinence. The Human Capital Curator's function fosters the accrual of social and organizational capital by nurturing an environment conducive to team and organizational identification among employees, thereby bolstering retention rates – a facet underscored by the significance of the Total Rewards Steward. Simultaneously, the Credible Activist and Strategic Positioner underscore employees' centrality to the organization's prosperity. Strategic amalgamation predominantly hinges upon robust social and organizational capital, which substantiates the organization's enduring competitiveness and viability.

The Total Rewards Steward determines the requisite fervor with which the "War for Talent" ought to be waged, acknowledging that perpetual talent acquisition endeavors may not yield victory for all entities. Strategic congruity encompasses not solely employee retention and recruitment at any expense but also a judicious blend of HR initiatives to confer a competitive edge. Consequently, the emphasis lies not merely on securing top-tier HR personnel but on cultivating a diverse and adept workforce to ensure sustained triumph over the long haul.

The Human Capital Curator and Total Rewards Steward also shoulder the onus of instituting an incentive framework for high-achieving personnel, achieved through the provision of comprehensive compensation packages comprising augmented salaries and supplementary perks like benefits, training avenues, and career advancement prospects. These incentives discernibly impact work quality and employee efficacy, thereby enhancing the organization's developmental capacity. Elevated remuneration further assumes pivotal import in employee retention, accentuating the strategic amalgamation of this function in the organization's enduring evolution (Senn, 2022, 558–566).

The involvement of the Human Capital Curator correlates closely with the roles of Credible Activists and Strategic Positioners within the domain of HR development, particularly concerning their significance for prospective achievements and congruence with organizational objectives. A Human Capital Curator plays a pivotal role in embedding human capital administration as an intrinsic component of the corporate ethos. This fosters a culture accentuating the significance of employee advancement, consequently facilitating enduring value generation for the enterprise. Credible Activists and Strategic Positioners actively champion the recognition of human capital across all echelons of the establishment. They contribute to ensuring that both frontline management and corporate stewardship grasp the significance of HR development and integrate it into strategic deliberations and blueprinting.

The correlation between the Human Capital Curator and Strategic Positioner is designed to ascertain that HR development is harmonized with the organization's enduring aspirations and requisites. Instruments such as the MBV, RBV, SWOT analyses, and environmental scans are employed to guarantee strategic congruence. Human Capital Curators endeavor to continuously adjust the framework of HR development in consonance with evolving organizational strategies to guarantee that employee advancement is synchronized with corporate objectives. To bolster strategic HR development, an enriched comprehension of human capital management is imperative. Human Capital Curators aid in this endeavor by furnishing training and resources to fortify the requisite competencies among Strategic Positioners.

Human Capital Curators facilitate the sustainable development of competitive advantages by ensuring that HR development is meticulously aligned with the company's specific needs and its external environment. Essential to this endeavor is their support for line management in cultivating a thorough understanding of the company's positioning, structures, and processes. A fundamental aspect involves continuously enhancing knowledge of operational processes and ensuring that employees possess the requisite competencies, skills, and abilities to secure a strategic and sustainable competitive edge. They identify gaps in human capital and design competency development programs. This identification enables the organization to transcend historical decisions and path dependencies, exploring novel strategies for effective and strategic HR development.

The Human Capital Curator performs potential analyses to optimize the utilization of human capital and mitigate risks, thereby achieving a strategic and sustainable competitive advantage. They identify talents capable of shaping the company's future and develop strategies for risk mitigation, such as talent pool development. The Human Capital Curator orchestrates learning processes within the organization to ensure that HR needs are fulfilled and conducts analyses on the qualitative and quantitative availability of HR. They develop training programs aimed at enhancing employee skills and preparing the organization for future changes.

The Human Capital Curator advances human capital management by credibly advocating for its enhancement and driving strategic assessment, evaluation, and utilization of HR. They elucidate to employees the criticality of their roles in the company's success and how their skills can be leveraged to achieve strategic objectives. The importance of social capital and organizational capital as determinants in HR utilization and development, as well as their impact on employee satisfaction, retention, and organizational success, is pertinent in this context. They facilitate the cultivation of relationships and networks within the organization to enhance collaboration and knowledge sharing. The Human Capital Curator persuades Business Partners of the significance and development of social and organizational capital for achieving corporate success and gaining a competitive edge. They illustrate the positive effects of investing in social and organizational capital on company performance and long-term success. The Human Capital Curator aids in embedding organizational and social capital into the corporate culture by ensuring that line management and corporate leadership acknowledge and exemplify their importance. They foster a culture of trust, collaboration, and knowledge transfer to bolster success and value creation (Winkler & Fink, 2022, 70–77).

The Human Capital Curator conducts strengths and weaknesses analyses through training and formulates strategies to enhance strategic positioning and targeted human capital management in alignment with corporate strategy to maximize employee potential. This includes augmenting the organization's innovation, agility, and flexibility by ensuring that employees possess the requisite skills and resources to adapt to changes and devise innovative solutions. As a Human Capital Curator, it is imperative to comprehend the company's strategic goals and opportunities. This understanding facilitates the targeted alignment of human capital and its development. Credible Activists and Strategic Positioners apply their knowledge of strategic goals to align HR development accordingly, ensuring it supports corporate objectives.

The implementation of the BSC facilitates credible advocacy for HR development while strategically positioning and orienting it. Credible Activists and Strategic Positioners employ the BSC as a control mechanism to ensure that the development of core competencies aligns with the company's strategic goals. Utilizing the ROI method underscores the strategic importance of HR development and considers strategic positions. By quantifying profitability and enhancing value-added contributions, Credible Activists and Strategic Positioners can substantiate the advocacy for HR development, ensuring efficient utilization of resources.

Assessing a learning organization allows for the evaluation of strategic positioning and credible advocacy for HR development. Credible Activists and Strategic Positioners leverage a systematic comprehension of relationships to refine HR development programs and methodologies, ensuring alignment with strategic objectives. The application of benchmarks secures strategic alignment, positioning, and control. Credible Activists and Strategic Positioners use benchmarks and indicators to adjust strategic development and alignment, guaranteeing that HR development aligns with the evolving needs of the company. The measurement of human capital forms the foundation for strategic development and HR evaluation. Credible Activists and Strategic Positioners utilize ROI methodologies and other evaluative approaches to assess the effectiveness of human capital, ensuring it supports the company's strategic objectives (Loebbert, 2019, 15–34).

The role of the Human Capital Curator is intrinsically linked to the responsibilities of Strategic Positioners in HR development, with the primary objective of ensuring the HR strategy's alignment with the corporate strategy. The Strategic Positioner leverages their expertise to comprehend the company's requirements concerning human capital and subsequently design the HR strategy to meet these needs. In light of the skilled labor shortage, it is imperative that the HR strategy focuses on attracting, developing, and retaining highly qualified professionals to fulfill corporate objectives. Recognizing the importance of human capital for corporate success is as crucial as its integration into strategic planning. This recognition implies that HR development should not be viewed in isolation but as an integral component of the corporate strategy, enhancing the company's agility and innovation capabilities.

The Strategic Positioner understands that human capital is central to improving agility and innovation within the organization. Therefore, they implement measures to develop and utilize human capital, ensuring the company's long-term success, despite the complexities involved in recognizing and evaluating the interrelationships in human capital development. These complexities stem from the challenge of qualitatively assessing human capital within the organizational system. Efforts are directed towards creating instruments and methodologies to better comprehend and evaluate these interconnections. The Strategic Positioner promotes a learning culture within the organization to support the networking and dissemination of knowledge, enabling employees to continuously develop and sustain their human capital, thereby contributing to corporate success. By employing techniques such as network analysis to measure social capital – and, consequently, human capital – within the company, it is possible to identify strengths and weaknesses in human capital and implement targeted improvement measures (Abbenhaus et al., 2023, 98–100).

9.2.3 The Connection between the Total Reward Steward and the Other Roles

The Total Rewards Steward serves as a crucial participant in HR development by overseeing various aspects of compensation and incentive systems, ensuring they align with the organization's strategic objectives while addressing the challenges inherent in the Credible Activist role. The Total Rewards Steward is responsible for developing salary structures and incentive systems designed to secure long-term employee retention. A well-balanced compensation policy combined with attractive incentives enhances employee loyalty. When designing bonuses and incentives, it is essential to ensure fairness by considering both the company's strategic objectives and the individual interests of employees. Transparent communication regarding bonuses and incentives is vital for fostering employee motivation and development. Transparency in the evaluation of salaries and incentives must be clearly articulated, utilizing well-defined criteria. Employees should understand how their compensation is calculated, enabling them to assess it more effectively. Total Rewards Stewards must advocate credibly and supportively for employer branding and the company's image in collaboration with Credible Activists.

The Total Rewards Steward crafts compensation packages that support the company's strategic goals and motivate employees to achieve these objectives. Adequate compensation promotes the retention and development of HR in alignment with corporate aims. Salaries and bonuses function as significant incentives to retain strategically important HR in the long term. The Total Rewards Steward takes these factors into account when designing compensation policies, ensuring they sufficiently reward employees' contributions to the company's value creation. The aim is to establish a balanced mix of salaries and bonuses that accurately reflect employees' contributions to value creation. A fair compensation policy encourages employees' willingness to develop in accordance with the corporate strategy. The Total Rewards Steward endeavors to create a reward system that not only offers financial incentives but also supports the company culture and fosters employee motivation. By aligning wage structures and bonuses with company values and strategic goals, HR management can be strengthened, and customer relationships improved (Hilmer, 2023, 8–13).

The Total Rewards Steward plays a pivotal role in designing a reward system that meets the diverse needs of multiple generations, thereby enhancing the company's attractiveness as an employer. By customizing compensation structures and benefits to the preferences of Generations Y, Z, and Alpha, they significantly contribute to elevating employee engagement. In addition to addressing generational preferences, it is crucial to secure leadership development through financial incentives and career opportunities, leveraging the multiplier effect and succession planning. Individual goals and performances must be integrated to boost motivation and engagement, with financial incentives tied to employees' personal objectives to foster effective employee development.

The objective is to formulate and implement a human development framework that supports employees in skill enhancement and professional advancement with appropriate rewards. This goal is grounded in the incorporation of flexibility and individuality in the reward system, through adaptable compensation structures that enhance the company's appeal as an employer and facilitate employee retention. Such a strategy is instrumental in retaining talented employees, particularly amidst skill shortages and intense job market competition.

Another objective of the Total Rewards Steward is to design a salary system that appropriately acknowledges employees' time and extra effort, incentivizing active participation in human development programs. Additionally, Credible Activists support these initiatives by underscoring the importance of fair compensation for training and performance enhancement, while Strategic Positioners ensure that the salary system aligns with the company's strategic goals and promotes long-term employee retention.

Moreover, Total Rewards Stewards foster an environment conducive to continuous learning and personal development by creating incentive systems that motivate employees to pursue further education and acquire new skills. Credible Activists advocate for a learning culture founded on trust, openness, and continuous improvement, while Strategic Positioners ensure that this culture aligns with the company's long-term goals and enhances competitiveness.

Furthermore, Total Rewards Stewards can establish incentives that motivate employees to adapt to changes and improve their resilience, such as rewarding engagement in training programs or the acquisition of new skills. Credible Activists highlight the significance of adaptability and resilience in a dynamic work environment and promote initiatives that enhance these capabilities, while Strategic Positioners ensure that employees' adaptability is consistent with the organization's strategic objectives.

Additionally, Total Rewards Stewards are pivotal in connecting HR development with career progression by creating incentive structures that reward direct promotions and professional growth. Credible Activists advocate for a transparent and equitable evaluation of competencies and performance to facilitate effective career advancement, whereas Strategic Positioners ensure that individual HR development and career progression align with the company's strategic goals and support long-term talent retention (Fließ, Dyck & Volkers, 2024, 332–339).

The Total Rewards Steward and the Strategic Positioner both play critical roles in HR development, particularly in linking wage systems and bonus design to a company's innovation capability, competitiveness, and agility. The Total Rewards Steward designs wage systems and bonuses to foster the company's innovation capability. By establishing an appropriate reward structure for innovative performance, employees are incentivized to generate and implement new ideas, thereby enhancing the company's competitiveness and agility. The Strategic Positioner integrates both external market data and internal work quality, along with the strategic positioning of the company, when determining market-based wages. Balanced compensation, in terms of quality and strategic alignment, attracts and retains talent, thereby further enhancing the company's competitiveness. The Total Rewards Steward evaluates and adjusts wage structures to ensure alignment with the company's strategy, goals, and culture. Aligning compensation with the company's overarching goals and culture supports coherent and targeted HR development, thereby strengthening the company's competitiveness.

Both the Total Rewards Steward and the Strategic Positioner incorporate employees' goal achievement in wage and bonus design. By clearly defining performance goals and linking them with appropriate rewards, a performance-oriented culture is promoted, thus enhancing the company's competitiveness. The Total Rewards Steward and the Strategic Positioner also recognize the importance of flexible work time models, such as the four-day workweek, for employee retention. However, this model must be integrated with the wage and bonus system to ensure that employee productivity and performance are not compromised. Adequate compensation and incentives help maintain employee motivation and the company's competitiveness (Senn, 2022, 558–566).

9.3 The Connection between the Role of the Credible Activist and the Strategic Positioner

The roles of Credible Activists and Strategic Positioners are crucial for advancing HR development within organizations. They facilitate the management of challenges and changes in complex business environments by acting as intermediaries across various levels of line management. This intermediary function not only enhances operational efficiency but also aligns HR development initiatives with strategic goals. Through the synergy between Credible Activists and Strategic Positioners, HR development is systematically and synchronously coordinated across different corporate levels.

Credible Activists and Strategic Positioners comprehend the significance of HR development in dynamic and challenging business contexts. They possess the ability to persuasively communicate the necessity of HR development investments for sustained business success. With their strategic insight and operational expertise, Credible Activists and Strategic Positioners ensure that HR development contributes tangibly to value creation. They understand the implications of organizational changes on required competencies and drive the adaptation of HR development measures accordingly. They identify the need for modifications in HR development processes and advocate for their advancement. Their role is pivotal in recognizing and implementing effective new approaches and methodologies.

Credible Activists and Strategic Positioners effectively engage line management, both as implementers of HR development measures and as key sources of information regarding development needs within the organization. They act as catalysts for new development initiatives and ensure that line management is actively involved in the HR development process. These roles contribute to embedding HR development and human capital advancement into the company's vision, mission, and culture. By demonstrating the ROI and value-added contributions, they ensure that HR development is strategically aligned.

These roles underscore the necessity for enhanced collaboration between Business Partners and line management. They facilitate the exchange of best practices and enable a comprehensive perspective on HR development across diverse domains. Credible Activists and Strategic Positioners underscore the long-term and strategic significance of HR development, particularly during periods of skill shortages. They illustrate that investments in employee development yield long-term corporate success. They advocate for a holistic approach to HR development, which incorporates a nuanced understanding of the unique needs and challenges within specific areas. This approach enhances credibility and amplifies the value-added contribution of HR development within the organization.

Credible Activists and Strategic Positioners serve as intermediaries between different management levels by communicating the importance of long-term HR development strategies in relation to short- and medium-term corporate objectives. They facilitate the alignment of perspectives and timeframes by demonstrating how investments in employee development can lead to sustained corporate success. Through their persuasive and communicative abilities, Credible Activists and Strategic Positioners address the diverse needs and viewpoints at various management levels, thereby emphasizing the role of HR development in augmenting the company's value creation. They customize their arguments to align with the goals and viewpoints of each management level to secure support and engagement (Huf, 2022, 160–162).

These individuals prioritize demonstrating the efficacy of HR development initiatives to fortify their credibility. Employing evidence-based methodologies and program evaluations ensures optimal resource utilization and goal attainment. Leveraging emotional narratives and individual success anecdotes aids in sensitizing line management to the effectiveness of HR development initiatives, fostering a personal connection and bolstering engagement.

Furthermore, Credible Activists and Strategic Positioners stress the collaborative responsibility shared by Business Partners and line management concerning HR development. They advocate for a culture of collaboration to underscore HR development as a company-wide imperative. Facilitating feedback loops and evaluation mechanisms supports continual enhancement and alignment of HR development programs with evolving organizational needs. Regular assessment guarantees the effectiveness of HR development strategies and their contribution to overarching corporate development objectives.

9.3 The Connection between the Role of the Credible Activist and the Strategic Positioner

Credible Activists serve as internal advocates and catalysts for change, disseminating the significance of HR development across hierarchical tiers and driving organizational transformations. Strategic Positioners possess a profound understanding of corporate strategic objectives, aligning HR development initiatives accordingly to bolster goal attainment. Through synergistic collaboration, Credible Activists and Strategic Positioners ensure uniformity in HR development approaches across all levels, facilitating coordinated and aligned measures.

Through the adept facilitation of HR development by Credible Activists and Strategic Positioners, line managers and executives are empowered to foster the progression of their teams and synchronize them with the strategic objectives of the organization. This empowerment equips them with lucid directives and requisite resources to proficiently nurture their personnel and augment their efficacy, thereby enhancing the overall performance metrics of the enterprise.

The collaborative efforts of Credible Activists and Strategic Positioners ensure the uniformity of HR development across all echelons of the organization and its strategic congruence. This collaborative synergy facilitates continual scrutiny and acknowledgment of the evolving essential proficiencies, ensuring that HR development remains attuned to the present and future exigencies of the enterprise.

Credible Activists and Strategic Positioners assume pivotal roles in assimilating HR development within the organizational ethos and strategic positioning. By accentuating the significance of HR development and ensuring its alignment with the strategic imperatives of the enterprise, they substantiate its entrenched status within the corporate strategy, portraying it as an indispensable element of business success (Dell & Dell, 2024, 68–74).

9.3.1 The Coordination Function of the Paradox Navigator

In the capacity of Paradox Navigators, the primary duty of Business Partners remains the integration and coordination of challenges stemming from the other eight roles. A pivotal aspect involves comprehending and analyzing company-specific contexts to systematically align HR development aspects. This role of Business Partnering becomes notably intricate when accounting for diverse temporal dimensions and their resultant implications.

Business Partners, acting as Paradox Navigators, are compelled to closely collaborate with counterparts from other roles to grasp developments, hurdles, and challenges, aiming to identify strategies for systematic enhancement. In this endeavor, they must not only accommodate the desires and expectations of the other eight roles but also deliberate on the efficient utilization of supplementary resources to ensure optimal deployment, fostering substantial value creation and systematic improvement. Efficient resource allocation by Business Partners hinges upon close collaboration and coordination with line management and corporate leadership. A formidable task for them lies in continually stressing the relevance and necessity of HR development within the role of Paradox Navigators, ultimately ingraining it deeply into corporate strategy, planning, and the consciousness of corporate leadership and line management.

The coordinating function for Business Partners as Paradox Navigators primarily materializes through collaboration, information acquisition, and processing with line management, corporate leadership, and fellow Business Partners. In practice, they shoulder the responsibility of mediating and coordinating between various interests, perspectives, and goals, both in substance and temporality. A fundamental prerequisite is that Business Partners, in their capacity as Paradox Navigators, not only possess extensive operational and strategic knowledge but also exhibit the ability to conduct goal-oriented and efficient analyses, deriving appropriate conclusions from them.

A primary necessity entails that Business Partners, in their capacity as Paradox Navigators, consistently evaluate the requisite competency advancements needed to execute a methodical, objective-driven, and value-optimized analysis, and derive implications from it. In addition to self-assessment, the competency levels within other roles of Business Partners also hold substantial importance, as they undertake numerous pivotal information and analytical tasks for the Paradox Navigator, who must rely on them. Analyses carried out by fellow Business Partners serve as indispensable decision-making frameworks for Paradox Navigators.

Considering that Paradox Navigators base their decisions on analyses of corporate management and line management or contribute to the strategic direction of the company, it becomes imperative for line management and corporate leadership to incorporate and contemplate aspects of HR management, particularly HR development. This is especially pertinent in firms where line management and corporate leadership possess acute awareness regarding the significance of HR development and acknowledge its noteworthy and strategic value contribution.

In the coordinating capacity of the Paradox Navigator, it is imperative to systematically consider HR development, wherein the value contribution and interrelations of HR development, HR strategy, and corporate strategy are effectively communicated, encompassing various viewpoints, interests, and temporal perspectives. It is crucial for Business Partners in their role as Paradox Navigators to underscore the impact on HR and their close integration with corporate strategy.

Business Partners acting as Paradox Navigators must articulate that HR development, as the foremost priority, aims to ensure the provisioning of appropriate HR resources at the precise time and location while maximizing their value contribution. They must recognize their significant contribution to the company's competitiveness through the strategic dimension of their role, exerting substantial influence on the company's trajectory. This holds particularly true in an evolving work milieu characterized by rapid changes in competency requirements, influencing factors, and dynamics, where human capital and thus HR development progressively emerge as strategic competitive assets. This directly correlates with the mounting significance of the nexus between HR strategy, particularly HR development, and corporate strategy.

10   Conclusion

The work environment has experienced substantial transformations over recent decades due to the advent of digitization. This phenomenon has precipitated a paradigmatic shift wherein conventional work methodologies are supplanted by automated processes and technological integration. Consequently, there is a heightened demand for adept professionals in domains such as information technology, data analysis, and AI. Concurrently, globalization has engendered intensified competition among enterprises worldwide for acquiring top-tier talents. These alterations have exacerbated the scarcity of proficient workers, as many organizations grapple with the challenge of filling vacant positions with suitably qualified candidates. This issue is compounded by a diminishing labor force potential, resulting in a sustained decline in the available workforce. Moreover, the availability of highly skilled professionals in numerous vocations often fails to align with the burgeoning demand and, in some instances, even diverges from it.

Given these circumstances, HR development emerges as a pivotal strategic tool for enterprises. Through targeted training initiatives, organizations can ensure that their workforce possesses the requisite skills and competencies to meet the exigencies of the evolving labor landscape. This facilitates the attainment of a competitive edge, as companies can boast a roster of adept and motivated personnel capable of devising innovative solutions and swiftly acclimatizing to new work dynamics. HR development not only enhances the immediate performance of employees but also fosters long-term value generation for the company. By continually nurturing their workforce, enterprises can guarantee access to the expertise necessary for accomplishing enduring strategic objectives. Furthermore, HR development assumes paramount importance as a competitive determinant, with companies that prioritize employee development enjoying a sustainable edge over their counterparts who neglect such initiatives (Hübschen, 2020, 326–335).

Ulrich's rationale underscores the pivotal role of harmonizing HR development with the exigencies of clientele and market dynamics. This underscores the imperative for employee enrichment to intricately correlate with the strategic imperatives of the enterprise. Employees are mandated to apprehend customer requisites and efficaciously furnish goods and services commensurate with such exigencies. By intimately intertwining HR development with customer and market centricity, enterprises can ascertain that their workforce harbors the requisite proficiencies and aptitudes conducive to enduring success. The evolution within the labor market and technological advancements concurrently present both prospects and challenges to HR development. On one facet, novel avenues emerge for pioneering pedagogical modalities and technologies, empowering enterprises to nurture their workforce with heightened efficacy. Conversely, these shifts necessitate a perpetual recalibration of HR developmental frameworks to ensure resonance with the evolving exigencies of the labor landscape.

Enterprises and their Business Partners are enjoined to cultivate and augment strategic HR developmental acumen to thrive. This entails a profound comprehension of extant and prospective labor market prerequisites, coupled with adeptness in conceiving and executing efficacious developmental initiatives. Through investment in employee advancement and nurturing an ethos of perpetual learning, enterprises and their Business Partners can fortify their arsenal with the requisite proficiencies and capabilities indispensable for enduring prosperity. HR development metamorphoses into a pivotal competency for sustaining enterprises' competitiveness. Enterprises that dedicate resources towards their workforce's enrichment can cultivate a sustainable competitive edge by nurturing a cadre of adept and motivated employees proficient in innovating and swiftly acclimatizing to novel operational paradigms.

The strategic significance of Business Partners within HR development resides in their capacity to establish a nexus between corporate strategy and HR strategy, thereby augmenting value optimization. Business Partners, equipped with suitable competencies in strategic HR development, assume a pivotal role in discerning, fostering, and retaining appropriate talents conducive to realizing the medium- and long-range objectives of the enterprise. Business Partners necessitate adeptness in comprehending the corporate strategy and transmuting it into a pertinent HR strategy, predicated upon a profound grasp of business aims, market dynamics, and labor market imperatives. By assimilating the corporate strategy and synchronizing the HR strategy accordingly, Business Partners contribute to the company's market sustainability. Furthermore, Business Partners must demonstrate proficiency in devising and executing an efficacious HR development strategy, predicated upon a comprehensive scrutiny of extant employee proficiencies and a prognostication of the company's prospective requisites. Grounded on this scrutiny, Business Partners must formulate developmental schemes that enable employees to acquire requisite proficiencies and abilities to meet forthcoming company exigencies. Via targeted HR development interventions, Business Partners can foster the maximization of the company's value proposition, ensuring that employees possess pertinent proficiencies and abilities in a timely manner to engender innovative solutions, operate effectively, and heighten customer contentment. This, in turn, not only amplifies the company's productivity and profitability but also fortifies its competitive stance in the market. Business Partners necessitate marked adaptability and nimbleness to promptly align themselves and HR development initiatives with shifting market dynamics, entailing perpetual vigilance of labor market and sales trends, coupled with regular reassessment and refinement of HR development schemes. By remaining pliant and responsive,

Business Partners can guarantee that the company is endowed with the appropriate talents requisite for sustained success.

In summation, Business Partners assume an indispensable role in optimizing the strategic import of HR development by identifying, nurturing, and retaining suitable talents to fulfill the company's long-term aspirations. By forging connections between corporate strategy, HR strategy, and HR development strategy, Business Partners contribute to the enhancement of value creation and fortification of the company's competitive standing in the marketplace, as delineated in Ulrich's model.

References

Abbenhaus, A.-C., Enzler, S., Fackler-Stamm, R., Gnann, F., Kho, N. & Luger, M. (2023). Integrale Betrachtung agiler Innovationsmethoden für den Kompetenzaufbau (98–118). In: Kauffeld, S. & Rothenbusch, S. (2023). Kompetenzen von Mitarbeitenden in der digitalisierten Arbeitswelt. Chancen und Risiken für kleine und mittlere Unternehmen. Berlin: Springer Gabler.

Armutat, S. (2021). Performance-orientierte Personalentwicklung (461–480). In: Haag, P. (2021). KMU- und Start-up-Management. Strategische Aspekte, operative Umsetzung und Best-Practice. Wiesbaden: Springer-Gabler.

Assies, K. S., Thiel, S. & Stulle, K. P. (2021). Innovative Personalentwicklung als Treiber und Unterstützer einer agilen Unternehmensentwicklung – Eine empirische Untersuchung innerhalb einer HR-Stichprobe (189–206). In: Karlshaus, A. & Wolf, A. (2021). Agiles Human Resources: Kundenzentriertes Denken und Handeln im Personalbereich. Wiesbaden: Springer Gabler.

Barbian, D. & Knabenbauer, K. (2023). Fachkräftemangel innovativ begegnen – mit Lösungen aus dem nachhaltigen Personalmanagement (409–427). In: Knappertsbusch, I. & Wisskirchen, G. (2023). Die Zukunft der Arbeit. New Work mit Flexibilität und Rechtssicherheit gestalten. Wiesbaden: Springer Gabler.

Bauer, W., Dworschak, B. & Zaiser, H. (2023). Weiterbildung und Kompetenzentwicklung für die Industrie 4.0 in KMU (125–148). In: Bauernhansl, T. (2023). Handbuch Industrie 4.0. Berlin: Springer Gabler.

Becker, F. G. & Bader, V. (2019). Transfersteuerung in der Personalentwicklung: Sine-qua-non der betrieblichen Wertschöpfung (431–450). In: Ulrich, P. & Baltzer, B. (2019). Wertschöpfung in der Betriebswirtschaftslehre. Wiesbaden: Springer Gabler.

Blaha, C. (2021). Bildungs-Controlling: Wir müssen Personalentwicklung messen, um sie weiterentwickeln zu können (65–84). In: Eschenbach, R., Baumüller, J. & Siller, H. (2021). Funktions-Controlling. Praxishandbuch für Unternehmen, Non-Profit-Organisationen und die öffentliche Verwaltung. Wiesbaden: Springer Gabler.

von Borcke, Y. P. & Plohr, N. (2024). Metaskills. Menschliche Kompetenzen für das Zeitalter der künstlichen Intelligenz. Wiesbaden: Springer Gabler.

Dell, M. & Dell, R. (2024). Unternehmenskultur als Motor für Innovation (67–90). In: Herget, J. & Strobl, H. (2023). Unternehmenskultur in der Praxis. Grundlagen – Methoden – Best Practices. Wiesbaden: Springer Gabler.

Dohmen, D. (2023). Berufliche Entwicklungserwartungen älterer Führungskräfte im Transformationsprozess eines Unternehmens. Eine empirische Untersuchung innerhalb der Finanzwirtschaft. Wiesbaden: Springer Gabler.

Einrahmhof-Florian, H. (2022). Fit für die jungen Generationen am Arbeitsplatz. Wie ticken sie und was macht sie aus. Wiesbaden: Springer Gabler.

Fallgatter, M. J. (2020). Management und Managementerfolg. Analyse, Prognose und Gestaltung von Wertschöpfung. Wiesbaden: Springer Gabler.

Fließ, S., Dyck, S. & Volkers, M. (2024). Management von Dienstleistungsprozessen: Service Co-Creation – Service Experience – Service Value. Wiesbaden: Springer Gabler.

Foelsing, J. & Schmitz, A. (2021). New Work braucht New Learning. Eine Perspektivreise durch die Transformation unserer Organisations- und Lernwelten. Wiesbaden: Springer Gabler.

References

Friedrich-Haßauer, J. (2023). Effizienz und Effektivität von Blended-Learning-Lernverfahren in der beruflichen Weiterbildung. Eine Analyse aus der Sicht der Lernenden. Wiesbaden: Springer Gabler.

Fritz, S. & Schneider, H. J. (2016). Total Compensation (331–346). In: Klaus, H. & Schneider, H. J. (2016). Personalperspektiven. Human Resource Management und Führung im ständigen Wandel. Wiesbaden: Springer Gabler.

Frodl, A. (2023). Personalmanagement im Gesundheitswesen: Instrumente wertschätzender Personalführung. Wiesbaden: Springer Gabler.

Gabathuler, J. & Bajus, S. (2021). Lern- und Lehrpsychologie, Bedeutung für die betriebliche Weiterbildung und Auswirkungen auf eine moderne betriebliche Bildung/Personalentwicklung (159–186). In: Blum, U., Gabathuler, J. & Bajus, S. (2021). Weiterbildungsmanagement in der Praxis: Psychologie des Lernens. Berlin: Springer Gabler.

Geissler, H.-G. (2023). Leadership und seine Erfolgsfaktoren in der digitalen Transformation (171–182). In: Kastner, C., Jacob, C., Hesmer, D. & Plugmann, P. (2023). Innovative Unternehmensführung. Erprobte Strategien, Techniken und Booster, die Unternehmen und Start-ups zukunftsfähig machen. Wiesbaden: Springer Gabler.

Germann, M. (2023). Wenn die Generation Z die Spielregeln neu definiert (65–84). In: Geramanis, O., Hutmacher, S. & Walser, L. (2023). Organisationale Machtbeziehungen im Wandel. Führung zwischen Zustimmung und Zwang. Wiesbaden: Springer Gabler.

Groß, M. (2023). Künstliche Intelligenz im Personalmanagement – Goldrausch im Spannungsfeld optimistischer Softwareanbieter und skeptischer Personalmanager (203–240). In: Vieweg, S. H. (2023). KI für das Gute: Künstliche Intelligenz und Ethik. Cham: Springer Gabler.

Grundei, J. (2024). Organization Design. Systematische Gestaltung der Unternehmensorganisation. Wiesbaden: Springer Gabler.

Guggenberger, A. (2021). Strategische und kompetenz-orientierte Personalentwicklung (309–318). In: Rosenberger, B. (2021). Modernes Personalmanagement Strategisch – operativ – systemisch. Wiesbaden: Springer Gabler.

Halene, V. (2022). Entlohnung gestalten (515–526). In: Kaudela-Baum, S., Meldau, S. & Brasser, M. (2022). Leadership und People Management: Führung und Kollaboration in Zeiten der Digitalisierung und Transformation. Wiesbaden: Springer Gabler.

Häring, K., Grandpierre, A. & Mynarek, F. (2023). Entwicklung von Selbstorganisationskompetenzen in der Industrie 4.0. (17–36). In: Kauffeld, S. & Rothenbusch, S. (2023). Kompetenzen von Mitarbeitenden in der digitalisierten Arbeitswelt. Chancen und Risiken für kleine und mittlere Unternehmen. Berlin: Springer Gabler.

Helmold, M. (2022). Leadership. Agile, virtuelle und globale Führungskonzepte in Zeiten von neuen Megatrends. Wiesbaden: Springer Gabler.

Helmold, M. (2023). Wettbewerbsvorteile entlang der Supply Chain sichern. Best-Practice-Beispiele in Beschaffung, Produktion, Marketing und anderen Funktionen der betriebswirtschaftlichen Wertschöpfungskette. Wiesbaden: Springer Gabler.

Helmold, M. (2024). Erfolgreiche Transformation zum digitalen Champion. Wettbewerbsvorteile durch Digitalisierung und Künstliche Intelligenz. Wiesbaden: Springer Gabler.

Helmold, M., Dathe, T. & Dathe, I. (2022). Entrepreneurship in Zeiten der Globalisierung und Digitalisierung. Für Startup-Gründer und solche, die es werden wollen. Wiesbaden: Springer Gabler.

Hendrischke, D. (2024). Vom Wandel des Lernens zur Implementierung von E-Knowledge. Eine Unternehmensperspektive (325–354). In: Kohne, A. (2024). Moderne Unternehmensführung. Einordnung und Umsetzungskonzepte von Managementtrends. Wiesbaden: Springer Gabler.

Hermann, K. & Bittner-Fesseler, A. (2024). Kennzahlen, strategische Entscheidungen und ihre Kommunikation und deren Einfluss auf soziale Nachhaltigkeit. Aktuelle Kennzahlen für soziale Nachhaltigkeit im Change anhand eines Praxisbeispiels (99–118). In: Hiller, M., Krüger, K., Riedel, T., Schempf, T., Steinhübel, V. & Zeitnitz, O. (2024). Finance-Perspektiven im Wandel. Digital, nachhaltig, resilient. Wiesbaden: Springer Gabler.

Hillebrecht, S. (2021). Perspektivenorientierte Personalwirtschaft. Einführung in das Personalmanagement aus Arbeitnehmer- und Arbeitgebersicht. Wiesbaden: Springer Gabler.

Hilmer, H. (2023). Willenskraft und Gewohnheiten im Personal Performance Management. So bleiben Sie auf Ihre Ziele fokussiert. Berlin: Springer Gabler.

Holtbrügge, D. (2022). Personalmanagement. Berlin: Springer Gabler.

Holtmeier, S. & Mertin, I. (2023). 360° Feedback-Varianten für faire Potenzialkonferenzen und ein effektives (Selbst-) Coaching (239–262). In: Stulle, K. P. & Justenhoven, R. T. (2023). Personalauswahl 4.0. KI, Machine Learning, Gamification und andere Innovationen in der Praxis. Wiesbaden: Springer Gabler.

Hübler, M. (2020). Die Führungskraft als Mediator. Mit mediativen Kompetenzen souverän führen und Veränderungen begleiten. Wiesbaden: Springer Gabler.

Hübschen, C. (2020). New Work: Digitale, agile neue Welt – Eine kleine Auswahl von Personalentwicklungsinstrumenten in einer Zeit, in der Geschwindigkeit und Wandel den Ton angeben (325-347). In: Wörwag, S. & Cloots, A. (2020). Arbeitskulturen im Wandel: Der Mensch in der New Work Culture. Wiesbaden: Springer Gabler.

Huf, S. (2022). Personalmanagement. Wiesbaden: Springer Gabler.

Hungenberg, H. & Wulf, T. (2021). Grundlagen der Unternehmensführung. Wiesbaden: Springer Gabler.

Ilic, P. (2024). Personalentwicklung und Unternehmenskultur (273–288). In: Herget, J. & Strobl, H. (2024). Unternehmenskultur in der Praxis Grundlagen – Methoden – Best Practices. Wiesbaden: Springer Gabler.

Jacob, C. (2023). Wie Ihnen agile Unternehmensführung und digitale Transformation helfen, eine zukunftssichere Organisationsplattform aufzubauen (229–238). In: von Hattburg, A. T. & de Grancy, C.-D. (2023). Agenda HR – Digitalisierung, Arbeit 4.0, New Leadership. Was Personalverantwortliche und Management jetzt nicht verpassen sollten. Wiesbaden: Springer Gabler.

Jensen, C. (2022). Personalmanagement in Non-Profit-Organisationen. Besonderheiten, Rahmenbedingungen und Herausforderungen. Wiesbaden: Springer Gabler.

Johannnsen, A. & Kant, D. (2022). IT-Governance-, Risiko- und Compliance-Management (IT-GRC) – Ein kompetenzorientierter Ansatz für KMU (275–294). In: Weber, K. & Reinheimer, S. (2022). Faktor Mensch. Wiesbaden: Springer Gabler.

Kaehler, B. (2023). Führen als Beruf. Andere erfolgreich machen. Berlin: Springer Gabler.

Karl, A. M. (2023). Future Skills, Future Leaders – Welche Zukunftskompetenzen Führungskräfte heute brauchen (331–347). In: Kastner, C., Jacob, C., Hesmer, D. & Plugmann, P. (2023). Innovative Unternehmensführung. Erprobte Strategien, Techniken und Booster, die Unternehmen und Start-ups zukunftsfähig machen. Wiesbaden: Springer Gabler.

Kaune, A., Glaubke, N. & Hempel, T. (2021). Change Management und Agilität. Aktuelle Herausforderungen in der VUCA-Welt. Wiesbaden: Springer Gabler.

Klaffke, M. (2022). Millenials und Generation Z – Charakteristika der nachrückenden Beschäftigten-Generationen (81–134). In: Klaffke, M. (2022). Generationen-Management. Konzepte, Instrumente, Good-Practice-Ansätze. Wiesbaden: Springer Gabler.

Kobi, M. (2021). Personal-Controlling: Eine verkannte Controlling-Dimension ganzheitlich angehen (365–388). In: Eschenbach, R., Baumüller, J. & Siller, H. (2021). Funktions-Controlling: Praxishandbuch für Unternehmen, Non-Profit-Organisationen und die öffentliche Verwaltung. Wiesbaden: Springer Gabler.

Kodalle, T. & Metz, M. (2022). Das Konzept Gamification als spielerisches Lernelement. (65–78). In: Becker, W. & Metz. M. (2022). Digitale Lernwelten – Serious Games und Gamification: Didaktik, Anwendungen und Erfahrungen in der Beruflichen Bildung. Wiesbaden: Springer Gabler.

Kolb, M., Burkart, B., & Zundel, F. (2010). Personalmanagement. Grundlagen und Praxis des Human Resources Managements. Wiesbaden: Springer Gabler.

Kollmann, T. (2022). Digital Entrepreneurship. Grundlagen der Unternehmensgründung in der Digitalen Wirtschaft. Wiesbaden: Springer Gabler.

Korn, O., Schulz, A. S. & Hagley, B. J. (2022). Gamification: Grundlagen, Methoden und Anwendungsbeispiele (43–64). In: Becker, W. & Metz. M. (2022). Digitale Lernwelten – Serious Games und Gamification: Didaktik, Anwendungen und Erfahrungen in der Beruflichen Bildung. Wiesbaden: Springer Gabler.

Kruse, C., Mecke, I. & Räss, A. (2024). Risikomanagement, wertschätzende Führung und digitales Recruiting. Anders wagen, anders gewinnen. Wiesbaden: Springer Gabler.

Lauer, T. (2019). Change Management. Grundlagen und Erfolgsfaktoren. Berlin: Springer Gabler.
Lay, C. & Niebling, C. (2023). Fachkräftemangel – Mythos oder Realität? (23–30). In: Knappertsbusch, I. & Wisskirchen, G. (2023). Die Zukunft der Arbeit. New Work mit Flexibilität und Rechtssicherheit gestalten. Wiesbaden: Springer Gabler.
Lebrenz, C. (2020). Strategie und Personalmanagement: Konzepte und Instrumente zur Umsetzung im Unternehmen. Wiesbaden: Springer Gabler.
Loebbert, M. (2019). Coaching in der Personal- und Organisationsentwicklung. Für selbstbestimmtere Mitarbeitende. Wiesbaden: Springer Gabler.
Lohmüller, E. K. & Greiff, K. (2022). Generationensensible Personal- und Karriereentwicklung – Ansätze und Instrumente für eine erfolgreiche Umsetzung in Unternehmen (225–242). In: Klaffke, M. (2022). Generationen-Management. Konzepte, Instrumente, Good-Practice-Ansätze. Wiesbaden: Springer Gabler.
Ludwig, A. (2024). Organisationales Lernen und Digitalisierung. Lernen von und in Organisationen unter dem Einfluss der digitalen Transformation. Wiesbaden: Springer Gabler.
Macharzina, K. & Wolf, J. (2023). Unternehmensführung. Das internationale Managementwissen. Konzepte – Methoden – Praxis. Wiesbaden: Springer Gabler.
Michl, J. (2024). Personalinformationssysteme in der Personalentwicklung und im Talent-Management. Eine empirische Untersuchung zum strategischen Einsatz und zur Rolle von Stakeholder*innen. Wiesbaden: Springer Gabler.
Nauendorf, W. (2023). Innovationskompetenz und Leadership. Eine Einführung in Mechanismen und Rahmenbedingungen. Wiesbaden: Springer Gabler.
Niehaus, M., Mocan, M. & Hansen, K. (2024). VUCA and Its Impact on Business Organizations (3–14). In: Prostean, G. I., Lavios, J. J., Brancu, L. & Sahin, F. (2024). Management, Innovation and Entrepreneurship in Challenging Global Times. Proceedings of the 16th International Symposium in Management (SIM 2021). Cham: Springer Gabler.
Nowoczin, J. (2023). "Wie statt Was" – Mit Methodenkompetenz Aufgaben effizient und erfolgreich managen. Berlin: Springer Gabler.
Obst, T. (2023). Historische Wende am Arbeitsmarkt in Deutschland – Wie der demografische Wandel das Wachstum bremst (13-22). In: Knappertsbusch, I. & Wisskirchen, G. (2023). Die Zukunft der Arbeit. New Work mit Flexibilität und Rechtssicherheit gestalten. Wiesbaden: Springer Gabler.
Peterke, J. (2021). Personalentwicklung als Managementfunktion: Praktische Grundlagen und zukunftsfähige Konzepte. Wiesbaden: Springer Gabler.
Rein, A. (2023). Agiler Organisationsaufbau. Die Entwicklung einer handlungsfähigen Organisation. Berlin: Springer Gabler.
Reinhardt, K. (2020). Digitale Transformation der Organisation. Grundlagen, Praktiken, und Praxisbeispiele der digitalen Unternehmensentwicklung. Wiesbaden: Springer Gabler.
Rittershaus, A. (2024). Führungspraxis für Ingenieure und IT-Experten. Der Werkzeugkasten für effektive Führungskräfte in der IT der Zukunft. Wiesbaden: Springer Gabler.
Romeike, F. & Hager, P. (2020). Erfolgsfaktor Risiko-Management 4.0: Methoden, Beispiele, Checklisten. Praxishandbuch für Industrie und Handel. Wiesbaden: Springer Gabler.
Rump, J., Kreis, L.-M., Schmoll, R. (2017). Personal strategisch planen: Bestandsaufnahme und Handlungsansätze (233–262). In: Rump, J. & Eilers, S. (2017). Auf dem Weg zur Arbeit 4.0. Innovationen in HR. Berlin: Springer Gabler.
Sagradov, O. & Müller, D. (2022). Verbesserung der Prognosequalität im Personalcontrolling. Praktisches Beispiel der Anwendung von multiplen linearen Regressionsmodellen, Regressionsbäumen und Extreme Gradient Boosting zur Vorhersage der krankheitsbedingten Abwesenheit (61–96). In: Kümpel, T., Schlenkrich, K. & Heupel, T. (2022). Controlling & Innovation 2022. Gesundheitswesen. Wiesbaden: Springer Gabler.
Sanabria, F. (2024). Neue Technologien und neue Kundenerfahrungen treiben Transformationen im privaten und öffentlichen Sektor voran. (351–364). In: Wollmann, P. & Püringer, R. (2024). Die Transformation von Organisationen im öffentlichen und privaten Sektor. Umsetzung eines nachhaltigen Zwecks, von einer Organisation auf der Reise und von Konnektivität für Resilienz. Cham: Springer Gabler.
Sander, E., Kröber, C., Anhalt, F. & Dick, M. (2023). Einfluss und Ohnmacht der Personalentwicklung in kleinen und mittleren Unternehmen (KMU). Impulse aus einer organisations-

ethnografischen Studie (251–268). In: Geramanis, O., Hutmacher, S. & Walser, L. (2023). Organisationale Machtbeziehungen im Wandel. Führung zwischen Zustimmung und Zwang. Wiesbaden: Springer Gabler.

Sass, E. (2023). Managementkompetenzen der Gegenwart und Zukunft. Welche Skills brauchen Führungskräfte? Wiesbaden: Springer Gabler.

Schermuly, C. C. & Graßmann, C. (2023). Erfolgreicher Einsatz von Coaching in der Führungskräfteentwicklung (203–216). In: Felfe, J. & van Dick, R. (2023). Handbuch Mitarbeiterführung. Wirtschaftspsychologisches Praxiswissen für Fach- und Führungskräfte. Berlin: Springer Gabler.

Schirrmacher, U. (2023). Kompetenzorientierte Personalentwicklung. Wie Sie in 9 Schritten ein individuelles Lernprogramm erstellen. Wiesbaden: Springer Gabler.

Schreyögg, G. & Geiger, D. (2024). Organisation. Grundlagen moderner Organisationsgestaltung. Mit Fallstudien. Wiesbaden: Springer Gabler.

Schreyögg, G. & Koch, J. (2020). Management. Grundlagen der Unternehmensführung. Wiesbaden: Springer Gabler.

Schreyögg, G. & Koch, J. (2023). Grundlagen des Managements: Basiswissen für Studium und Praxis. Wiesbaden: Springer Gabler.

Schüll, A. (2020). Das Triade-Konzept der Personalentwicklung. Instrumente und Maßnahmen zu einer ganzheitlichen Personalentwicklung. Wiesbaden: Springer Gabler.

Schwarz, D. (2010). Strategische Personalplanung und Humankapitalbewertung. Simulationen anhand der Cottbuser Formel. Wiesbaden: Springer Gabler.

Schwengber, J. G. (2024). Organizational Learning as Relational Governance. Cham. Springer Gabler.

Senn, P. (2022). Personal entwickeln. Individualisierung – Prozessorientierung – Kompetenznutzung (557–568). In: Kaudela-Baum, S., Meldau, S. & Brasser, M. (2022). Leadership und People Management. Führung und Kollaboration in Zeiten der Digitalisierung und Transformation. Wiesbaden: Springer Gabler.

Stettes, O. (2023). Wenn digitaler auf demografischen Wandel trifft – Welche Chancen und Risiken birgt die digitale Transformation bei einer schrumpfenden und alternden Erwerbsbevölkerung (31–37). In: Knappertsbusch, I. & Wisskirchen, G. (2023). Die Zukunft der Arbeit. New Work mit Flexibilität und Rechtssicherheit gestalten. Wiesbaden: Springer Gabler.

Stulle, K. P. & Thiel, S. (2023). Digitalisierung der Eignungsdiagnostik für Personalauswahl und Potenzialeinschätzung als Grundlage für anschließende Personalentwicklung (239–264). In: Schulte, S. & Hiltmann, M. (2023). Eignungsdiagnostische Interviews: Standards der professionellen Interviewführung. Wiesbaden: Springer Gabler.

Thommen, J-P., Achleitner, A.-K., Gilbert, D. U., Hachmeister, D., Jarchow, S. & Kaiser, G. (2023). Allgemeine Betriebswirtschaftslehre. Umfassende Einführung aus managementorientierter Sicht. Wiesbaden: Springer Gabler.

Tolimir, E.-M. (2022). Lebenszyklusorientierte Karriereplanung. Ein Weg für Frauen in Führungspositionen. Wiesbaden: Springer Gabler.

Treier, M. (2019). Wirtschaftspsychologische Grundlagen für Personalmanagement. Berlin: Springer Gabler.

Troger, H. (2018). Die Führungskraft als Personalmanager. Eine neue Rollenverteilung zwischen Führungskräften und HR-Management. Wiesbaden: Springer Gabler.

Ulrich, D. (1997). Human Resource Champions. The Next Agenda for Adding Value and Delivering Results. Boston, MA: Harvard Business School Press.

Ulrich, D., Allen, J., Brockbank, W., Younger, J., & Nyman, M. (2009). HR Transformation. Building Human Resources from the Outside In. New York, NY: McGraw Hill.

Ulrich, D. & Brockbank, W. (2005). The HR Value Proposition. Boston, MA: Harvard Business School Press.

Ulrich, D., Kryscynski, D., Ulrich, M., & Brockbank, W. (2017). Victory Through Organization. Why the War for Talent Is Failing Your Company and What You Can Do About It. New York, NY: McGraw Hill.

Vollendorf, I. & Jansen, M. (2023). Virtual Reality in Personalauswahl und Personalentwicklung (97–114). In: Stulle, P. & Justenhoven, R. T. (2023). Personalauswahl 4.0. KI, Machine

Learning, Gamification und andere Innovationen in der Praxis. Wiesbaden: Springer Gabler.
Voß, E. & Würtemberger, S. (2023). Vielfalt im Employee Lifecycle. Diversity Management in HR-Prozessen. Wiesbaden: Springer Gabler.
Wagner, D. N. (2021). Augmented Human-Centered Management – Personalentwicklung für hochautomatisierte Geschäftsfelder (305–327). In: Altenburger, R. & Schmidpeter, R. (2021). CSR und Künstliche Intelligenz. Berlin: Springer Gabler.
Weber, P. J. & Feistel, K. (2019). Talent Management durch Weiterbildung und seine Veränderung durch die Digitalisierung (198-204). In: Busold, M. (2019). War for Talents. Erfolgsfaktoren im Kampf um die Besten. Berlin: Springer Gabler.
Wegerich, C. (2015). Strategische Personalentwicklung in der Praxis. Instrumente, Erfolgsmodelle, Checklisten, Praxisbeispiele. Wiesbaden: Springer Gabler.
Wienkamp, H. (2021). Psychologische Anforderungsanalysen. Anforderungsprofile für Management, Arbeit und Business. Berlin: Springer Gabler.
Winkler, K. & Fink, J. (2022). Personalentwicklung in der digitalisierten Arbeitswelt – Das individuelle, lebenslange Lernen im Mittelpunkt (61–87). In: Cloots, A. (2022). Hybride Arbeitsgestaltung: Herausforderungen und Chancen. Wiesbaden: Springer Gabler.
Wirtz, B. W. (2024). Digital Business. Strategien, Geschäftsmodelle und Technologien. Wiesbaden: Springer Gabler.
Wißfeld, S. (2023). Employer Branding auf dem Arbeitsmarkt der Zukunft – Was müssen Unternehmen Arbeitskräften bieten? (315–322). In: Knappertsbusch, I. & Wisskirchen, G. (2023). Die Zukunft der Arbeit. New Work mit Flexibilität und Rechtssicherheit gestalten. Wiesbaden: Springer Gabler.
Wollmann, P. & Püringer, R. (2024). Allgemeine Einführung (3-18). In: Wollmann, P. & Püringer, R. (2024). Die Transformation von Organisationen im öffentlichen und privaten Sektor. Umsetzung eines nachhaltigen Zwecks, von einer Organisation auf der Reise und von Konnektivität für Resilienz. Cham: Springer Gabler.
Zayats, M. (2020). Digital Personal Branding. Über den Mut, sichtbar zu sein. Ein Guide für Menschen und Unternehmen. Wiesbaden: Springer Gabler.
Zimmermann, W., Richter, F. & Stuer, A. (2024). Sustainability Leadership. Wie Führungskräfte mittelständischer Unternehmen Nachhaltigkeit verankern können. Wiesbaden: Springer Gabler.